# Get a FREE eBook

To register this book, scan the code or go to
**www.manning.com/freebook/demauro**

## By registering you get

- **FREE eBook copy**
  download in PDF and ePub
- **FREE online access**
  to Manning's liveBook platform
- **FREE audio**
  read and listen online in liveBook
- **FREE AI Assistant**
  it knows the book and what you are reading when it answers
- **FREE in-book testing**
  fun tests to lock in your knowledge

In Manning's liveBook platform you can share discussions and comments with other readers, add your own bookmarks and highlights, insert personal notes anywhere on the page, see color versions of all the book's graphics, download source code and other resources, and more!
To register, scan the code or go to www.manning.com/freebook/demauro

MANNING

# Grokking
# AI Applications

## An illustrated guide for programmers and other curious people

Andrea De Mauro

Illustrated by Ines Schweigert
Foreword by Rodrigo Nader

MANNING
SHELTER ISLAND

For online information and ordering of this and other Manning books, please visit www.manning.com. The publisher offers discounts on this book when ordered in quantity. For more information, please contact

Special Sales Department
Manning Publications Co.
20 Baldwin Road, PO Box 761
Shelter Island, NY 11964
Email: orders@manning.com



Manning Publications Co.
20 Baldwin Road
Shelter Island, NY 11964

Development editor: Rebecca Johnson
Technical editor: Rohit Agarwal
Review editors: Radmila Ercegovac and Kishor Rit
Production editor: Kathy Rossland
Copy editor: Julie McNamee
Proofreader: Keri Hales
Typesetter: Dennis Dalinnik
Cover designer: Marija Tudor

ISBN: 9781633435872
Printed in the United Kingdom by CPI Group Ltd

*To my son, Suraj*

# brief contents

# contents

# foreword

Building AI applications is a fundamentally different kind of engineering. In traditional software, you write deterministic logic—sequences of functions where inputs map predictably to outputs, and bugs live in the codebase. With agentic pipelines, you're designing systems where an LLM makes decisions on your behalf. You don't control the output directly; you influence it through prompt design, retrieval strategies, tool orchestration, and careful observation of how the system reasons. This shift demands new skills, new tools, and a new way of thinking.

That's one of the problems we set out to solve when we created Langflow. The idea was straightforward: give people a visual, open source environment where they could compose AI applications by connecting building blocks—models, agents, data sources, tools—without being forced to write everything from scratch. Not because code doesn't matter, but because the real complexity in AI development has moved. It's no longer just about implementation. It's about designing the right flow, testing how an agent behaves, inspecting its reasoning, and iterating quickly until the system works reliably. Whether you're a software engineer building a multi-agent pipeline, an analyst automating document classification, or a product team prototyping a customer support bot, the challenge is the same: you need visibility, control, and speed.

What I've seen over the past few years is that the people building the most impactful AI applications are the ones who understand their domain, who can think in terms of systems—connecting context, reasoning, and action into coherent workflows—and who have access to tools that let them move fast without sacrificing control. The democratization of AI development isn't just real—it's happening blazing fast, right in front of our eyes. Jobs will change, techniques will evolve, and those who keep up with the convergence of where all of this is heading will be the ones who make the most out of it.

This is what makes Andrea's book so timely. It puts you in front of real problems—a customer service assistant, a marketing advisor, a travel planner—and walks you through constructing each one step-by-step. Along the way, you learn the techniques that matter most: prompt and context engineering, RAG, agentic design, and tool integration. They are the foundational patterns of how AI applications are built today and will likely continue to be built for years to come.

In the book, Andrea interestingly covers the nature of LLMs—the nondeterminism, the statelessness, the opacity. He gives you the intuition to understand what's happening inside the black box, then hands you the practical techniques to work with it effectively. That balance between understanding and pragmatism is what a new generation of builders needs.

We're still early. Agents will become more autonomous, retrieval systems more intelligent, and development environments will increasingly blur the line between writing software and conversing with it. The people who thrive will be the ones who know how to compose AI systems with intention and creativity. This book starts with that foundation.

—Rodrigo Nader
Cofounder of Langflow

# preface

Artificial intelligence is *big* these days.

It hardly fits into the typical boundaries of other technology upgrades in the digital space—and, it shouldn't. AI is a general-purpose technology, like steam power, electricity, the internet, and all the other novelties that sparked industrial revolutions and made the world better in certain aspects, worse in others, and undoubtedly different from before.

This forces many of us to think and talk about AI. For better or worse, we find ourselves immersed in an ongoing debate on social media about artificial intelligence, its magical promises, and embarrassing shortcomings. Yet, only a few people are actually in a position to go beyond the "talk" and the more or less grounded opinions about AI, and to know enough about AI to build something useful with it, test it themselves, feel its limitations, and anticipate its real potential. It's like the world is split into two different groups: those who *talk* about AI and those who *make* something useful with it. I wrote this book to empower people to move to the second group.

AI is one of those things that you only fully understand when you find yourself building with it. Let me give you an example. Everyone talks about AI agents these days. Beyond the shallow promise of AI agents "automating stuff," there's a much more profound, complex, and certainly more promising opportunity to rethink the way companies and individuals operate. But the only way to visualize how this is done is to try to do it yourself. In the case of agentic AI, for instance, you need to understand the looped behavior of agents, their need for context, and the requirement to create a versatile toolbox for them to operate in the real world. In this book, you learn how agents think, how to give them instructions, and how to provide them with the right context; you build tools for them to act in the real world; and you create groups of agents and experiment with them to see how they can cooperate on what really matters to you. To be clear, you can't have a custom behavior with a general-purpose tool such as ChatGPT, Copilot, or Claude: you need to build a custom application to see agentic AI serve a specific, repeatable need. This is what you'll learn to do in this book.

From my experience as an AI advisor, researcher, and teacher, when you build something custom with AI, most of the time is spent on what you wouldn't expect. Firstly, you spend a significant amount of time ingesting and preprocessing documents and datasets (definitely more time than you want, given that this part isn't the sexiest and might be boring). Secondly, you invest a lot of time visualizing how the application should operate, its logical flow, and the order and composition of the prompts and instructions required at each step. The actual coding is somewhat of a consequence of this high-level design. Of course, AI coding assistants can also help write code, provided you have a very good idea of how the application should work, what data and knowledge it should use, and what output it should produce. This is why instead of writing a *coding-first* book (listing the ever-changing Python libraries supporting AI development), I decided to write a *design-first* book where the focus is to understand what really matters (primitives of AI applications, including agents, tools, retrieval-augmented generation [RAG], prompt engineering), make it happen with a low-code application (such as Langflow), and then deploy it or see how it could be rendered with Python code.

This isn't just to make it easier for you. I followed this approach because I've seen with former students that it really unleashes their creativity and potential, regardless of their technical background or coding literacy. Actually, I've noticed that business experts, such as marketing managers, sales representatives, web designers, HR professionals, lawyers, and so on, are often best positioned to design AI applications that meet their specific needs. This book enables them to move from an idea to a prototype rapidly.

I hope you're enjoying the feeling of getting your hands dirty in AI. By the last page of this book, you'll have crafted a list of projects to bring to life over the next weeks and months. Ultimately, this is why I wrote this book—to make you a *maker* of AI applications.

Enjoy the ride!

# acknowledgments

As I started writing this book, I knew it would be no easy quest. The topic has been (and will be) evolving so rapidly that it has required continuous effort to balance offering solid frameworks with exploring technical novelties. No doubt I would never have been able to make it work by myself. At the end of the ride, I feel pervaded by a strong sense of gratitude and debt toward the many people who made this happen.

Writing this book has been possible only thanks to the eye-opening input, the rigorous feedback, and the heartfelt encouragement of so many wonderful people. Although writing the names of some of them doesn't do them full justice, let me thank Dimitrios Skoufakis, Michele Pacifico (how could I do without his brilliant advice?), Adam Graham, Alessio Villardita, Giuseppe Papaianni, Michael Berthold, Daniele Abbate, Jamilya Baimukhambetova, Roberto Bellotti, Marcello Lando, Fabio Pistilli, Gilberto Grasso, Leonardo Fenizi, Mario Galietti, Nicola Lopez, Antonio Fazzari, Luca Merlo, Nicolas Kerling, Paolo Palazzo, Lorenzo Ricciardi Celsi, Rosaria Silipo, Ermanna Maiuri, Marcin Czajkowski, Alberto Montanari, Tom Davenport, Michelangelo Ferraro, Guy Peri, and all the other amazing friends, colleagues, and leaders who have passionately worked alongside me to create sustainable value by putting AI and data analytics genuinely at the service of people and the real problems they face at work.

It would have been impossible for me to address this subject without having the opportunity to investigate it systematically alongside my many precious partners in academic research and university teaching: my fellow faculty members at LUISS Guido Carli and the other universities and business schools where I teach—Irene Finocchi, Davide D'Emiliano, Alessio Di Leo, Enzo Peruffo, Paolo Peverini, Mauro Sozio, Giuseppe (Pino) Italiano, Simone Malacaria, Mario Miozza, Antonio Gatto, Adham Kahlawi, Valentina Poggioni, Mohamed Almgerbi, Andrea Sestino, Paola Demartini, Cristiano Ciappei, Luca Petruzzellis, Pasquale Del Vecchio, Gaetano Cascini, Nikos Tsourakis, Domenico Vistocco, Dogan Duven, Marco Greco, and Michele Grimaldi. A deeply heartfelt, separate thank you goes to my dear students, whose questions, curiosity, hard research work, and thoughtful challenges in the classroom have taught me far more than I could ever teach them.

The team at Manning has proven to be a well-oiled "machine" of quality knowledge creation. As an author, I felt greatly supported throughout the entire process. The number and the quality of people involved have exceeded all of my expectations. Starting with Michael (Mike) Stephens, my acquisitions editor: he managed to make the idea behind this book grow and pivot dramatically to be always aligned with what matters to the readers, keeping them at the core of everything we put in the book. Rebecca Johnson, my development editor, has guided me through the process and shown a great deal of patience with me and my writing. I also want to thank the author of the foreword, Rodrigo Nader, one of the true visionaries of modern GenAI, whose contribution to this book has been genuinely enriching. I am equally indebted to the technical editor, Rohit Agarwal, whose precise, complete, and remarkably thorough work made the book far more robust. He could hardly have been a better fit for the role: as Chief AI Officer at Bizom, where he leads a team of data scientists and software engineers focused on transforming retail analytics through advanced GenAI and deep learning techniques, Rohit sees every day how AI applications make a real difference.

My gratitude extends to Julie McNamee, Kathy Rossland, Aleksandar Dragosavljevic, Aira Dučić, Christina Rudloff, and the many reviewers who have improved the text: Ademílson F. Tonato, Adetunji Onafuwa, Afshaan Mazagonwalla, Aidas Liaudanskas, Aishwarya Ray, Alex McLintock, Alexander Blinov, Alfons Muñoz, Andrew Freed, Ankush Rastogi, Avinash Tiwari, Banani Mohapatra, Brandon Abshire, Christopher Brousseau, Dana Robinson, Denis Chiriac, Diganta Sen Gupta, Erico Lendzian, Eugen Istschuk, Felipe Provezano Coutinho, Fernando Kobayashi, Govind Tatachari, Hanusha Durisety, Heather Ward, Hongming Zheng, Jay Mehta, Jerry Kuch, Jose Joaquin Morales Aragon, Joseph Godfrey Nixon Homer, Julien Pohie, Karl-Gustav Kallasmaa, Karsten Strøbaek, Lin Zhang, Meetu Malhotra, Michael Scarborough, Michele Santoro, Najam Uddin, Naveen Krishnan, Nicolas Bievre, Oluwatoyin Rebecca Aromokeye, Pankaj Verma, Peter Bishop, Rajeev Kumar, Roberto Infante, Rodney Weis, Rolando Madonna, Sai Chaitanya, Sanjay Devnani, Sanjeev Jaiswal, Sarayut Nonsiri, Srinath Chandramohan, Stefan Papp, Sumeer Basha Peta, Thomas Tellner, Tom Calhoon, Wei-Meng Lee, Yanqi Luo, and Zorodzayi Mukuya.

A very special thanks goes to Ines Schweigert, the artist of the brilliant illustrations for the book: a software developer and automation expert with the rare gift of holding clarity, humor, and technical depth all at once. Ines has been the closest creative partner this book could have ever wished for, and I'm sure that, without her art, these pages would have been infinitely less fun and effective.

Finally, my deepest thanks go to my family and—above all—Sławka, for her patience and for being the great, inspirational writer she is. Without her support, this book would simply not have been possible.

# about this book

This book is a hands-on, design-first guide to understanding AI and building real AI applications. From chapter 2 onward, each chapter includes a full, step-by-step tutorial that takes you from a blank canvas to a working app: a virtual customer service assistant, a marketing advisor, a travel planner, a CRM-powered personalization engine, and more. The goal is for you to learn by doing—experiencing firsthand what it means to design, build, and deploy end-to-end AI solutions that solve problems.

The focus is on the durable parts of AI development. Prompt engineering, retrieval-augmented generation (RAG), agentic structures, tool design, and orchestration are the "primitives" of any AI application, and they will outlast any specific library or framework. By mastering them, you give yourself a foundation that stays relevant as the technology around you keeps changing.

To keep the journey enjoyable, fast, and accessible, the tutorials are built using two low-code environments: Langflow and KNIME. The concepts and patterns you'll learn translate naturally to any tool or codebase you choose to work in later. By the last page, you'll have a portfolio of working apps you can adapt to your own needs and a clear mental model for designing many more.

## Who should read this book

The book is written for two primary categories of readers:

- The first group includes individuals with computer literacy and a keen interest in AI, but without specialized AI coding skills. They may be web programmers, data enthusiasts, or Python coders without experience in developing AI applications. Typical roles include web developers, AI hobbyists, aspiring data scientists, and tech professionals looking to expand their skill set into AI development quickly.

- The second group includes nontechnical readers who want to understand how LLM chain design and orchestration work, so they can apply AI in their jobs. They aren't looking to switch careers; instead, they want to partner more effectively with AI in their existing professions. They also want firsthand experience with the potential of AI so they can guide their technical colleagues on what they need. This group includes managers and other non-IT staff in various industries who view AI as a strategic asset in their work and seek hands-on experience partnering with machine intelligence.

For the Python developers among you, every chapter from chapter 2 onward includes a "What if we coded it?" section that translates the chapter's tutorial into a fully commented Python script, so you can immediately reapply the concepts in your own code and pick up the relevant libraries along the way.

## How this book is organized: A road map

Your journey in building AI applications is organized in eight chapters, designed to take you by the hand through a gradually steeper path.

- In **chapter 1**, you get a first peek inside Large Language Models, the "engines" of AI applications that generate text. Instead of going through the complex math behind these models, you build an intuition of how they are built so that you're aware of both their potential and inherent limitations, which stem from their probabilistic nature.
- **Chapter 2** gets you straight into the game: it introduces system messages, which let you customize your app's behavior and gives you a head start with Langflow, the environment we'll use throughout the book. By the end of the chapter, you'll have built your first virtual assistant with a customized personality.
- In **chapter 3**, you'll learn the "art and science" of prompt engineering, going through a proven methodology to write effective prompts and a series of enhancement techniques to boost their performance. You'll build a more complex assistant that uses two adversarial roles to refine the AI's output until it meets your precise needs.
- **Chapter 4** introduces retrieval-augmented generation (RAG), a fundamental technique that grounds AI answers in real documents. The chapter takes you through the full process of ingesting documents of any type into a vector database; by the end, you'll have built a customer assistant that answers questions related to a specific business.
- In **chapter 5**, you enter the world of agentic AI to extend your app's capabilities. You'll learn how agents behave, what tools are, and how to equip agents with multiple

tools; you'll build a virtual travel operator that autonomously builds travel itineraries, surfing the web and consulting Wikipedia.

- **Chapter 6** takes agents to the next level, showing you how to build agentic structures—groups of agents that interact with each other to solve complex problems. Like an HR director, you'll assemble agentic teams, and you'll put this into practice by building a full virtual copywriting team that generates coherent social media marketing posts.
- In **chapter 7**, you'll explore how to integrate GenAI flows into complex data sources and systems. By using both Langflow and KNIME, you'll build an application that systematically pulls data from an external database and uses a large language model (LLM) to do something useful with it—specifically, a machine that taps a customer relationship management (CRM) database to generate hyper-personalized messages for each individual customer.
- Finally, **chapter 8** shows you how to deploy your applications in the real world so that everyone can use them, how to monitor their behavior continuously (with the help of observability tools), and how to use agent protocols to connect your applications to existing environments and reuse capabilities. The final tutorial pulls together some of the assistants you've built throughout the book into a more complex service that emails travel itineraries along with matching recipes.

The chapters are organized in order of increasing complexity and build on each other, so I recommend you follow their order and complete all of the tutorials included. Even if you might not see immediate value in a particular tutorial—for example, an agent that writes recipes—all the tutorials serve as templates you can reuse and adapt to build custom applications tailored to your specific needs. I strongly suggest you do them all.

## About the code

This book contains many examples of source code both in numbered listings and in line with normal text. In both cases, source code is formatted in a `fixed-width font like this` to separate it from ordinary text. Sometimes code is also **`in bold`** to highlight code that has changed from previous steps in the chapter, such as when a new feature adds to an existing line of code.

In many cases, the original source code has been reformatted; we've added line breaks and reworked indentation to accommodate the available page space in the book. In rare cases, even this wasn't enough, and listings include line-continuation markers (➥). Additionally, comments in the source code have often been removed from the listings when the code is described in the text. Code annotations accompany many of the listings, highlighting important concepts.

From chapter 2 onward, you'll find at least one Python script at the end of each chapter that implements the tutorial. The script is heavily commented, so you can follow what's going on and connect each step with what you've seen in the chapter.

Source code is available in the book's accompanying GitHub repository, https://github.com/laibniz/GrokkingAIapplications. The repository contains the following:

- The input files (Word documents, PDFs, CSVs) required for the tutorials
- All the executable Python scripts, organized by chapter, following the naming convention (`CHn-xxx.py`)
- A markdown document (`SCRIPT_GUIDE.md`) that extends the "What if we coded it?" sections from the book, so Python developers can see exactly how the Langflow projects translate into code

Star the repository and check back regularly—I'll use it to post updates, errata, and any supplementary material that may become useful over time.

You can get executable snippets of code from the liveBook (online) version of this book at https://livebook.manning.com/book/grokking-ai-applications. The complete code for the examples in the book is also available for download from the Manning website at www.manning.com/books/grokking-ai-applications.

## liveBook discussion forum

Purchase of *Grokking AI Applications* includes free access to liveBook, Manning's online reading platform. Using liveBook's exclusive discussion features, you can attach comments to the book globally or to specific sections or paragraphs. It's a snap to make notes for yourself, ask and answer technical questions, and receive help from the author and other users. To access the forum, go to https://livebook.manning.com/book/grokking-ai-applications/discussion.

Manning's commitment to our readers is to provide a venue where a meaningful dialogue between individual readers and between readers and the author can take place. It isn't a commitment to any specific amount of participation on the part of the author, whose contribution to the forum remains voluntary (and unpaid). We suggest you try asking the author some challenging questions lest his interest stray! The forum and the archives of previous discussions will be accessible from the publisher's website as long as the book is in print.

## about the author

**Andrea De Mauro** is a seasoned executive advisor and fractional CDO. He has held leadership roles at Vodafone and Procter & Gamble, shaping data-driven strategies at scale. He teaches Marketing Analytics and Applied AI at Luiss University in Rome and other top European universities. Recognized in *CDO Magazine*'s "Forty Under 40" list, he is also a prolific researcher, exploring the fundamental forces behind Big Data as a phenomenon and the transformative impact of AI and data analytics on businesses and society. His latest books in English include *The Financial Times Guide to Data-Driven Transformation* (FT Publishing International, 2024) and *Data Analytics Made Easy* (Packt Publishing, 2021), bridging the gap between AI theory and business impact.

## about the illustrator

**Ines Schweigert** (born Dedović) is a machine vision expert and a senior software developer at Jonas & Redmann. Occasionally, she does side projects to stay connected to the scientific and art communities. She illustrated several other Manning books, including *Algorithms and Data Structures for Massive Datasets* and *Hugo in Action*.

# Peeking inside the black box | 1

## In this chapter

- what's needed to develop useful generative AI applications
- how large language models work

While it feels natural to *use* tools like ChatGPT or Copilot these days, you realize what a strange animal a generative AI (GenAI) application can be when you try to *build* one yourself. How can AI systems communicate in fluent, human-like language? Does ChatGPT really *think* like we do, or is something else at play? In this book, we'll explore what makes GenAI so unique, mysterious, and fascinating.

Before diving deeper into what makes GenAI applications such an exciting new species, it's worth taking a moment to clarify the approach of this book and what you should expect from here.

## Our journey ahead

The *primary goal* of this book is to help you understand how GenAI applications are built. Instead of going through mathematical proofs or model architecture internals, we focus on what truly matters when you want to design real-world apps: the main building blocks, how they fit together, the problems they solve, and their limitations. By the end of the book, no matter which tools or frameworks you choose to use, you'll have a clear mental model for designing and reasoning about GenAI applications.

The *secondary goal* is to enable hands-on practice. You'll build real applications using a low-code tool called Langflow. Although we use Langflow, the concepts are intentionally tool-agnostic. Prompts, chains, retrieval, tools, agents, deployment, and observability are ideas that transcend any specific library or vendor. These concepts have a long shelf life and can be applied across many different technologies.

Low-code tools such as Langflow make learning concrete and accessible, allowing you to focus on design and reasoning rather than syntax. Visual components and flows let you quickly experiment, fail, adjust, and iterate—the perfect mindset for building GenAI systems.

If you're not a Python expert, you can still build meaningful applications right away. If you're a Python developer, Langflow becomes a rapid prototyping tool, helping you explore architectures and get a head start on more complex projects. Visual flows often make architectural decisions clearer than code alone: trust me—you'll see the benefits of this approach soon.

Starting in chapter 2, each chapter concludes with a short "What if we coded it?" section that translates the low-code solution into Python, with helpful comments explaining what's happening. If you don't want to code, skip these parts. If you do, you'll see how visual design connects to code, giving you reusable patterns for your own projects.

To begin our journey, let's take a look at the fundamental characteristics that set GenAI applications apart and make our ride worth the effort.

## The uniqueness of GenAI programming

Let's consider the key differences between programming a traditional application and a GenAI application. Both aim to define application behavior that provides useful output given an input, but they achieve this in very different ways.

In traditional programming, you instruct a machine to perform certain steps in a specific order, forming a logical workflow that transforms your input into the desired output. These steps are described through code, resulting in mainly deterministic behavior. This codification uses a formal language with defined syntax and semantics, such as Python, Java, or C, that developers use to write programs.

In GenAI programming, an additional element enters the picture: the Large Language Model (LLM). At some point in your workflow, you pass through this "magic black box," which takes text as input and generates text as output. As you design the workflow, you must learn to craft the right text input for the LLM. This input is not written in a programming language but in natural languages, such as English or Italian. The LLM is a black box that operates probabilistically, so no matter how carefully you craft your prompt, you cannot be certain of the exact output you will receive. This probabilistic process introduces inherent randomness into the GenAI application's behavior.

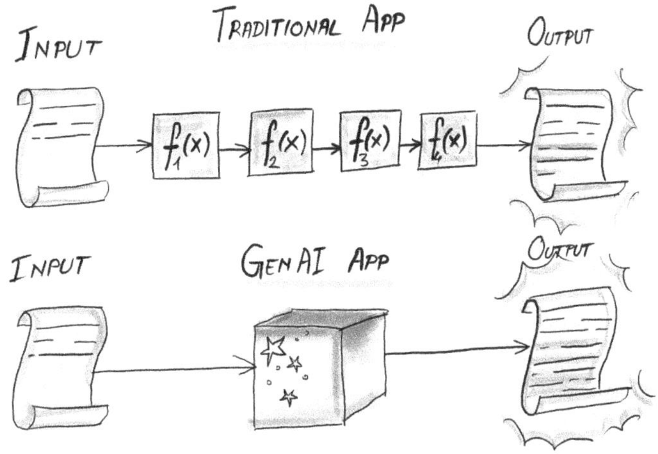


**Figure 1.1** GenAI applications have an LLM (magic black box) somewhere.

What a strange animal, indeed. To "tame the beast," we must learn to effectively manage the randomness of nondeterministic behaviors and the subtleties of natural language.

Some of these probabilistic elements are present even outside of LLMs and GenAI. For example, in AI applications (not specifically generative), we also contend with the unpredictable behavior of probabilistic models. For instance, when a model predicts whether a customer will buy a product, it doesn't follow a fixed rule that guarantees a certain answer. Instead, it estimates the likelihood of different outcomes based on patterns learned from data—for example, predicting a 72% chance that the customer will make a purchase. In GenAI, we must *always* deal with both challenges: natural language instructions and probabilistic behavior. So, we need to become very good at managing them effectively, as we'll learn throughout this book.

## AI, ML, and GenAI: What's the difference?

Artificial Intelligence (AI) refers to technology replicating human-like intelligence traits, such as finding patterns, reasoning, or learning. Machine Learning (ML) empowers AI by enabling machines to replicate one remarkable aspect of human intelligence: the ability to learn autonomously from data, rather than following fixed rules. Generative AI (GenAI) is a specialized area within ML where machines learn something specific: how to generate content, such as text, images, or code, that is coherent, relevant, and human-like. Tools like ChatGPT are GenAI systems—meaning they belong to a subset of ML, a subset of AI. While people often say "AI" when referring to ChatGPT, it's important to remember that these tools represent just one (very impressive) part of a much broader field.

# Dealing with LLMs

Natural language instructions and probabilistic behavior are intrinsic to GenAI because of the component that turns a generic application into a GenAI application: the LLM. We'll explore how LLMs work later. For now, as mentioned earlier, think of an LLM as a magic black box that takes some text as input and generates some other text as output, as shown in figure 1.2.

**Figure 1.2** The magic black box gets text as input and generates text as output.

This box has several features that affect how the output text is generated:

- *The behavior of an LLM is inherently nondeterministic.* You can't be sure what you'll get for any given input because LLMs work with probabilities, not with set logical rules.
- *LLMs are not explanatory.* Because it's a black box, you don't know what's happening inside, and you'll never know why you got a specific output.
- *LLMs are stateless.* They don't retain memory between calls. Every time they are called and produce an output, they return to their original state as if nothing happened. They have no memory and start from a clean slate each time.
- *LLMs are pretrained.* They have some fixed knowledge hardwired into their "digital brains" that can't change as they are used. The way LLMs work is set during their training phase: from then on, they can't accept new knowledge (unless you build a different LLM).

If we compare our daily experience as GenAI users with what we just described, something doesn't add up. The LLM limitations of being stateless, pretrained, and so on aren't present in real-world applications.

For example, the iconic ChatGPT by OpenAI (debuted in 2022) doesn't seem to be affected by such restrictions, although it's clearly based on LLMs. ChatGPT appears to have some memory: it remembers what we said earlier in a conversation and builds upon it. It doesn't seem truly stateless. The OpenAI engineers working on ChatGPT managed to overcome the memoryless limitation.

Similarly, GenAI applications used in the workplace, such as Microsoft's Copilot, seem able to "learn" from your documents and provide answers based on specific knowledge that wasn't available when the underlying LLM was built. In other words, their understanding of the world doesn't seem limited to what they were pretrained on; it appears expandable.

The reason is that real GenAI applications do not rely on the LLM alone. They combine the model with additional components—such as memory, external data sources, and tools—that extend the model's capabilities beyond its original training.

### Beyond OpenAI

This chapter refers to OpenAI's GPT-3 and ChatGPT as examples. GPT-3 is now obsolete, but it's used here as a historical reference because it marked a turning point in the public adoption of GenAI. Fortunately, many newer LLMs are now available, making it impossible to provide a fully updated and comprehensive list. At the time of writing, some of the most notable LLMs include Google's Gemini, Meta's LLaMA, DeepSeek's R models, Anthropic's Claude, and X's Grok. The good news is that the techniques we'll learn in this book are entirely agnostic to the specific LLM used.

## Building GenAI applications that extend LLMs

When building GenAI applications, we combine LLMs with additional components that extend what the model alone can do. Engineers at OpenAI and Microsoft have done this with ChatGPT and Copilot, respectively, and as GenAI application designers, we'll do the same. Let's explore what this involves through some examples.

### Overcoming the "stateless" barrier

LLMs have no built-in memory; they start from scratch with each prompt. If you want your application to appear as if it "remembers" earlier parts of a conversation, *you* must provide that memory. Your app must keep track of previous user inputs and LLM outputs and then package them with each new request.

Let's see how this works with an example.

## Try it yourself

You can test the following examples using your preferred GenAI assistant (e.g., ChatGPT or Copilot). Many platforms now include features that remember information across sessions to personalize responses. In most cases, you can disable memory or personalization controls in the assistant's settings (e.g., in ChatGPT via Settings > Personalization > Memory). You may also need to clear existing saved memories separately for a truly stateless interaction. Note that the interface and availability of memory controls can vary by plan and deployment, so the exact steps may differ.

**INPUT** `Hi, I'm Andrea. How are you?`

**OUTPUT** `Hello Andrea! I'm doing well. How can I assist you today?`

Now, if you open a brand-new chat (with all memory features disabled) and ask the following:

**INPUT** `What's my name?`

**OUTPUT** `I'm not sure. You haven't told me your name.`

Notice that the second question was asked in isolation, without referencing the initial introduction. The LLM had no memory of the previous conversation because, under the hood, a new call to the LLM was made with a clean slate.

**Figure 1.3** In LLM relationships, every chat is a first date.

When ChatGPT appears to "remember" your name, it's actually the ChatGPT application resending your entire prior conversation to the LLM each time. As a GenAI application designer, you'll do something similar: your system will capture and forward relevant snippets to preserve context between interactions.

For example:

**INPUT**

```
What's my name?
Previous conversation history:
<User: Hi, I'm Andrea. How are you?>
<Agent: Hello Andrea! I'm well. How can I assist you today?>
```

**OUTPUT**

```
Your name is Andrea, and I'm here to help!
```

By appending the `Previous conversation history` block to our input, the LLM could answer correctly. This needs to happen in GenAI applications: we need to manage memory so that each call to the LLM is self-sufficient.

## Providing fresh knowledge in prompts

LLMs are pretrained on fixed datasets and don't automatically know about new or private information. If you need answers based on up-to-date company policies or newly released product details—information not present in the LLM's original training data—you must include these details in your prompt each time they're needed.

Let's look at an example:

**INPUT**

```
When does your office open?
```

**OUTPUT**

```
I don't have an office, but I'm here to help 24/7! Let me know what
you need assistance with.
```

Nice try, LLM! The answer was generic because the LLM didn't have the specific knowledge required. Let's see what happens when we include relevant information in the prompt:

**INPUT**

```
When does your office open?
Relevant knowledge:
<Our office hours are 9 AM to 6 PM from Monday to Friday.>
<The office address is 3180 18th St., San Francisco, California.>
<The office number is +1-800-242-8478.>
```

**OUTPUT**

```
Our office opens at 9 AM on weekdays.
```

Here, the LLM uses the extra `Relevant knowledge` text we provided to craft an appropriate response. Without that snippet in the prompt, the LLM wouldn't know your specific office hours. Notice that we provided more information than the user needed (the address and phone number were also included), but the LLM was able to identify and use only the relevant part.

A natural question is how can an application equip the LLM input with the proper knowledge? We'll explore techniques for this in later chapters. For now, consider two simple options: always attach the full knowledge to each query (if the knowledge base is small)—for example, by inserting the relevant documents directly into the prompt sent to the model—or run a deterministic search on a document repository to find and attach only the relevant sentences (such as those containing the word 'office').

We'll come back to this topic. In chapter 4, we'll learn how to consistently retrieve and attach relevant context using a powerful technique called Retrieval-Augmented Generation (RAG)—for now, you got the gist.

## How this book helps you build real-world GenAI applications

These examples demonstrate that building a GenAI application requires more than just *forwarding* a user message to the LLM. When building an interface to interact with an LLM, you need to do the following:

- *Manage conversation state.* Store and forward previous user messages and model outputs to provide context for subsequent requests, as we saw in the first case. We will learn how to do this later in our journey.
- *Use the right prior knowledge.* Pull in the right snippets—company data, user-specific info, or any external resources—to keep the model's responses accurate and updated, as we've done in the second case. Learning to ingest and properly store the right knowledge is essential for retrieving the correct information. This is easier said than done, so we'll need several chapters to perfect this ability.

But there's more to building real-world applications than these two skills. For example, you'll also need to do the following:

- *Trigger actions.* Learn how to handle any tasks the LLM suggests, such as sending emails or retrieving additional data, by integrating your application with external tools (for programmers, this means working with APIs).
- *Customize the behavior.* Ensure the LLM's responses align with the desired tone, style, and objectives of your application. This is where the art and science of writing a good prompt (we call it *prompt engineering*) comes in, helping you fine-tune and control outputs. Chapter 3 will be devoted to this.

- *Design agentic structures.* LLMs enable the creation of systems with multiple specialized agents working together. This involves assigning roles, responsibilities, and organizational structures, similar to how an HR manager designs an org chart. We'll explore how to do this efficiently in the final chapters.

GenAI solutions such as ChatGPT, Microsoft Copilot, and others perform many of these tasks behind the scenes. As you progress through this book, you'll learn how to replicate these strategies, tailoring them to your specific domain or industry. By the end, you'll be equipped to tame the beast of GenAI yourself (figure 1.4) and design a helpful, context-rich, and interactive user experience.

**Figure 1.4** Taming the GenAI beast

# Inside the LLM

The source of all the strangeness of GenAI programming is the magic black box—the LLM. Given its centrality, it makes sense to understand what happens under the hood and how the LLM can generate coherent text.

Just as you don't need to know how an engine works to drive a car, you don't need to master every detail of an LLM to build generative AI applications. In the following pages, you'll learn how large language models work, with complex concepts broken down into simple, digestible explanations.

## Learning how to speak

First, it's important to clarify that an LLM is built by applying several machine learning algorithms in order. Machine learning algorithms are computational methods that learn patterns from data to make predictions or decisions without being explicitly programmed for each rule. Each algorithm plays a distinct role in processing and generating language. For example, the pioneering ChatGPT is the result of multiple stages of machine learning training, each refining its ability to hold meaningful conversations with human users.

## Three types of machine learning

Machine learning algorithms fall into three main types: unsupervised, supervised, and reinforcement learning:

- Unsupervised learning finds patterns and structures in data without labels, like children grouping similar toy shapes on their own.
- Supervised learning predicts outcomes by learning from past examples, or labels, much like a child learning colors with an adult's guidance.
- Reinforcement learning interacts with an environment to achieve goals through trial and error, much like a child learning to walk by trying different movements and adjusting based on success or failure.

**Figure 1.5** The three types of machine learning: unsupervised, supervised, and reinforcement

We can understand the learning process behind a tool such as ChatGPT by considering three ML stages, as illustrated in figure 1.6. The first component of ChatGPT is GPT (Generative Pretrained Transformer), an unsupervised model that completes sentences by predicting the most likely next word. Additional steps, or fine-tuning, enable the model to sustain conversations with humans. These further human refinement steps are achieved through supervised and reinforcement learning steps, where the initial output is improved to enhance conversational capabilities, making it ideal for use as a chatbot.

**Figure 1.6** The learning stages of ChatGPT

This is what happens during the three learning stages:

1. In the first stage, GPT learns to "speak" human language by reading a massive library of documents. This is accomplished through unsupervised learning, where the model learns grammar and predicts the next word without direct supervision. The ML algorithms find their own rules for creating coherent sentences and selecting appropriate word completions.
2. In the next phase, the model undergoes supervised refinement where it's fine-tuned for meaningful dialogue by training on examples of human conversations. This supervised learning process helps the model operate in a question-and-answer (Q&A) fashion. The model, originally able to complete sentences generically, is now trained to find completions that result in coherent, relevant dialogue, improving its conversational effectiveness.
3. The final step uses a technique called *Reinforcement Learning from Human Feedback* (RLHF). Human reviewers provide feedback on the model's responses, indicating which answers are effective and which are not. This feedback loop helps the model improve through trial and error, making it progressively better at human-like conversations. When users interact with chatbots, they often provide feedback on the responses, further refining the model to produce better answers over time.

This combination of unsupervised learning, supervised refinement, and reinforcement through human feedback enables ChatGPT to understand and generate human language effectively.

## Where everything starts: Sentence completions

Let's dive into the first component of ChatGPT: GPT. This model excels at generating coherent, contextually appropriate continuations of a given text. It effectively predicts and completes sentences by anticipating the "next best word."

Think of GPT as a supercharged autocomplete engine. You've likely seen this in action when typing a search query in Google or composing a message and suggestions pop up to complete your sentence. GPT works similarly, but with far more power because it doesn't just guess the next word, it can complete entire thoughts, paragraphs, or even full documents based on what you've already written.

If you run the completion step repeatedly, you get an additional word each time. Such a model is called *autoregressive* because it is applied over and over, using the previous iteration's output as input to build more complex completions—creating complete sentences, paragraphs, poems, tales, or entire reports.

Let's build an intuition for how GPT works by understanding how it represents text. In GPT, phrases are "tokenized," meaning they are split into units called *tokens*. A token can be a word, part of a word (some more complex English words are represented as a composition of multiple tokens), or a punctuation mark. These tokens are then translated into numbers through a process called *embedding*.

Let's use a simplified example of a basic GPT that uses a dictionary of just eight words: "The," "capital," "of," "Italy," "is," "Paris," "Rome," "London." Each word in the dictionary is associated with three numbers (its embeddings) and can be visualized in a 3D space, as figure 1.7 shows. Don't worry about where these numbers come from—you'll see that later in the chapter. For now, imagine that the words lie in a 3D space, and the coordinates (x, y, z) might reflect their meaning along intuitive axes such as width, depth,

| Word | x | y | z |
|---|---|---|---|
| The | 0.1 | 0.3 | 0.1 |
| capital | 0.6 | 0.4 | 0.3 |
| of | 0.2 | 0.1 | 0.3 |
| Italy | 0.5 | 0.6 | 0.1 |
| is | 0.4 | 0.1 | 0.5 |
| Paris | 0.2 | 0.5 | 0.8 |
| Rome | 0.6 | 0.5 | 0.4 |
| London | 0.3 | 0.3 | 0.9 |

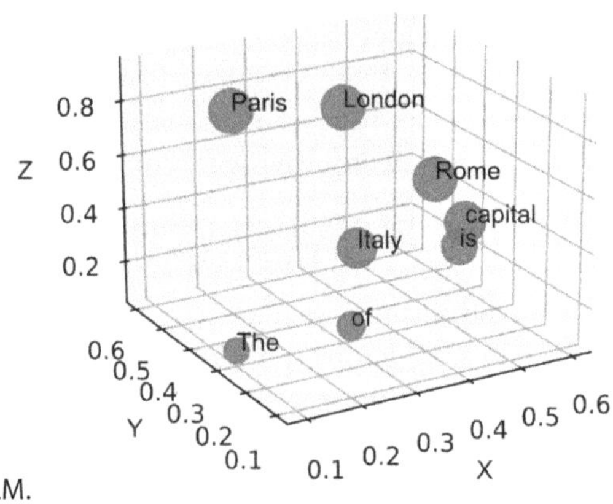


**Figure 1.7** Words are numbers in the eyes of an LLM.

or height in this imaginary space. These tuples of numbers, the *embeddings*, will be the atomic units used for computations.

If you look at the figure, you'll notice that words with similar meanings tend to be closer together. For instance, the city names—Rome, Paris, and London—appear grouped in the upper part of the space, while more functional words—"The", "of", and "is"—are positioned lower. This spatial layout reflects semantic similarity, even in this made-up example.

Let's move to the next step: completing a sentence. For example, imagine we want to complete the following sentence: "The capital of Italy is . . . ." In LLMs, the sentence to be completed is called a *prompt*.

What does the GPT algorithm do? First, it builds a *context* from the prompt using calculations based on the embedding coordinates. For instance, by calculating the arithmetic mean, coordinate by coordinate, of the words in the prompt, we obtain a new tuple of numbers called the *context*.

As shown in figure 1.8, the x-coordinate of the context is computed by taking the average of the x-coordinates of the words in the prompt (i.e., summing those x-values and dividing by the number of words). This is, of course, a simplification of the actual calculation process happening within GPT, but let's use it for now to help us build our intuition about how this seemingly magical process works.

| Word | x | y | z |
|---|---|---|---|
| The | 0.1 | 0.3 | 0.1 |
| capital | 0.6 | 0.4 | 0.3 |
| of | 0.2 | 0.1 | 0.3 |
| Italy | 0.5 | 0.6 | 0.1 |
| is | 0.4 | 0.1 | 0.5 |
| Paris | 0.2 | 0.5 | 0.8 |
| Rome | 0.6 | 0.5 | 0.4 |
| London | 0.3 | 0.3 | 0.9 |

| | x | y | z |
|---|---|---|---|
| Context | (0.1+0.6+0.2+0.5+0.4)/5 = **0.36** | (0.3+0.4+0.1+0.6+0.1)/5 = **0.30** | (0.1+0.3+0.3+0.1+0.5)/5 = **0.26** |

**Figure 1.8** Given a prompt, you can calculate the context.

Now you have a tuple representing the context of the sentence to complete and some candidate words in the dictionary that can complete it. For simplicity, let's imagine that only "Paris," "Rome," and "London" (the words not yet used in the sentence) are candidate words (typically, every word in the dictionary is considered a possible completion). By combining the embeddings of the candidate words with the context, you can determine which word needs to be added as the completion.

In the example shown in figure 1.9, the coordinates of the candidate words are combined with the coordinates of the context by comparing their numbers coordinate by coordinate and combining them into a single score. Technically, this operation is called an *inner product*. The word with the highest score wins. In this case, "The capital of Italy is" yields "Rome" as its best completion, as the resulting probability for "Rome," 0.47, is higher than what the other candidate words get. Well done to our simplified GPT for having guessed the right completion!

| Word | x | y | z |
|---|---|---|---|
| The | 0.1 | 0.3 | 0.1 |
| capital | 0.6 | 0.4 | 0.3 |
| of | 0.2 | 0.1 | 0.3 |
| Italy | 0.5 | 0.6 | 0.1 |
| is | 0.4 | 0.1 | 0.5 |
| **Paris** | **0.2** | **0.5** | **0.8** |
| **Rome** | **0.6** | **0.5** | **0.4** |
| **London** | **0.3** | **0.3** | **0.9** |

| | x | y | z |
|---|---|---|---|
| Context | **0.36** | **0.30** | **0.26** |

| Word | Probability | |
|---|---|---|
| **Paris** | 0.2*0.36+0.5*0.30+0.8*0.26= **0.43** | |
| **Rome** | 0.6*0.36+0.5*0.30+0.4*0.26= **0.47** | ← winner |
| **London** | 0.3*0.36+0.3*0.30+0.9*0.26= **0.43** | |

"The capital of Italy is **Rome**"

**Figure 1.9** Guess the next best word by combining embeddings with context.

Let's quickly recap to help the core ideas stick. Here's a summary of how GPT figures out the best completion for a sentence:

- The text is split into atomic units called *tokens*. A token corresponds to a word or part of a word. The possible tokens are included in a dictionary.
- Every token in the dictionary is represented by an *embedding*, which is a set of numbers. In our case, we had a dictionary of eight tokens, each described by an embedding corresponding to a set of three decimal numbers.
- The phrase to complete is the *prompt*. By combining the embeddings of the words included in the prompt, you obtain a set of numbers called a *context*.
- By combining the context with every token in the dictionary, you can calculate the probability that each token completes the prompt. The token with the highest likelihood is chosen by GPT as the output and becomes the completion of the prompt.
- You can continue generating longer completions by repeating the previous two steps: this time, the previous completion is added as part of the new prompt. You get an updated context, calculate the next completion, and keep going. Figure 1.10 summarizes this sentence completion process.

This process of breaking down phrases, converting them into numerical representations, and iteratively predicting the next token forms the backbone of how LLMs generate text.

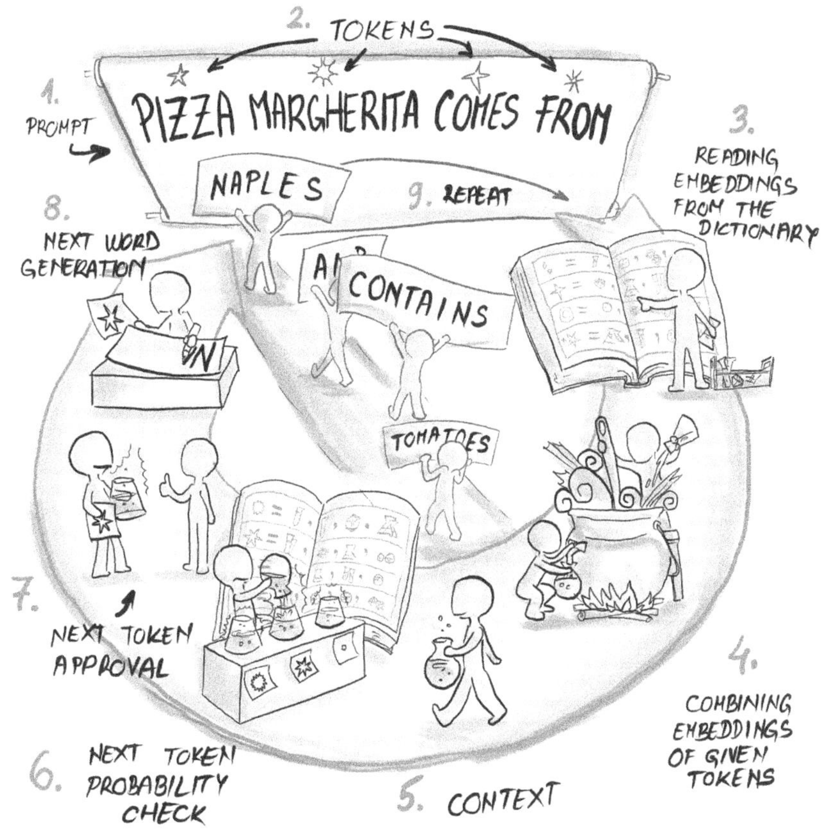


**Figure 1.10** The GPT sentence completion process

# Understanding GPT: How a real LLM works

Now, if the process we just described looks too simple to be true—it is. The simplified process uses basic calculations that could, in theory, be done with pen and paper because linear combinations only involve multiplications and sums. With a dictionary of only eight tokens and embeddings of 3 numbers per token, we need just 24 numbers to perform the completion calculations.

Modern LLMs, specifically GPT-3, the model used in the first versions of ChatGPT released in 2022, are much more complex. We focus on GPT-3 because it marks a significant milestone in the evolution of LLMs, and, crucially, its architecture, scale, and parameters are relatively well documented and publicly available. While newer models build on and extend these ideas, they are often less transparent about their internal details.

Let's dive into the complex reality of GPT-3 by examining three key aspects of the simplified methodology we discussed earlier: the dictionary of embeddings, the calculation of the context, and the calculation of the next best word.

You'll encounter many new concepts and technical terms in the next few pages. But don't worry, you don't need to become an expert on every detail of modern LLM architectures. Think of this as a look under the hood to see what's actually happening. While specific numbers and implementations may vary in newer models, the core concepts you'll learn here still apply. If some sections feel too dense, feel free to skim or even skip ahead to the final section, "Keeping the model knowledge up-to-date," without missing the bigger picture.

## Embeddings

In our simplified example, we used a dictionary with three numbers per word and an eight-word vocabulary. This minimal setup is indeed straightforward and easy to grasp. By contrast, GPT-3 operates on an entirely different scale:

- *Simplified example*—3 numbers per token, 8-token dictionary
- *GPT-3*—12,288 numbers per token, 50,000-token dictionary

To put this into perspective, while a 3D chart could easily represent our simplified dictionary, it would be impossible to visualize GPT-3's embeddings in the same way. You would need more than 12,000 dimensions to describe a single word. Instead of just "up/down" or "left/right" like in our earlier city example, each new dimension could capture something different, such as how formal a word is, how modern it sounds, or whether it relates more to geography or emotion. In the space of embeddings, words with similar concepts stay close to each other, while unrelated ones are far apart. With so many dimensions to position words, GPT-3's embedding mechanism captures intricate nuances of meaning and context far beyond the capabilities of simpler models. Now imagine how many subtle shades of meaning you could capture with 12,000 such dimensions, and you start to see how GPT-3 achieves such an impressive grasp of language.

## Context calculation

In the simplified example, the context of a prompt is calculated as the simple average of the words. This straightforward approach works well for basic illustrations but falls short in real-world applications:

- *Simplified example*—The context of a prompt is calculated as a simple average of the words. The position of each word in the sentence is ignored. For example, "The dog bit the man" and "The man bit the dog" produce the same context.
- *GPT-3*—Context is the result of applying prompt tokens to deep neural networks with 96 layers and 175 billion parameters. The position of each word in the prompt significantly affects the calculation of the context.

If you're new to deep learning, neural networks are complex systems inspired by the human brain, consisting of layers of interconnected nodes, called neurons. Each neuron takes inputs from the neurons in the preceding layer, combines them with its own set of parameters, and relays its outputs to the neurons of the following layer. Neurons are stacked one upon each other, forming a deep hierarchical architecture (this is why the ML subfield that develops neural networks is called *deep learning*). The context calculation in GPT-3 uses these deep learning techniques, taking into account not only the words but also their positions in the text. This positional awareness is achieved through a mechanism known as *transformers*.

## Deep learning and transformers

**Deep learning** involves training large neural networks with many layers, enabling them to learn hierarchical representations of data. This approach allows models to understand complex patterns and relationships. **Transformers** are a type of neural network architecture designed to handle sequential data, such as text. They use a mechanism called *attention*, which helps the model focus on the most relevant parts of the input sequence, making it particularly effective for natural language processing tasks. For example, when answering the question "What is the capital of Italy?" the attention mechanism allows the model to focus more on the word "Italy" (rather than "what" or "is")—leading it to correctly predict "Rome."

For completeness, note that the number of tokens you can use in a single GPT-3 prompt is limited by the model's context window. For GPT-3, the maximum is 2,048 tokens in your prompt. This is called the *context window size* and limits the amount of text you can insert into the LLM at once. For an "old" model such as GPT-3, that meant a maximum of nearly three pages. Modern models have much larger context windows, sometimes accommodating entire books, and this limitation may eventually disappear.

Clearly, processing an ordered set of prompt tokens through deep neural networks with billions of parameters is far more complex than simply averaging token embeddings. This is what it takes to build an LLM that seems confident about what it is talking about, whatever the subject.

### Combination process

The final step in our process is to combine the context with candidate words to select the next best word. In our simplified example, this is done with an inner product:

- *Simplified example*—The combination is just an inner product.
- *GPT-3*—The combination is performed by another neural network with two layers and 1.2 billion parameters.

This additional neural network layer adds another level of depth and sophistication. It ensures the selected word fits the immediate context and aligns with the broader narrative the model is constructing. This layered approach allows GPT-3 to generate coherent and contextually appropriate continuations, from sentences to entire paragraphs.

Figure 1.11 shows how a GPT architecture can be broken down into three main blocks. First, incoming words or tokens are converted into embeddings—large sets of numbers

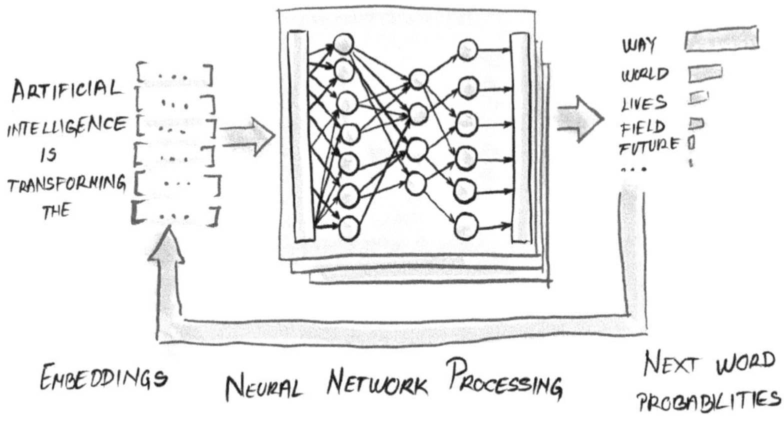


**Figure 1.11** How a GPT architecture generates sentences

that capture their meaning. Next, these embeddings pass through deep neural networks (the Context Calculation and the Combination steps), which use attention and positional information to produce a probability distribution over all possible next tokens. Finally, the token with the highest probability is selected and added to the prompt. That expanded prompt then reenters the cycle, generating new embeddings, an updated probability distribution, and so on.

Reality proves to be way more complex than our naïve example. GPT-3 uses a matrix of around 12,000 rows and 50,000 columns for its dictionary: notice that we're talking about more than half a billion numbers, which means over 1 GB of data when stored in a single file. This is just the simplest part: converting text into numbers via a static dictionary. The subsequent neural networks come with plenty of neurons packed with parameters—about 175 billion numbers this time. In total, if you "stored" all the numbers GPT-3 needs for completing sentences, you would need roughly 350 GB of disk space. Additionally, you need solid computing power (your laptop wouldn't make it, I'm afraid) to combine these billions of numbers every time a single new word needs to appear on the screen as the completion of your prompt.

This scale explains why LLMs require specialized infrastructure rather than running directly on a typical PC.

## When smaller is better: Small language models

While we focus on LLMs such as GPT-3, Claude, or Gemini, many of the same principles apply to small language models (SLMs). These are considerably cheaper and smaller, typically with just a few billion parameters at the time of writing, but still powerful enough for many real-world tasks. SLMs are gaining popularity as practical choices for smart assistants running locally on smartphones, document summarization, and other specific tasks that don't require the breadth and depth of LLMs.

## Pretraining the model

There are two main stages in the life cycle of an LLM like GPT-3: model training and inference. During *model training*, the model learns the optimal set of parameters to predict word completions. During *inference*, these parameters are applied to a prompt to generate a completion.

We have so far focused on the inference stage. In the previous steps (translating words into numbers, calculating context, and combining it with the prompt), a *given* set of parameters is applied to the input (the prompt) through complex computations. But where do these parameters come from? How do we obtain the precise set of numbers that produce "Rome" as the completion for our sentence about the capital of Italy?

This is what happens during the first stage of the LLM life cycle: model training. The "P" in GPT stands for *pretrained* because the parameters used during inference are found once and for all during the preliminary training process. Let's see how this stage works.

To start, let's build an intuition for how neural network models are trained. Neural networks start with random parameters, which are numbers that influence how the network makes decisions. Think of it like a student with no prior knowledge guessing answers. Initially, these guesses are often wrong, but with each new piece of information (or training example), the student adjusts their guesses to get closer to the correct answer.

This adjustment occurs through iterative learning passes, often described as "backward" learning or *backpropagation*. Here's how it works: the neural network makes a prediction based on its current parameters. If the prediction is wrong, the network adjusts the parameters slightly to improve future predictions. This process repeats many times, with the network constantly adjusting its parameters to reduce errors.

Training requires a lot of human-readable text. Each time the network sees a new piece of text, it learns to better predict and complete sentences. To train effectively, the dataset must cover diverse subjects and disciplines. This helps the network learn to handle a wide variety of contexts and topics.

For GPT-3, OpenAI used a massive dataset totaling 45 TB of text. This dataset included content from various sources, such as websites (using pages "scraped" from blogs, forums, news portals, etc.), books, the whole of English Wikipedia, and academic articles, providing a rich and varied dataset for training. By processing this extensive text, the neural network's parameters gradually converged to values that enable accurate and contextually appropriate text completions.

To perform these countless adjustments efficiently, specialized hardware is needed. In particular, graphics processing units (GPUs) are a key component of modern AI training. Originally designed for graphics rendering through parallel processing (this is why they're an essential part of any gamer's kit), GPUs are also ideal for the matrix operations at the heart of neural network training. In 3D graphics, similar operations, such as inner products between vectors, are used to compute lighting, shading, and object orientation. Because neural networks carry out billions of simultaneous mathematical operations, especially matrix multiplications, which internally involve many inner products, GPUs provide the speed and scale required to make model training feasible.

## The massive power it takes to train an LLM

Floating-point operations per second (FLOPS) measures a computer's performance, with a petaflop equaling 1 quadrillion (1,000,000,000,000,000) operations per second. Training GPT-3 required a total of 3,640 petaflop-days of computation, meaning it used the equivalent of a computer performing 1 quadrillion calculations per second for 3,640 days. By comparison, a high-end gaming laptop, which at the time of writing can include a GPU capable of 100 teraflops, or 0.1 petaflops, would take around 100 years to train the same model. The energy required would be similar to that used by 120 households in a year.

Now we have a complete picture of how GPT-3 works, as summarized in figure 1.12. The process begins with a massive collection of training text, which the model uses to learn and develop its parameters. This model training phase equips GPT-3 with the ability to understand and generate human-like text. When a prompt is given to the trained model during inference, it processes the input using the learned parameters and produces a generated completion.

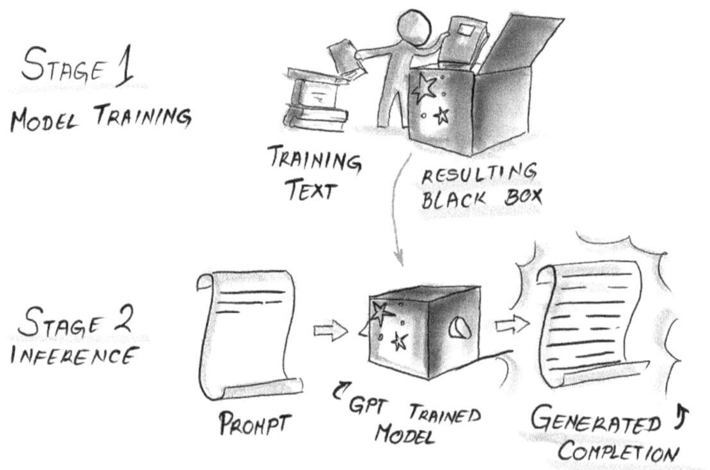


**Figure 1.12** The two stages of GPT-3. First, it gets trained, and then the sentence completion is inferred.

### Keeping the model knowledge up-to-date

Now that we understand how a real LLM works, we can better appreciate its inherent static knowledge limitation and envision how to solve it. It's important to distinguish between the static and the dynamic in an LLM. Model training occurs once, which is why GPT is called "pretrained." This static training means the model's knowledge is fixed up to a specific date, reflecting the latest documents in its training set. Consequently, when interacting with an LLM, you may see disclaimers stating that the model's knowledge is current only up to a certain date, referred to as the *knowledge cutoff* date. To incorporate recent or real-time knowledge into our GenAI applications, we must enable the model to retrieve up-to-date information from the web, a topic we'll explore further in this book.

Conversely, the inference process occurs in real time based on the user's prompt. Before calling the LLM, the prompt must be enriched with any additional or updated information, using specific prompting techniques, as you'll learn in this book. We need to equip the LLM with mechanisms, devices, and customizations to integrate its pretrained knowledge with whatever else it needs.

Another important concept is *fine-tuning*, which allows us to enhance or specialize a pretrained model (see figure 1.13). Fine-tuning involves taking a pretrained neural network, such as GPT-3, and conducting additional training with new, specific, or more relevant data. This process can yield multiple benefits: it can make the LLM more adept at specific tasks by tailoring it to particular sets of instructions, or it can integrate specialized knowledge from domains that were underrepresented in the initial training data, such as a specific branch of medicine. Additionally, fine-tuning can improve the model's ability to maintain dialogues with humans, as demonstrated by ChatGPT, which fine-tuned GPT-3 for better conversational capabilities.

This fine-tuning process follows a typical supervised learning approach. The model is provided with numerous prompts and the desired completions, so that it can learn from those given examples. The neural network adjusts its parameters to converge toward the desired completions through backpropagation-like learning passes, enhancing its performance and applicability.

**Figure 1.13** Enhancing a pretrained model through fine-tuning

## Summary

- GenAI programming is fundamentally different from traditional coding and requires us to handle nondeterministic outputs and natural-language inputs.
- Building real-world GenAI applications involves orchestrating multiple supporting components (e.g., memory management and updated knowledge retrieval) around the core LLM.
- Transformer models, such as GPT-3, generate text one token at a time by leveraging embeddings, huge neural networks, and massive pretraining.
- LLMs have fixed, pretrained knowledge and are stateless by default, but we can work around these limits with fine-tuning and additional architectural elements.

# Building your first GenAI app 2

## In this chapter

- using the low-code development platform Langflow to create GenAI applications
- creating your first working chatbot

In this chapter, you'll become acquainted with your travel companion in GenAI programming. Meet Langflow, a low-code development platform specifically designed for GenAI applications. By the end of this chapter, you'll have a fully functioning development environment and will have created your first simple but working chatbot, the unmissable Hello, World!

This is the first chapter of many where you'll need to be in front of a computer. We'll get our hands dirty, so make sure you have one handy as you get started.

## Wait a minute, low code?

I often see Python developers turn their noses up when they hear about low-code programming tools. As we unveil Langflow, it makes sense to dispel some myths and clarify why low-code programming is highly suitable for developing GenAI tools, regardless of your coding proficiency.

First, using low-code programming tools is the natural consequence of a long-term technology trend: the level of abstraction used for programming has been constantly increasing over time. If you had the opportunity (for some, it might have been the misfortune) to write code in the 1980s, you might have written it in assembly language. In assembly, every line of code had to deal with basic operations at a specific part of the processor.

Writing the code for multiplying numbers in assembly for the Intel 8086 processor implied several lines of code. Nowadays, writing a multiplication in a modern high-level language like Python is as simple as `c=a*b`. The level of abstraction will continue to grow, and low-code tools are a natural step in this journey. As abstraction increases, the programmer is increasingly freed from low-level concerns—like syntax, memory management, or framework intricacies—and can focus instead on solving the actual problem and delivering value. Soon, we might be able to program using only natural language, which is the ultimate level of abstraction from a human interface perspective.

**Figure 2.1** Old-school coding in the 1980s: developers battled memory addresses and registers line by line.

Using low-code programming for GenAI has many perks:

- *Prebuilt components*—As mentioned in chapter 1, building a GenAI application means assembling a workflow with multiple components, including the call to the LLM. In GenAI development environments such as Langflow, the components you typically need around the LLM are well implemented for us. We can focus on selecting, configuring, and connecting them without investing time in learning the technical details of a specific framework or language. This allows us to concentrate on designing the application flow, where we can create real value.
- *Graphical design*—Low-code environments are ideal for visually designing complex logic blueprints. When building a chat-based assistant, for instance, we can "visualize" our input message entering the left side of a flow and exiting on the

right end after all the necessary steps. These steps might include enriching the user's message with relevant context, formatting it into a more detailed prompt, or filtering certain inputs before passing them to the LLM. Or, when building agentic structures, as mentioned in chapter 1, visually organizing the different agents makes the process faster and more effective. Even if we had to write code, we would first sketch what we want to achieve and how the agent's interactions should work. Low-code programming makes this step smooth and natural.

- *Simplified debugging and collaboration*—Building a workflow in a low-code editor such as Langflow simplifies debugging (you can "see" what happens at each step) and improves collaboration among programmers. Minimal commenting is needed to enable others to reuse portions of your workflow.
- *Efficient prototyping*—Programming GenAI often involves frequent interactions with API calls and specialized libraries. Not much hardcore custom programming is required; most time is spent understanding how specific libraries work and making API calls. Prebuilt low-code nodes in environments such as Langflow dramatically speed up the design of quick prototypes.

All in all, low-code environments are a very good choice, especially for GenAI applications, where you need to combine, or, as we can say, *orchestrate*, specialized components.

One last note for programmers: although we'll build everything visually in Langflow, this book is meant to be equally useful if you prefer thinking in code. Starting with this chapter, you'll find a short *What if we coded it?* section at the end of each chapter. In it, we mirror the flow we just built with a Python script, step-by-step, so you can see the one-to-one correspondence between our low-code components and the equivalent code constructs.

**Figure 2.2** You don't necessarily need to tame Python to write code for GenAI applications.

At the time of writing, there are a few alternatives to Langflow, including Flowise, n8n, and KNIME. You can check them all out if they trigger your curiosity. Still, we're going to use Langflow in our path to discover GenAI because it has some unique points of difference:

- Langflow is open source and completely free to use. You can download and install it on your laptop or host it on your cloud infrastructure (as you'll see in chapter 8).
- Although you can use all the built-in components without writing any code, Langflow allows you to edit each component's Python code. This gives you limitless customization power in your development.
- You can instantly deploy your GenAI application using the built-in API. For example, you can easily publish a newly created chatbot on your website in minutes.

Although we'll use Langflow for the rest of the journey, the fundamental concepts, methods, and techniques you'll learn in this book are tool-agnostic, so they can be applied to whatever platform you need to use.

Let's get started with our new friend, Langflow.

## Intro to Langflow

Langflow is an open source, low-code tool that builds customized LLM orchestration flows and agentic structures. There are three ways to start using Langflow quickly:

- *Download the Langflow Desktop app for free.* Langflow offers native desktop applications for macOS and Windows users. You can download them from www.langflow.org. This is the easiest way to get started because dependencies are included and setup is simplified.
- *Use a public sandbox.* This lets you play with the tool on a public server without any authentication, but it doesn't guarantee privacy or the permanent storage of your data. You can reach a sandbox at https://tiny.cc/langflow-sandbox.
- *Install Langflow locally through Python.* You can run Langflow on your computer or a cloud-hosted virtual machine (we'll cover how to deploy Langflow on the cloud in chapter 8). This option gives you maximum flexibility and is best suited for production-level applications.

### Installing Langflow with Python

You can install the Langflow Python package on your machine in a few steps:

1. Download and install Python (versions 3.10 to 3.14) from www.python.org. Follow the website's instructions to complete the installation for your operating system (Windows, macOS, or Linux; they are all good).

2. Langflow uses uv, a fast Python package manager and runner that also helps manage virtual environments. If you don't have uv installed yet, install it once by running:

```
pip install uv
```

3. I recommend creating and activating a virtual environment first so the installation remains isolated from other Python projects. Do this by running:

```
uv venv
source .venv/bin/activate
```

4. Once the environment is active, install Langflow with this command:

```
uv pip install langflow
```

5. Start Langflow by typing this command:

```
uv run langflow run
```

6. Open your browser and go to `http://127.0.0.1:7860`.

You should be able to see the Langflow home page.

Some steps might change as new versions are deployed. For the latest instructions or troubleshooting tips, search "Install Langflow" and follow the instructions.

Let's now dive deep into Langflow and see what it can do. In the next few pages, we'll introduce many new Langflow keywords that we use often throughout the book. They're shown in *italics* at their first appearance to make sure you notice them.

## What you can do with Langflow

Langflow lets you design a GenAI application by constructing a *flow* that outlines how your application will function. Imagine this process as building with Lego bricks, where each brick, which Langflow calls a *component*, represents a specific functionality. These components can be linked via *connections*, allowing you to combine various functionalities to create a powerful solution tailored to your needs.

Langflow offers ready-made components for you to assemble your Lego construction. For example, if you want to build an AI chatbot that answers questions based on the knowledge described in several PDF documents, you'll need to piece several components together, as illustrated in figure 2.3:

- *Connecting to an LLM*—First, you need to implement a connection with your magic black box, the LLM. Langflow offers components to connect with your chosen LLM, whether it's OpenAI's ChatGPT, an LLM hosted on AWS Bedrock, or a local model running on your system. Drag and drop the appropriate component into your workspace and configure its parameters, and you're ready to link your LLM.
- *Managing memory*—To provide a better user experience, you might want your application to retain context from earlier parts of a conversation. Langflow offers

**Figure 2.3** Piecing bricks together to get a GenAI app

memory management components that implement various strategies to ensure continuity in user interactions.

- *Storing and processing PDFs*—To make your chatbot capable of answering questions based on external documents, Langflow provides components for multiformat file *ingestion* and creating a vector store. A *vector store* is a specialized database that stores *chunks*—smaller, processed pieces of text found in your PDF content—as *embeddings*. Connecting this to your LLM lets your application dynamically perform queries to retrieve relevant knowledge.

Many more components are available in Langflow for complex GenAI operations, such as implementing agentic structures or interacting with external applications. Langflow has you covered with components that can be mixed and matched to get what you need. Each component can be configured (by setting some *parameters* using your mouse and keyboard) and connected to one or more components to combine different functionalities for a common objective.

One of Langflow's standout features is its ability to test your GenAI application during development. This is done through the *Playground*, a testing environment where you can interact with your application and observe the results in real time. For example, while building your AI chatbot, you can toggle memory components on and off to compare how they affect the user experience. The low-code nature of Langflow lets you make quick adjustments, iterate rapidly, and debug efficiently, far surpassing the speed of traditional code-based development.

Lastly, Langflow allows you to "host" your GenAI application. For example, you can embed a chatbot built in Langflow into a webpage using a snippet of HTML code (more to come). You can also use Langflow to create an API endpoint that lets other applications *call* the flow you built and use it in the background. This is very handy when the LLM-based logic you've built is just one part of a more complex application that does more.

## API: Making applications speak with each other

An *application programming interface* (API) is a set of rules that enables different software applications to communicate. When an application makes an API call, it sends a request to a specific endpoint, essentially an internet address (URL) that the API exposes. This request often includes parameters that specify what data or action is needed. An API key is typically required to authenticate the request. After the API processes the call, it returns the necessary data or performs the requested action, allowing seamless interaction between different software systems. In Langflow, you can use nodes that "wrap" API calls to interact with external applications. You can also implement API endpoints to enable other applications to speak with yours.

**Figure 2.4** An API key is typically required to authenticate the request.

Langflow's ability to graphically design applications, test them quickly, iterate, and deploy, makes it an amazing companion in our quest to learn GenAI programming. Let's examine Langflow's user interface (UI) to understand its components.

## Navigating through Langflow without getting lost

Langflow is a web application accessible through any modern browser (unless you're using the desktop version, which offers a similar interface). Upon entering it—and logging in if necessary—you'll be greeted by the home page, which is shown in figure 2.5 (note that the precise look and feel may vary slightly in newer versions). Here's a quick guide to help you navigate the interface when you encounter it for the first time.

At first, the home page will appear empty, but you can imagine that your new flows will show up in the *central panel* (1) and can be nicely organized within *projects*: they are like folders, which are listed on the left side of the screen (2). If you click on the user icon in the top-right corner (3), a drop-down menu will appear, allowing you to access Settings (4) to customize your experience and manage credentials.

To open your first flow, click + New Flow (5) to begin building your first project.

**Figure 2.5** The Langflow home page.

When you click New Flow, a wizard pops up (you can get an idea of what it looks like in figure 2.6), offering various templates to choose from if you don't want to start your flow from scratch.

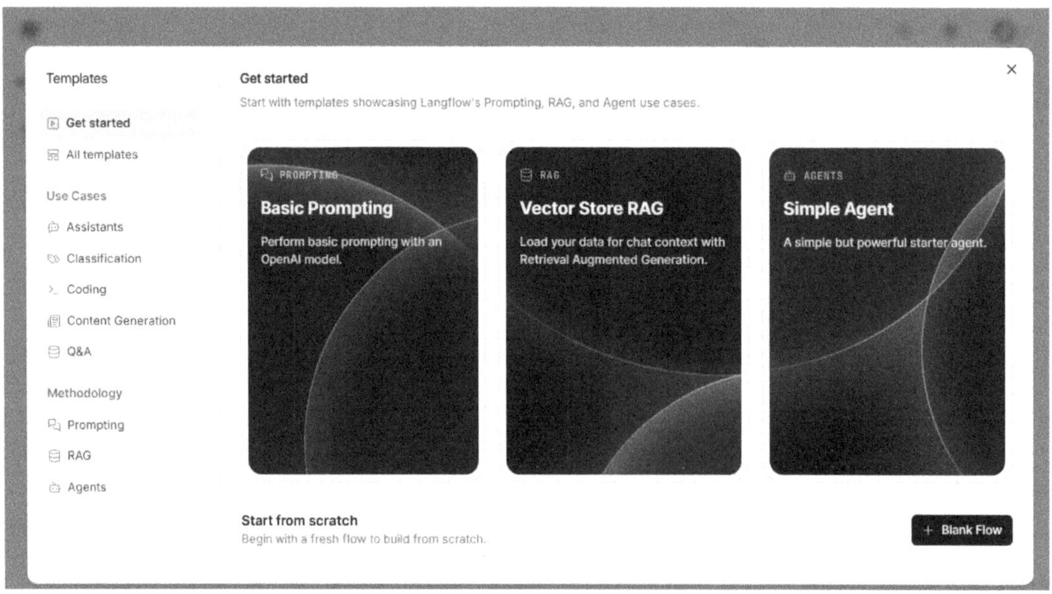


**Figure 2.6** Templates to get started in Langflow

These templates are grouped by use cases, such as these:

- *Basic prompting*—For simple LLM interactions.
- *Vector store RAG*—For retrieval-augmented generation (RAG) applications. We'll build this in chapter 4.
- *Simple agent*—For creating agentic structures. We'll get started with agents in chapter 5.

Alternatively, you can start from scratch with a blank flow and design your project step-by-step. We'll do this shortly.

For now, close this window so you can go back to the main page and open the Settings page to familiarize yourself with it.

The Settings page, shown in figure 2.7, allows you to

- Change your profile picture by selecting from a variety of icons. (1)
- Manage global variables, which you can reuse across all your flows. For example, you can set API keys as global variables to connect your flows with external applications. (2)

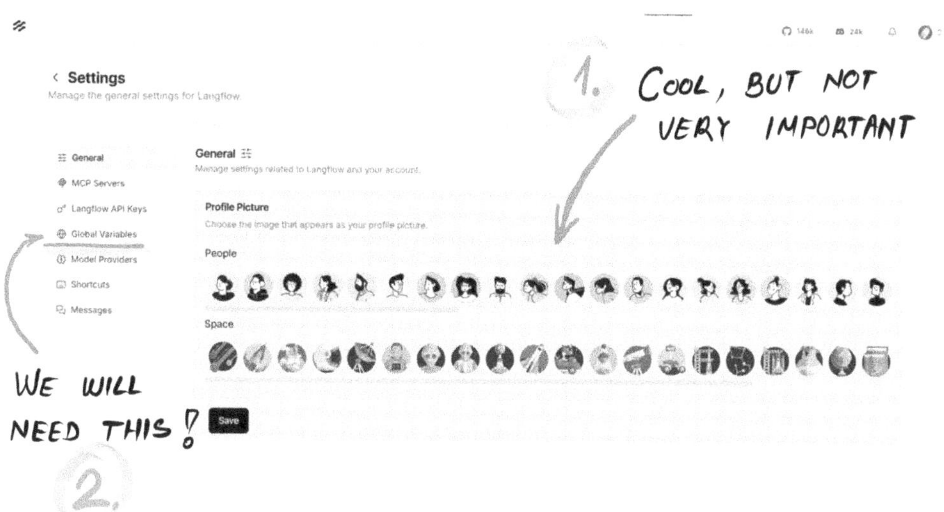


**Figure 2.7** The Settings menu in Langflow

Going through the folders available on the Langflow main screen gives us an idea of all the cool things we can build with it. I hope you're excited to learn how to use them all during our journey ahead.

Let's discover Langflow's other functionalities by getting our hands dirty. We'll learn by doing as we build our first flow from scratch!

# Hello, World! Our pirate chatbot

Let's imagine we want to build a simple chatbot that will interact with us in a rather peculiar way: speaking in Pirate English. Besides the somewhat eccentric objective, our pirate-sounding chatbot will be an opportunity to learn how to deal with several recurring steps in every GenAI application we build in this book, such as implementing and connecting nodes, creating an API key, and so on.

**Figure 2.8** A pirate virtual assistant—how useful

First, let's create a blank chat flow. From the home page, click + New Flow > + Blank Flow to start from scratch. Once you do that, the white canvas will appear, which is encouraging.

## Using the flow editor

The flow editor is the workspace to design and orchestrate your GenAI applications in Langflow. As you can see in figure 2.9, this editor window gives you all you need to make the magic happen.

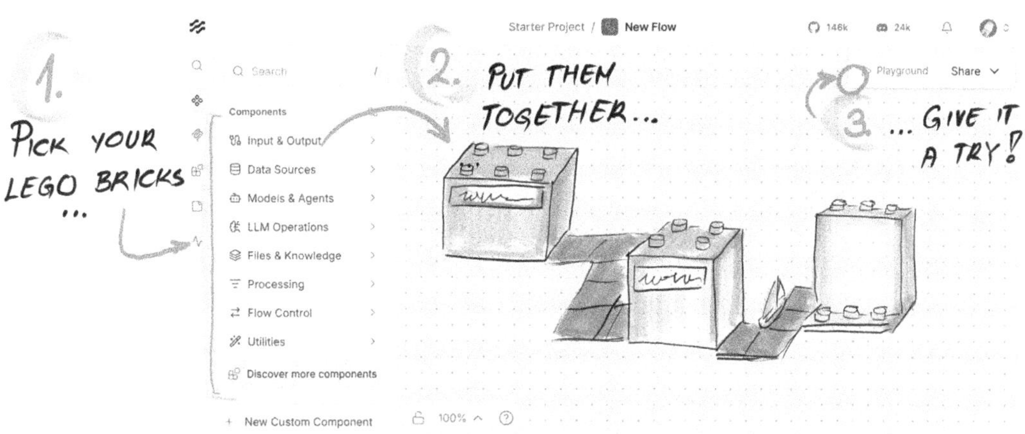


**Figure 2.9** The flow editor in Langflow

You can pick your components on the left (1). They're nicely organized into sections, which we'll explore later, so you know where to find the Lego brick you need. Then, you can mix and match the components on the central canvas (2), connecting them as you please to combine their functionality. Notice that you have a few icons in the upper right (3). The Playground lets you try what you've built. For instance, you can start a conversation with the assistant you've built. The other icons let you share your creation with others and embed it on your website or in a broader application through the API mechanism. This page lets you play with your construction and test as you go—sweet!

Let's explore the components on the left and see what we can find across these sections.

## Exploring Langflow components

Let's see what bricks we have available in this repository by exploring the sections. You can see what's inside a section by clicking its header:

- *Input & Output, Data Sources, and Files & Knowledge*—Here are the components that connect your application with the real world. It's not hard to imagine that a chatbot flow will start with a chat input and end with a chat output. Everything between these two components decides how the chatflow should respond to a given user input. The data section includes components that let your flow use data from outside, such as an API, a saved file, or a web page at a given URL. The Files & Knowledge section includes components to read, write, and structure knowledge sources used by the flow.
- *Models & Agents*—This is where our magic black box lies! These components let us seamlessly connect with the most popular LLMs, send them text, get a response, and forward it in our flow.

- *Processing*—This section lets you transform text and data, such as splitting and parsing snippets of text and combining them to craft the right prompts that will ultimately be sent to the LLMs. The components in this section give us the flexibility we need for the flow to do exactly what we want it to do.
- *Flow Control and Utilities*—These are useful components that let us give superpowers to our virtual assistants through execution logic and supporting functions. This is where you can implement conditions and loops or provide extra custom functionality that LLMs can't do by themselves, such as tools to make calculations or run custom code.
- *Discover More Components*—This area lets you explore collections of components that can be added to Langflow from external libraries or third-party integrations. These components extend Langflow beyond its built-in capabilities, for example, by adding components for sending emails (such as through Gmail), performing web searches, or interacting with external services. We'll use some of these components later in the book.

By quickly reviewing these component sections, we start getting excited, anticipating the many things we can build together with so many colorful Lego bricks at our fingertips!

Enough wandering around: let's pick the components we need for our pirate friend.

## A pirate's blueprint

As with many projects in life, planning what to do before doing it gives us an advantage. Now that we have an idea of what Langflow is capable of, let's spend a few minutes envisioning our first product.

We want to build a chatbot, or virtual assistant, that answers questions using a specific language: Pirate English. We can assume that our magic black box, the LLM, has learned many languages as part of its extensive pretraining phase. The LLM will have been exposed to movie scripts and other fiction works with pirates involved and will have read web pages of pirate aficionados who have codified a Pirate English dictionary and described it formally (if you don't believe this, search for "pirate words and phrases" and be amazed).

So, the LLM can speak Pirate English if we ask. What we need to do then is "tweak" the LLM's default behavior by adding a constant guideline, such as "use Pirate English in your responses."

This is similar to what we tried to do in chapter 1 when we added extra instructions to the LLM calls to obtain some nondefault behavior from the LLM. We could add a constant custom command (some extra text) each time we send the LLM a message to remind it to speak in Pirate English. Ideally, we'd get something like this:

**INPUT**
```
How are you doing?
System message: Always reply in Pirate English.
```

**OUTPUT**
```
I be feelin' as fine as a ship sailin' on a calm sea! How be ye farin'
on this fine day?
```

So, we need to add a `system message` like the one in the previous example to the component calling the LLM. When we looked at components, we noticed one called "OpenAI"; maybe we can use that one to make the LLM calls. Then, we connect our chat inputs and outputs to the LLM so that everything the user writes gets forwarded to the LLM, with the only tweak being the system message, which "primes" the AI behavior. Then, whatever the LLM comes back with is sent back to the user. In our first tour of the components, we saw that the Chat Input and Chat Output components can do just that: route messages in and out of our flow.

Ultimately, we need to "wire" those three components as figure 2.10 shows.

**Figure 2.10** The blueprint of our pirate chatbot

That's not a bad sketch design for our first chatbot flow! By connecting just three components, we get what we need. The original message, as captured in the Playground chat window, gets sent to the LLM with a custom system message. The magic black box will output something (hopefully piratey enough), and this output is displayed back to the user in the Playground window.

### Building our first flow

Enough about planning, let's make this happen.

Open the Input & Output section of the Components panel on the left by clicking on it. Drag and drop the Chat Input component onto the flow editor, as shown in figure 2.11. Once dropped, you'll see your first component right in the middle of the canvas.

> **Editing a component**
>
> If you want to change the title or description of the component (as a way to "document" what's happening in your flow), double-click it. If you click a component and then click the Code button that appears on top, you can even edit the code behind each individual component. We don't need any of this now, but it's helpful to know that you can deeply customize any component in Langflow with the click of a button.

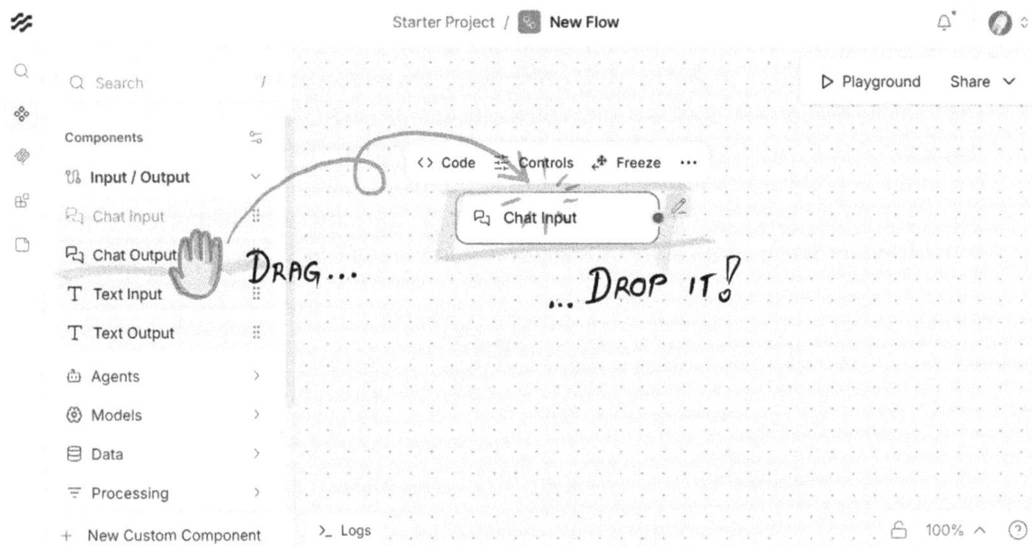


**Figure 2.11** Drag and drop a component to build with it.

Let's now implement the second component, the smart, magic LLM! Use the search box to look for a component called "OpenAI". Then, drag and drop it onto the canvas, placing it to the right of the Chat Input.

Notice that we could have also used the generic component called Language Model, which you can find within the Models & Agents section on the left. Language Model lets you choose among various providers, such as OpenAI, Anthropic, and Google.

Once implemented on the canvas, we noticed a few interesting features that are recurrent in most components, as you can see in figure 2.12.

Notice that it has an icon, OpenAI as the title at the top, and a description that reads "Generates text using OpenAI LLMs." This is encouraging because it's exactly what we wanted it to do.

The colorful dots on the components' left and right sides are their *ports*. They serve as "connectors" with other components. You have input ports on the left (they "bring in" data or text from previous components in the flow) and output ports on the right (they "send" data or text to the following components in the flow). The color tells us about the type of data flowing through that connector. Most ports are indigo blue and refer to strings of text or messages. Some other ports are red, indicating that they carry data such as numeric tables, or yellow, which carry data such as embeddings.

You have input controls within each component, such as text boxes and radio buttons, that let you adjust component parameters to configure their behavior as needed. For instance, in the OpenAI component, you can customize the System Message or specify the API Key required for the LLM call.

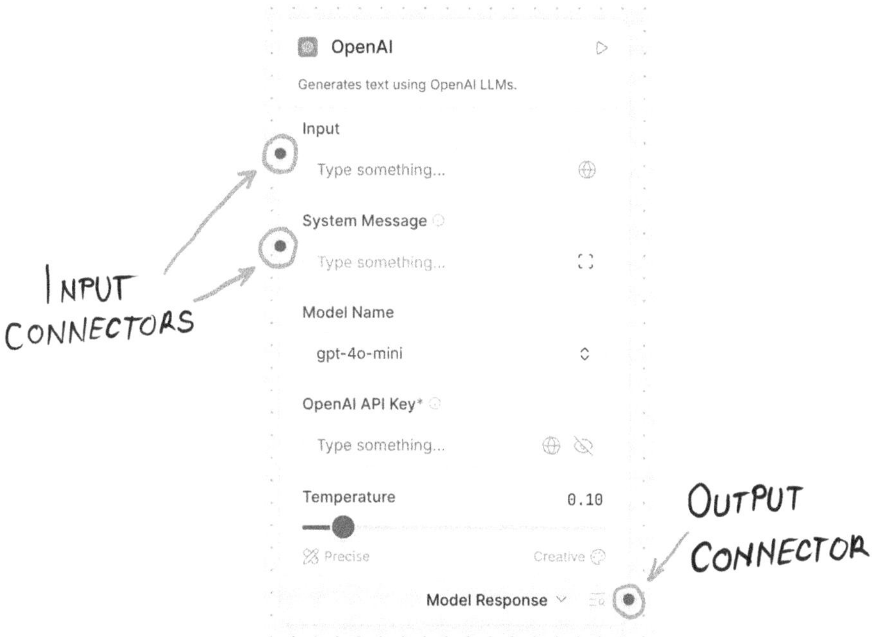


**Figure 2.12** The OpenAI Model component: our gateway to the magic black box

You'll notice that some parameters are linked to an input port. This means that the values of those parameters can be set manually (by entering some text in the control box) or controlled by an external component through a variable.

Now that we've implemented our first two components, we can link them together. We want the message from the Chat Input to be used as input for the LLM call. To do so, click the output port of the Chat Input component (named Message) and drag it to the input port of the OpenAI component (the first port). When you release the mouse button, you'll see a connection linking the first two components. Whatever is written in the Playground chatbot will be forwarded smoothly to the OpenAI component as an input message.

Let's go back to the second component because we need to manually configure a parameter of utmost importance for our pirate assistant to work. We want to set the custom system message for the LLM call to customize all of its responses. To do so, click the System Message textbox in the OpenAI component and type something like "`Always reply in Pirate English.`"

Another key parameter to set is the OpenAI API Key. To invoke the LLM, the component needs to establish a connection with the OpenAI servers by means of an API call. Langflow makes this step simple for us. The OpenAI component works out the intricacies of the API connection under the hood. It knows the protocol required for making the call and receiving the response from OpenAI. The only configuration the node needs from us is the credentials to connect with OpenAI. To obtain those credentials, you must create an account with OpenAI, generate an API key, and ensure that your account has enough credit to use.

## LLM API costs and how to avoid them

Invoking a proprietary LLM such as OpenAI GPT or Google Gemini has some related costs. These costs are minimal for the applications we'll build throughout the book. Some providers offer free credit in some countries. If this isn't an option for you, you'll have to do the minimum credit top-up (USD $5, in most cases) to get started. Alternatively, you can run an open source LLM locally using open source tools like Ollama. Check out the Ollama component to try this cost-free approach. Because performance is generally lower, we'll use proprietary LLMs throughout the exercises in the book, but you know there is an alternative if you don't want to spend the extra pennies.

If you don't have an OpenAI key yet, you can create one by going to the API Keys section of your Personal dashboard (available at https://platform.openai.com/api-keys; you need to sign up for an OpenAI Platform account if you don't have one yet) and clicking Create New Secret Key, as shown in figure 2.13.

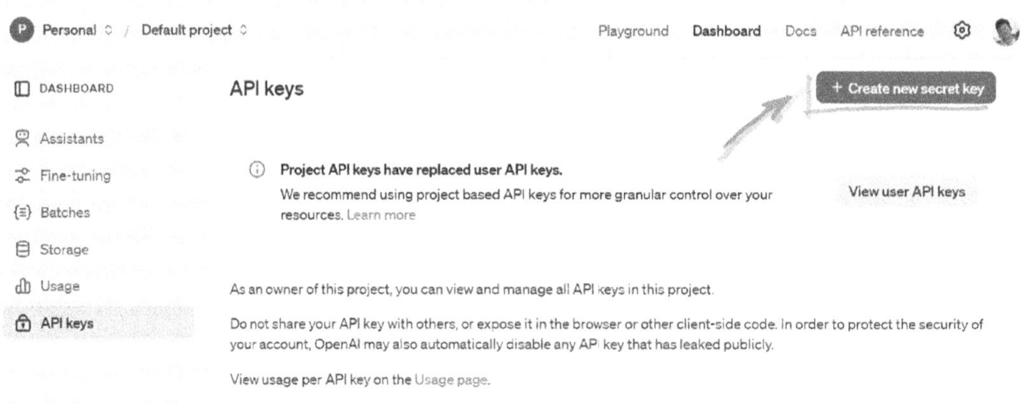


**Figure 2.13** This is how you generate an API secret key to call OpenAI LLMs.

When prompted, you can give your new secret key a name, as shown in figure 2.14. This is handy because it helps you track the costs related to its usage. If your application will rely on OpenAI keys, you can estimate your costs once the users grow by checking the costs linked with a specific key.

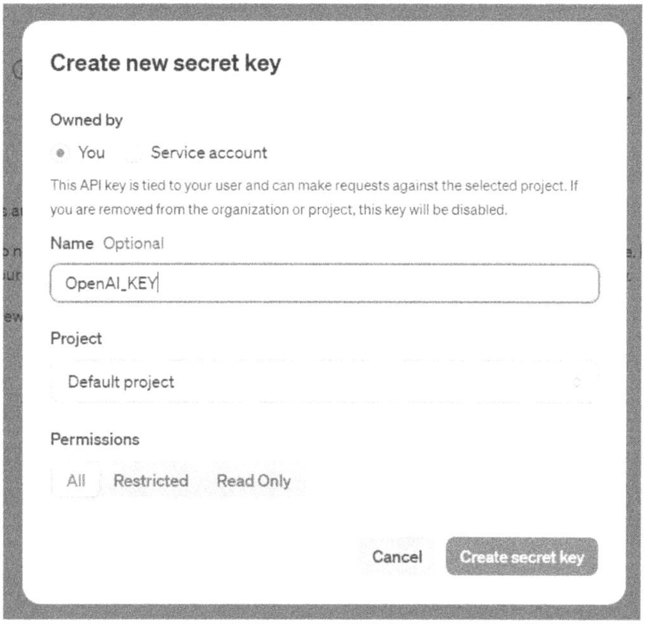


**Figure 2.14** You can give a name to your OpenAI secret key.

As the next step, you need to copy the newly created key (paste it somewhere safe so you can reuse it if needed) and enter it in Langflow. You should set this key as a Langflow global variable so that you can reuse it across multiple flows without entering it again. To do so, click the globe icon in the OpenAI API Key parameter of the OpenAI component (refer to figure 2.12), and then click Add New Variable. The Create Variable window, shown in figure 2.15, lets you define the variable's name (you can enter something like "OpenAI Key") and paste your key in the Value box. You can select whether the variable is generic or a credential by using the Type dropdown menu. Credentials are encrypted by Langflow, so as a general security best practice, always store your API keys as credentials. Just click Save Variable when you're done, and you'll be good to go.

All global variables can be managed (updated, deleted, or displayed, if they haven't been encrypted) by using the Global Variables menu in Settings. Remember, you can always access Settings by clicking the user icon in the top-right corner of any screen in Langflow.

For now, we can leave all the other settings (the Model Name and the Temperature) at their default values and move to the final part of our flow: the chat output.

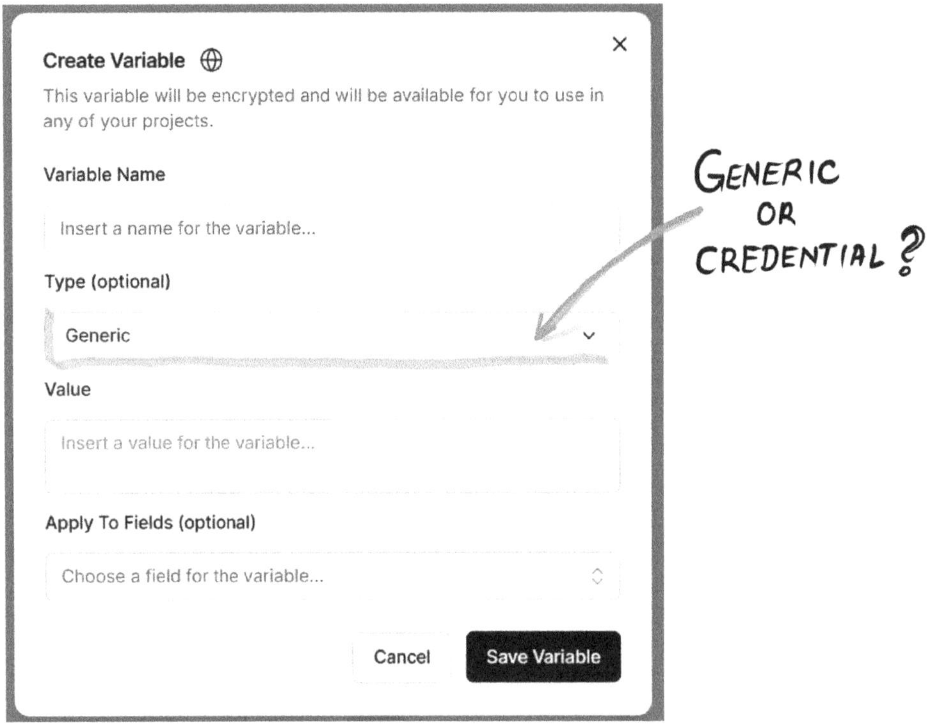


**Figure 2.15** You can save all of your keys as global variables and reuse them as needed.

## Managing model providers centrally

Langflow lets you manage model provider settings centrally across your instance. As an alternative to the OpenAI component, use the generic Language Model component instead. In that case, first choose the provider from the Language Model dropdown. The first time using a provider, click Manage Model Providers, select the one you want (such as OpenAI), enter the API key, and save. This way, the provider configuration can be reused across flows and components instead of managed separately inside each individual LLM component. This is conceptually equivalent to storing the key as a global credential variable in Langflow. For simplicity and consistency throughout this book, we'll usually use provider-specific components, but you can use the generic Language Model component instead if you prefer. You can always update provider-specific keys later through Settings > Model Providers.

Find the Chat Output component within the output section of the panel on the left. Drag and drop it somewhere east of the OpenAI component. Here, you don't need to configure anything. To send the LLM output back to the user Playground chat window, create a connection between the first output port of the OpenAI component (called "Text") and the sole input port of the Chat Output component.

That's it! With three components and a couple of connections across them, we arranged our first flow, shown in all its beauty in figure 2.16.

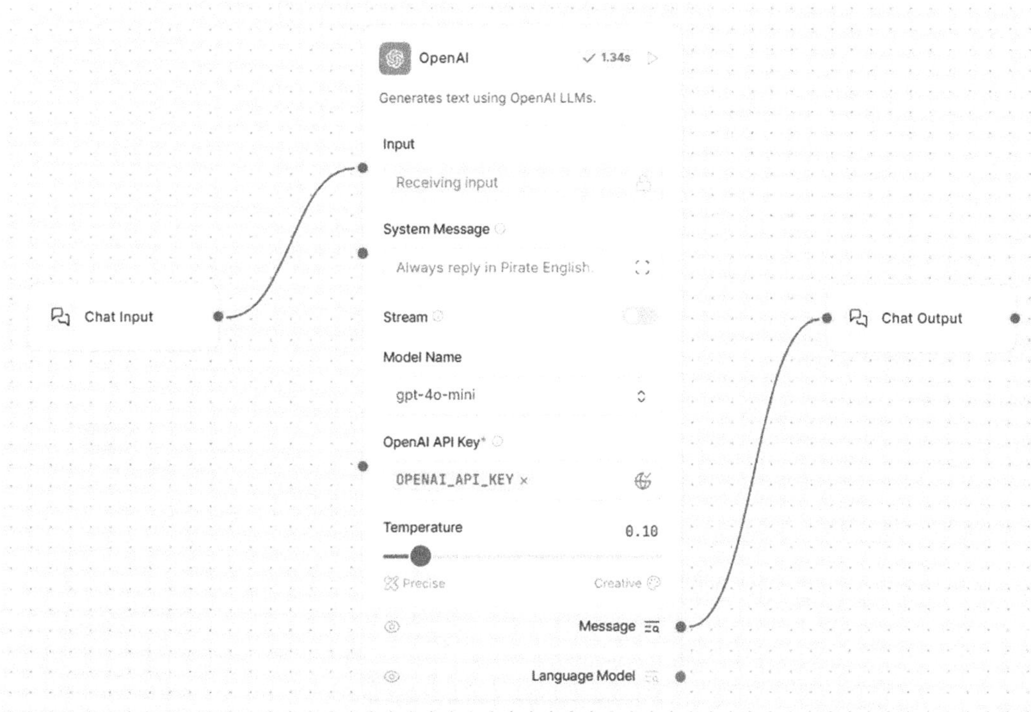


**Figure 2.16** Our first Langflow creation is ready to chitchat.

Let's save and give our flow a name. Click its current (untitled) name in bold at the top, and then click Flow Settings. In this window, you can edit its name (how about "Hello, World!" or "Ahoy, Matey!" as a title) and description, and then save it by clicking the Save button at the bottom. Then, click the Playground icon in the top right and give it a try.

Hopefully, you now feel the thrill of chatting with an assistant you generated yourself. Of course, we're now entering the world of probabilistic models, whose output is influenceable but is inherently unpredictable. Your answers will differ from those I received, which are shown in figure 2.17. This is normal and part of the game. LLMs might answer differently even when given the same input.

The answers coming back from the AI after our initial "Hello, World!" greeting are a consequence of the configuration we put in the LLM component, more precisely, the System Message. We told it to speak with pirate English and its usage of *Ahoy!* and *Arrr!* seems to be in line with what we asked. The assistant also identifies itself as AI, which is what we expected.

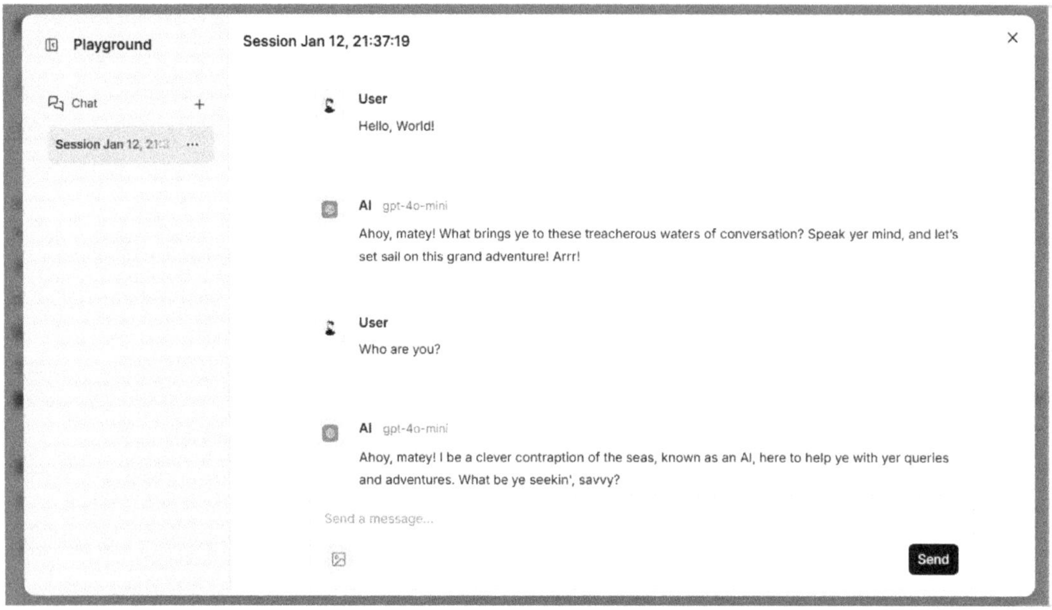


**Figure 2.17** A piratey chat, generated by our first creation in Langflow

Notice that our AI counterpart seems a bit forgetful. In this specific example, repeating the "Ahoy, matey!" greeting at the beginning of each sentence is a sign that our virtual assistant isn't equipped with any memory! And, indeed, we haven't added a memory mechanism. But hey, this is our very first creation in Langflow. Let's leave something for the next steps of our journey, shall we?

Feel free to play around with your new pirate assistant. Try changing the System Message from the OpenAI component and see how its behavior changes.

## What if we coded it?

Before closing this chapter, it's helpful to go back to its beginning, when we discussed the perks of using a low-code environment.

Everything we built in this chapter could've been implemented using good old-fashioned lines of code. Up to this point, we've deliberately stayed inside Langflow, using a visual, low-code approach to build our very first GenAI application. This was intentional: Langflow is designed to help you reason in terms of building blocks and data flowing between them, without worrying about syntax or code.

Under the hood, however, Langflow is not doing anything magical. It is built on top of *LangChain*, a Python framework that provides abstractions for working with language models, prompts, messages, tools, and chains of operations. Every box you placed on the canvas in this chapter—Chat Input, the OpenAI model, and Chat Output—maps very naturally to LangChain concepts.

LangChain revolves around the idea of *chains*: ordered sequences of steps that take some input, transform it, and produce an output. Graphically, this is almost identical to how you think about a Langflow flow. The main difference is that, in Langflow, you draw the chain; in Python, you write it. Conceptually, though, you're doing the same thing.

To make this explicit, the following script mirrors the Hello World pirate chatbot we've built in Langflow, but implements it directly in Python using LangChain. The goal here isn't to replace Langflow, but to help you see the one-to-one correspondence between the visual tutorial and its code-based equivalent, which is especially useful if you later want to integrate your prototype into a larger Python application.

If you don't code in Python, feel free to skip this section entirely. Nothing else in the book depends on it. If you do code, read it as a translation exercise: this Langflow flow, expressed as Python.

You'll find this and all other chapters' scripts readily available in a GitHub repository (https://github.com/laibniz/GrokkingAIapplications/), which also includes all sample files and documents used in the book. In the repository, you'll find this chapter's script, named `CH2-HelloWorld.py`.

```
"""
Install dependencies once:

    pip install langchain-openai langchain-core python-dotenv

Before running the script, make sure your OpenAI API key is available.
You can either:
- add it to a local `.env` file as OPENAI_API_KEY=...
- or paste it inline below (not recommended for real projects)
"""

import os
from dotenv import load_dotenv
from langchain_openai import ChatOpenAI
from langchain_core.messages import SystemMessage, HumanMessage
```

LangChain's ChatOpenAI is the Python analog to Langflow's OpenAI component.

System/Human message objects reproduce the prompt nodes from the canvas.

```
load_dotenv()
# os.environ["OPENAI_API_KEY"] = "REPLACE_WITH_YOUR_KEY"
```

`load_dotenv` reads the local .env so you don't copy keys into code.

Pull the OpenAI key once the environment is hydrated.

```
api_key = os.getenv("OPENAI_API_KEY")
if not api_key:
    raise RuntimeError("Set OPENAI_API_KEY before running this script.")
```

Fail fast if the key is missing, mirroring Langflow's settings check.

Instantiate GPT-4o mini with the chapter's pirate-chat parameters.

```
llm = ChatOpenAI(model="gpt-4o-mini", temperature=0.1)
system_msg = SystemMessage(content="You only answer in Pirate English.")
```

Keep the pirate persona text as a reusable system prompt.

Wrap the chat loop for reuse in tests or other scripts.

```
def chat_loop() -> None:
    """Replicates the Langflow chat node by streaming prompts from stdin."""

    try:
        while True:
            user_input = input("User: ")
            response = llm.invoke([system_msg, HumanMessage(content=user_input)])
            print("AI:", response.content)
    except KeyboardInterrupt:
        print("\nGoodbye, matey!")


if __name__ == "__main__":
    chat_loop()
```

Invoke the LLM with the ordered system + user messages.

Mirror Langflow's chat UI by streaming the assistant reply to stdout.

Catch CTRL-C so the terminal chat ends cleanly.

Standard entrypoint guard so imports stay side-effect free.

Start the chat loop when running the file directly.

As you can see from the annotations, there's a 1:1 equivalence between the design steps we took during the chatbot's creation (setting up the OpenAI key, writing a custom system message, and so on) and the code we would have written in Python. This highlights how the fundamental logic remains consistent, whether we're working in a traditional coding environment or a low-code platform.

When dealing with more complex GenAI features, such as incorporating multiple agents, advanced memory structures, or custom API integrations, the Python code can quickly become dense and harder to follow. It requires careful attention to detail and a deep understanding of the codebase and the underlying frameworks. Debugging in such scenarios often involves tracing through extensive logs, dealing with potential edge cases, and ensuring that each component interacts as expected.

On the other hand, although the Langflow visual design might also grow more intricate as we add complexity, its graphical nature provides a significant advantage. The ability to visually map out and connect components in a drag-and-drop interface makes the logic easier to follow. It reduces the cognitive load associated with understanding the data flow and decisions within the system. This visual approach becomes especially powerful when debugging; you can visually trace the flow, see where things might be going wrong, and adjust the setup without delving into lines of code.

This is the core reason this book on GenAI programming went "low-code": the ambition is to decouple the complexity of writing code from the complexity of building superior GenAI apps using powerful but difficult-to-handle probabilistic models. In the rest of the book, we'll learn the art and science of this strange animal called GenAI. We'll focus on the creative and strategic aspects of building GenAI applications that do the job. We'll leave everything else outside.

At the end of the day, the equivalence between the Langflow project and the corresponding Python code will always be there (and you can read the corresponding code behind each component, as we said earlier). If you know how to code in Python and prefer building your GenAI apps that way, you should absolutely do so. Just enjoy the rapid prototyping environment Langflow offers to sketch out your GenAI creation in style. But if you'd rather avoid the complexity of code-based programming and the technical intricacies of specialist libraries, you can simply rely on Langflow, and this book will guide you every step of the way.

**Figure 2.18** Meet Langflow, the wizard of GenAI apps.

# Summary

- Low-code development is the next step in programming abstraction, making GenAI tools more accessible and faster to prototype.
- In Langflow, a flow is built by connecting premade, Lego-like components, each of which handles a specific task, from user input to LLM output.
- Each component has input and output ports that let you chain it with other components, and you can customize its behavior by tweaking its parameters.
- Langflow offers a wide range of prebuilt components, connecting to popular LLMs, vector stores, embeddings, and agent tools, so you can build GenAI apps with minimal coding overhead.
- System messages (such as "Always reply in Pirate English") shape how your LLM responds, guiding the style or function of its output.

# Writing the right prompt | 3

## In this chapter

- recognizing the elements that make a prompt effective
- crafting the right prompt based on your specific needs
- building and customizing prompt templates in Langflow

Writing the right prompt is the single most important skill you need to develop a GenAI application successfully. The "art and science" that lets you do that is called *prompt engineering*.

It's *science* because we understand the theory behind what makes a prompt clear or ineffective, and we use proven frameworks to guide us. It's *art* because there are multiple ways to get the job done. Natural language is intricate, so you must stay creative, experiment, test, and be open to trying something new. I can tell you that prompt engineering is one of the most engaging and inherently "human" parts of GenAI. I hope you enjoy this chapter, which is all about the art and science behind the right prompts.

## What makes a good prompt?

Technically, a prompt is the input received by a large language model (LLM) that generates the corresponding output. Practically, well, the prompt is the foundation of *everything* we build in GenAI.

We called the LLM a magic black box, but it's not actually magical. Sadly, it can't read your mind as a user. One rookie mistake that people experimenting with GenAI often make is sending the most generic prompt, hoping the LLM will be smart enough to amaze them with the output. Sure, you might be lucky and get a *decent* response. But as GenAI users today, we have high expectations: we don't aim for just a *good enough* answer; we want an *exceptional* one. To get there, we need to master the art of "asking the right questions." The prompt is literally the only thing we share with the LLM, so everything depends on it. We need to be good at writing the right prompt—as simple as that.

### The right length

Size matters in prompt engineering. If the prompt is extremely concise, chances are that the LLM won't have enough context to give a useful output. It will be easier for the LLM to *hallucinate* and go off on a tangent in directions that we don't want it to.

> **What are hallucinations?**
>
> In GenAI, hallucinations occur when an LLM generates incorrect or nonsensical information because of its probabilistic nature, often triggered by insufficient context or vague prompts. You can minimize these hallucinations with well-crafted prompts, verification layers, or integrated external checks, but they remain an inherent limitation of LLMs.

On the other hand, if we use a very long prompt full of useless details, we increase the likelihood of our command being misinterpreted. Imagine explaining a task to a new colleague at work: if you're too vague, they might deliver something coarse or misaligned with your expectations. If you overwhelm them with excessive information, they'll struggle to identify what's truly important. The same principle applies to LLMs: provide what's necessary, no more, no less.

**Figure 3.1** Like pirates, GenAI can also suffer from hallucinations.

Let's also not forget that we have technical limitations regarding how long our prompts can be. As we discovered in chapter 1, LLMs have a finite context window, a maximum number of tokens they can process simultaneously. Although modern models offer increasingly longer context windows, research shows that excessively long prompts degrade response quality beyond a certain length.

So, now we know that size matters in prompt engineering, and finding the right length is essential to crafting effective prompts.

## The right structure

Good prompts are also structurally clear. Different parts of a prompt should be easy to distinguish. For example, if you're asking the LLM to translate text, the prompt should specify the target language and present the text to be translated in an easily recognizable format.

When chatting with a close friend, you might use shorthand or lingo that relies on shared understanding. With an LLM, that approach won't work. Remember what we discussed in chapter 1: LLMs are *stateless*, resetting with each interaction. You must provide all the necessary context, history, and background, and do so in a way the model can easily parse. Structured prompts are essential for this.

## The standard template

Although prompt engineering isn't pure science, we can rely on a general template that shows what elements a good prompt should have. Many good models have been shared, and many have some merit. But if we boil them down to the most essential elements, we can identify four, which form the following prompt *standard template*:

**INPUT**
```
Acting as [ROLE], complete
this [TASK] so that
[FEATURES], as in [EXAMPLES].
```

This is simple, but it makes so much sense! We have four structural elements: [ROLE], [TASK], [FEATURES], and [EXAMPLES]. When we combine them, we maximize our chances of being clear.

Let's review each one and use examples to try this ourselves with an LLM of our liking.

**Figure 3.2** The standard prompt template in action—for a thoughtful daughter

### Role

We'll get better responses if we explain to the LLM the human role it should impersonate when responding.

This sounds bizarre initially, but it has a clear rationale. LLMs are exposed to many human-written texts during pretraining, such as webpages, articles, and more. Many of these documents clarify the author or context in which they were written. If we specify in our prompt that we want an answer that an experienced marketing manager would give, we're more likely to receive a response reflecting the critical thinking and expertise of a seasoned professional.

This also applies if we clarify the role of the intended audience rather than the author. For example, if we ask an LLM to explain an atom as if speaking to a five-year-old, we'd get a simplified description with child-friendly analogies. This is because the LLM, having read books and stories for children during pretraining, recognizes patterns that suit young audiences.

You can get very creative in specifying a possible role for your LLM. For example, consider these:

- A marketer
- A 35-year-old female consumer
- An experienced data scientist
- A journalist
- A serial entrepreneur
- A bestselling fiction author
- A nonnative English speaker

Defining the role in a prompt is crucial because it shapes the tone, expertise, and depth of the response based on the LLM's training. To find the right role to assign, think carefully about your ideal assistant for that task. Who would you trust most to handle the task you have in mind? Who would you hire for that? Aim high if need be; the cost doesn't change.

### Task

If we tell the LLM precisely what to do, it's more likely to achieve the desired result.

Be crystal clear and assertive in your prompts, using active verbs that specify what the LLM should do (e.g., "make a summary" or "generate an email") rather than passively describing the expected result (e.g., "a summary" or "an email").

Be as specific as you can in the description of your task. Here are some examples of task descriptions:

- Write an email.
- Generate a list based on "X."
- Build a table.

- Write a video script.
- Make a summary of "X."
- Write a blog post.
- Write the documentation for "X" code.
- Generate 10 possible names.

Notice that sometimes a task needs to be applied to an object. For instance, if you need an email summary, the text of the email will have to be included with the prompt. In this case, make sure that the object to which your task needs to be applied is identifiable. You can use explicit delimiters as we did in the examples by putting quotation marks around the X object (`"X"`), or you can use explicit variables like `translate TEXT into Italian. TEXT=Hi there`. If you use delimiters, they need to be used only as delimiters. So, if your object is a piece of code that might contain quotation marks, you can't use single quotation marks as delimiters; you might want to use double quotation marks as an alternative in this case.

### Features

If we list the expected features of your desired outcome, we'll get more accurate responses.

Don't make assumptions about what the output should be. Imagine what it should look like in terms of format, length, content, and any other characteristics, and clearly state those features in your prompt. Don't be shy: the stricter you are in your prompt, the better your responses will get. The LLM likes to receive assertive and precise directions, so keep it happy and be firm.

If you don't, the LLM will make assumptions about the output, leaving it freer to use broader paths within the underlying neural networks, which may result in off-track answers or, worse, hallucinations.

In this part of the prompt, you may also explain the language style the LLM should follow or any other attributes related to the language to use. Because of how they're built, LLMs are good at translating or adapting text to specific styles, so take advantage of this feature and state the style of the output.

Here are some examples of features in prompts:

- It is one page long.
- Includes approximately 300 characters.
- It has two columns: "X" and "Y."
- Makes the following points: "X."
- Is in English.
- Uses CSV format.
- It is authoritative and friendly in style.

- Focuses on practical examples.
- Nontechnical readers can understand it.
- Your goal is to maximize "X."

Some elements of tone and language level can also result from the role you ask the LLM to impersonate or the audience you want to target. So there might be some overlap with the Role section, and that's OK. In fact, if a feature is very important to follow, stating it twice in different terms won't hurt. Some LLM experts call this technique *double-down*, which means stressing essential elements of the prompt multiple times in the same prompt. We'll come back to this point later.

#### Examples

Sharing specific examples of the output we want will increase our chances of getting a useful answer.

LLMs are good at reusing patterns. Some have called them (although improperly, in my opinion) stochastic parrots. Because of how they function, LLMs have the innate ability to mimic observed patterns. So, after explaining what we want, let's share one or a few examples or cue them in the direction we want them to take. For instance:

- "A good title would be something like 'X'."
- "The format should look like: [NAME]: [DESCRIPTION]."
- "We initially thought we'd do 'X' and 'Y' but need better alternatives."
- "If the input is 'X', a good output would be 'Y' while a bad one would be 'Z'"

When we provide an example, the LLM learns what type of answer is most appropriate. Prompting techniques that involve providing examples are commonly referred to as *shot learning*. Instead of training the neural network to fine-tune its behavior, we can quickly provide examples (or "shots") of what we need so the LLM knows what to emulate.

More specifically, we can recognize the following cases:

- *Zero-shot prompting*—You don't provide any examples; you just explain the task and the expected features. This is the simplest approach, but often far from the best.

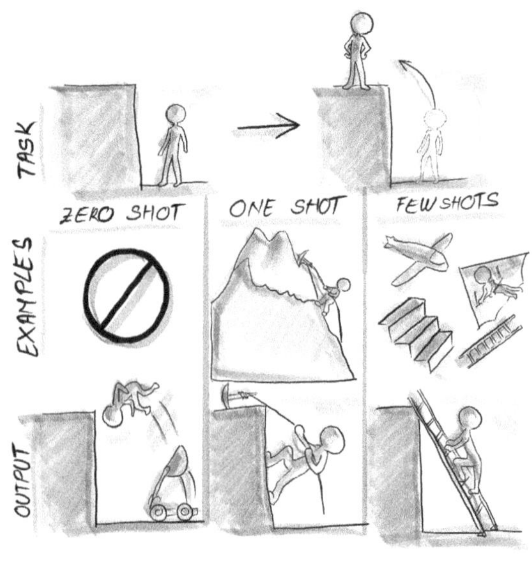


**Figure 3.3** The more examples you give the LLM, the easier the climb.

- *One-shot learning*—You include a single example of the desired response in your prompt: "Provide a concise summary of this document. For example: [Sample summary]" or "A good title would be [Sample]."
- *Few-shot learning*—You provide multiple examples to help the LLM understand the diversity of possible directions it can take and the nuances of the formatting template. This approach takes more time, as it requires preparing several examples, but it leads to the best results.

One-shot and few-shot learning can be very successful and force us, as humans, to carefully consider the type of output we need at each part of the flow in a GenAI application. I encourage you to add examples to your prompt and observe the difference it can make.

**Figure 3.4** Role, Task, Features, and Examples—elementary, my dear Watson

# Prompting enhancement techniques

In addition to using the general four-part prompting template, we can use several *prompting enhancement techniques* that experts have found helpful. These techniques fine-tune the interaction with LLMs, making responses more accurate and better aligned with our needs:

- *Double-down.* As the Latin saying goes, *repetita iuvant* (repetition helps). Repeating critical instructions within a prompt reinforces key points for the LLM. For example, provide guidance before and after your main content, or restate crucial directions in slightly different terms to ensure clarity.

- *Give the LLM a way out.* Specify an alternative response if the task can't be completed. For instance, when querying a specific text, include a fallback: "If the answer is not found, respond with 'not found'." This prevents the model from generating inaccurate or misleading information.
- *Break the task down.* Complex tasks are more manageable for LLMs when split into smaller steps. For example, instead of asking, "Help me create a business plan," try, "List the key sections of a business plan. Then, outline the goals for each section." This approach ensures the response aligns with structured reasoning and avoids confusion.
- *Use Chain of Thought (CoT).* This technique builds on breaking tasks down. Instruct the model to reason step-by-step in its response. For example, "Explain your reasoning for each step and provide a final answer." CoT improves the logical flow and coherence of the response. Even though many modern models perform internal reasoning automatically, explicitly asking for structured reasoning is still one of the best ways to make the model show its work in business settings.
- *Ask for self-validation.* Prompt the LLM to verify or cross-check its response, for example, "Provide your answer and explain why it makes sense." This encourages the model to reflect and justify its reasoning, improving accuracy and transparency.

By combining these techniques, you can maximize the effectiveness of your prompts and achieve more reliable, high-quality responses from the LLM.

## Give it a try

How about we test these techniques out? Let's go through some examples together. Open your favorite LLM-based assistant and try these prompts yourself. Then, modify them to suit your style and experiment freely to see the difference these techniques can make.

Suppose we want the LLM to help us develop a tagline for the energy drink that our company is about to launch. If we were lazy (or too optimistic that the magic black box could read our mind), we could go ahead with a basic prompt:

**INPUT** `Give me a tagline for an energy drink.`

**OUTPUT** `Stay energized!`

Not very creative, right? It's generic and cheesy. It's hard to imagine such a response helping with our creative task.

Now, let's craft a prompt that uses the standard template. We need to force ourselves to think about several aspects of the response we'd like to receive:

- Who is best placed to generate our tagline? What's their *role*? Maybe a `seasoned branding expert`.
- What's the specific *task* to be executed? It would be good to have some alternatives, so let's ask it to `generate three taglines`.
- What *features* should our answer have? We should provide the LLM with context about the brand (for example, that it's `targeted at athletes` and that it `should convey high energy, endurance, and a bold lifestyle`) or about the characteristics of the tagline (for instance, that it should be `between 2 and 4 words` long).
- Is there an *example* to adhere to or to stay away from? We might explain that we already pursued a specific tagline, which `sounded cliché`.

Instead of a simple line, the prompt will now look like a structured paragraph:

**INPUT**
```
Acting as a seasoned branding expert, generate three catchy,
unique taglines for an energy drink targeted at athletes.
The taglines should convey high energy, endurance, and a bold
lifestyle, and be between 2 and 4 words. We had an idea,
'Fuel Your Fire,' but it sounded cliché.
```

**OUTPUT**
```
Here are three fresh and unique taglines for your energy drink:
  'Unleash the Edge' (conveys boldness, competitive advantage, and
  peak performance)
  'Endurance Ignited' (highlights stamina and sustained energy with a
  powerful twist)
  'Relentless Power' (evokes unstoppable energy and determination for
  bold lifestyles)
These options aim to break away from clichés while appealing to
athletes who value high energy and resilience.
```

The template improved the result significantly by specifying the role (branding expert), the target audience (athletes), and the desired features (energy, endurance, and boldness). Adding examples gave the LLM a clear sense of direction, leading to a tagline that's much more tailored and effective. The LLM shared an explanation behind each proposal by building on our stated expectations.

This might be further improved using some of the prompt enhancement techniques we went through, for instance:

- *Double-down.* Reiterate the key aspects, such as the brand's target consumer, to reinforce their importance. The prompt might end with something like this:

"`... Make sure that the taglines strongly resonate with athletes.`"

- *Give the LLM a way out.* Specify an alternative response if the task can't be properly completed. For example, it could ask for additional data points if it struggles to generate strong taglines. The prompt should also have a sentence like "`... If you think you don't have enough context information to generate a quality response, answer 'Not enough data' and then suggest a list of additional information you might require.`"

**Figure 3.5** This drink better be magic.

- *Break the task down.* Split tagline generation into smaller, manageable steps to ensure more focused and structured responses. You can add such instructions at the end of your prompt: "`... First, generate a list of 10 words that fit this brief. Then, use the best-fitting words to create three taglines.`"
- *Chain of Thought (CoT).* Instruct the LLM to explicitly describe its reasoning for each tagline and maybe assign each one a fitness score. This helps provide transparency in the generation process and ensures the results align with the given criteria. You can append instructions like: "`... For each tagline, explain the fit with the brief and target audience. Summarize results in a table having 4 columns: Tagline, Brand fit, Audience fit, Overall fit score (1-10).`" Asking the LLM to produce structured descriptions of its generation, such as tables, can make a real difference.
- *Ask for self-validation.* You can ask the LLM to autonomously validate specific boundaries before sharing the output by adding a request like "`... Before sharing the taglines, double-check that they are actually between 2 and 4 words long.`"

As you can see, there are many options to move from good enough answers to exceptional ones! You can use the standard prompt template as a solid foundation. You can then improve your response by using the prompting enhancement techniques we discussed.

The only way to make this a habit—and become the GenAI pro you aspire to be—is to practice! So, I suggest you allocate a few minutes to perform a simple but very helpful exercise. Pick 3 out of the 10 scenarios from the list following these instructions, open your favorite LLM assistant (or even try more than one), and start experimenting. Follow these steps:

1. Input the basic version of the prompt *as is*.
2. Invest a few minutes crafting a longer, well-structured prompt where you implement the four parts of the *standard template* (role, task, features, examples).
3. Incorporate at least two *enhancement techniques* and see how much they elevate the quality of the response.

Trust me, if you do this exercise, you'll have a better chance of memorizing the art and science of prompt engineering. So, let's get started!

Here are 10 basic prompts to pick from for your exercises:

- Write a goodnight story.
- Advise me on whether I should quit my job.
- Let me understand how quantum computers work.
- Generate a thank-you note for my colleague.
- Create a tagline for a fitness app.
- Suggest a recipe for tonight's dinner.
- Draft a motivational speech for a sports team.
- Explain climate change in simple terms.
- Recommend a book for someone interested in history.
- Plan a one-week itinerary for visiting Rome.

Once you've completed the exercise, you'll have experienced firsthand how much of a difference the prompt makes. You'll also feel reassured that, yes, there is a way to write effective prompts. The key lies in keeping these techniques in mind while staying open to experimentation.

I told you prompt engineering is a fascinating field, and now you have the proper toolkit to embrace it fully.

## Prompt templates in Langflow

Now that we've laid the foundations of prompt engineering, let's get our hands dirty with building and using the right prompts in Langflow.

As we've seen so far in this chapter, prompts are structured pieces of text. To build them systematically, we need to implement a repeatable structure that can be reused as needed. In other words, if we want to industrialize prompt creation, we need to construct *templates*, composed of parts, that will be dynamically assembled into the final prompt sent to the LLM.

## Using variables in prompt templates

To build composite prompts of this kind (a prompt made of various parts), we need a way to dynamically insert different text values into a prompt template. This is done using what in computer science is called a *variable*, a placeholder that can be replaced with real input when the prompt is executed. In Langflow, variables are recognized by the curly brackets around them. For example, in the prompt `"What color is this {breed} dog?"`, the label `breed` inside the brackets is a variable name, so it can be anything you choose. If the user types `"hound"`, the final prompt becomes `"What color is this hound dog?"`. If the user types `"sheep"`, it becomes `"What color is this sheep dog?"`

We've already seen something like this in previous chapters. For instance, in chapter 2, when we built our pirate chatbot, the actual prompt sent to the LLM was a mixture of input from the user and special text we used to prime the behavior of the LLM, called the *system message*, to make it speak Pirate English only. So, the overall prompt looked like the juxtaposition of two parts:

```
           User: {User_message}
System message: {System_message}
```

If we expand on this idea, we can create complex prompts by hierarchically integrating multiple variables, each forming a prompt that leads to another prompt.

Langflow is great at designing and using prompt templates. A fundamental component called Prompt Template allows us to implement this mechanism easily. Let's see this useful component in action by making a small but significant improvement to our pirate assistant: adding memory to the conversation.

## Adding memory to pirate assistants

Go to the Langflow home page and open the Hello, World! flow that we built in chapter 2.

We want to modify the flow to enrich the text sent to the LLM with the history of the conversation up to that point. For example, if I introduced myself to the pirate by providing my name in step 1 of the conversation, I should be able to ask what my name is in step 2 and receive the correct answer. This is possible if I include the previous exchanges when making the call in step 2, as illustrated by figure 3.6.

Let's imagine that the whole conversation history is saved somewhere (and, fortunately, it is conveniently saved in Langflow, as we'll see). To use it, we need to send the LLM a composite prompt that looks like this:

```
                 User: {message}
Conversation history: {history}
```

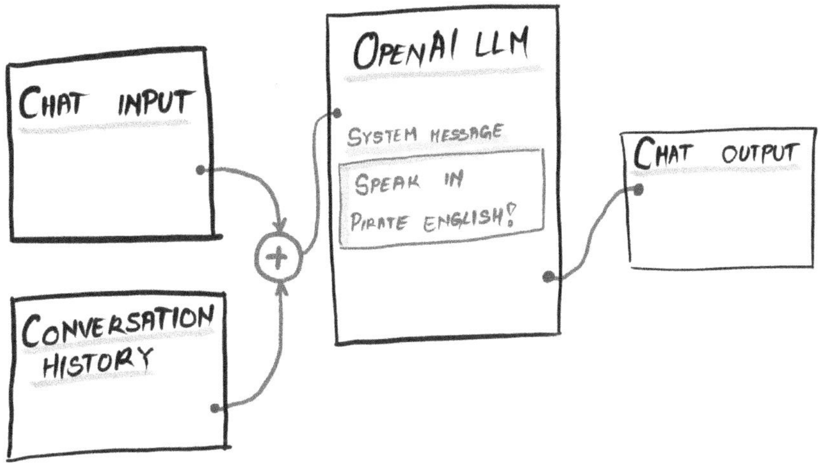


**Figure 3.6** To give memory to our LLM, we'll combine the user message with the conversation history.

In this example, `{message}` is the latest message that we want to send to the LLM, while `{history}` is the conversation's history—as simple as that.

**Figure 3.7** We equip LLMs with memory by sending them the whole history every time.

To create a composite prompt like this, we need to implement the Prompt Template component in our flow. To do so, select Models & Agents > Prompt Template from the components panel on the left, or just search for "prompt" in the search box. Then drag and drop the component onto your flow somewhere on the left.

Once the component is on the flow, click on the Template text box to open the Edit Prompt window, as shown in figure 3.8.

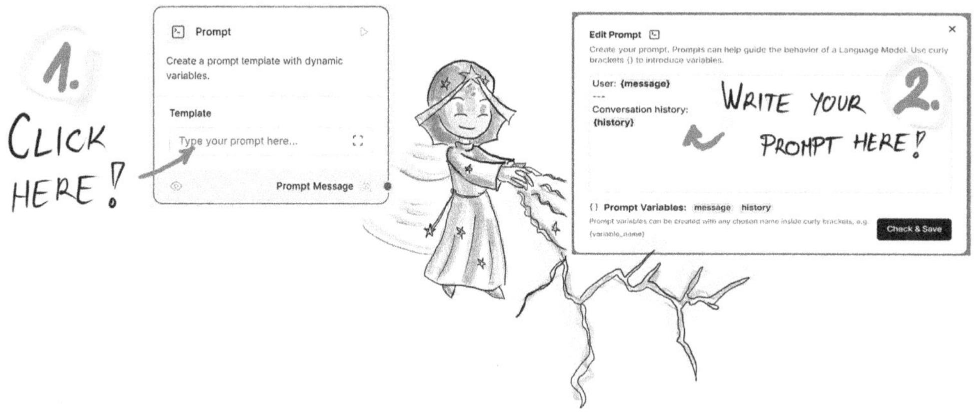


**Figure 3.8** Design your prompt in style with the Prompt Template component.

Now we can finally build our prompt template by mixing static text with any variable. Implementing variables is as easy as putting curly braces around any keyword, as in `{new_variable}`.

Let's write the prompt template we drafted earlier. As we write the variables in curly brackets (`{message}` and `{history}`), Langflow recognizes them and creates a list of variables in the Prompt Variables section at the bottom of the window.

After we click the Check & Save button, we notice that the Prompt Template component has changed. As shown in figure 3.9, it now has two input connectors, one per variable. This means we can connect other components to control the variable's value in the prompt.

It would be nice to use the latest message entered by the user in the chat as the variable `{message}` in the prompt. To do so, let's remove the current connector between the Chat Input and OpenAI components and create a new connection between the output of Chat Input (the latest message entered by the user) and the `message` input connector of the prompt template.

One last thing remains for us to do: connect the history of the previous conversation to the prompt template component. Fortunately, there's a handy component that does just that.

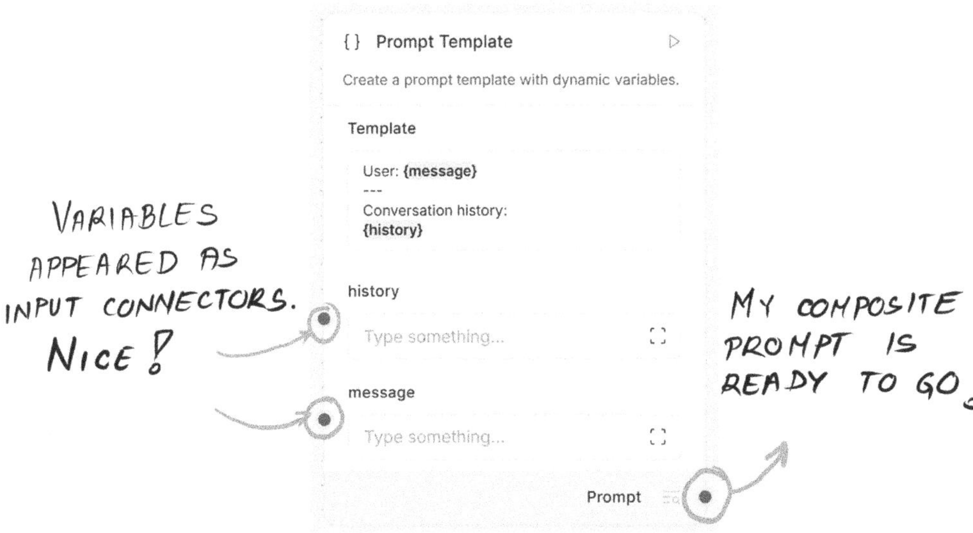


**Figure 3.9** The Prompt Template component has one input connector for each required variable.

Look up the Message History component and drop it in the flow. Just connect the output of the new component to the `{history}` input connector of the Prompt Template component. Langflow automatically stores the conversation as a message history so we can use it for any prompt we like.

Now the Prompt Template component can do its job because all variables are connected. Our Prompt Message output connector now has the text that combines all the variables together into a nice prompt, ready to go to our LLM. As the last step, let's connect the output of the Prompt Template component with the Input connector of the OpenAI component (or whatever model you're using), obtaining the final flow shown in figure 3.10.

That's it! With the help of a couple more components, we've equipped our pirate assistant with a memory of the previous parts of conversations.

## When chats get too long. . .

Passing the full conversation history to your prompt is useful—but not always possible. LLMs have a limited context window, so long chats can quickly hit the limit. A smart workaround is to use a *summary memory*, where an LLM summarizes key points after each exchange and updates the memory accordingly (can you think of a prompt that would do this?). This way, only the most relevant information is retained—making longer conversations possible.

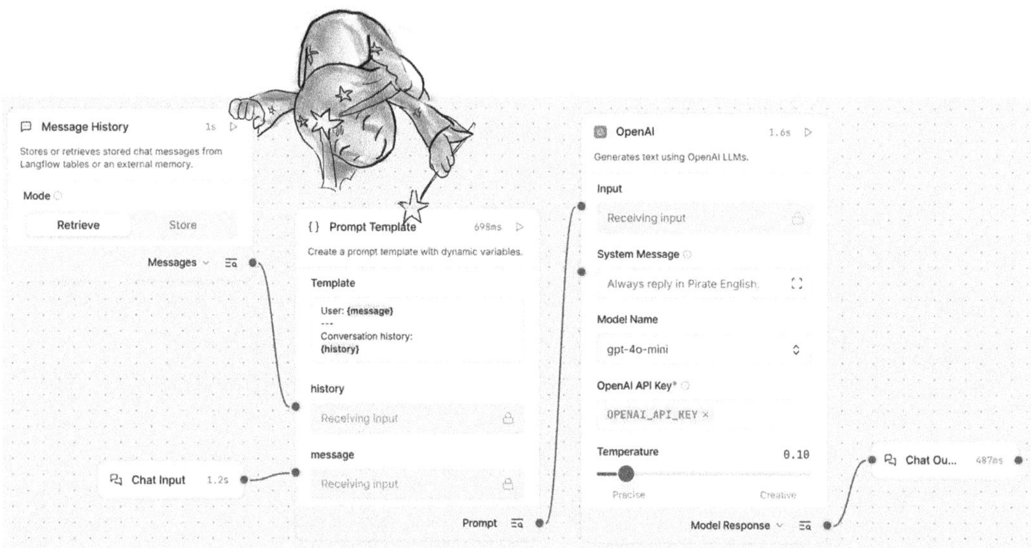


**Figure 3.10** Our Pirate Assistant 2.0 may still drink rum nonstop, but it now remembers conversations.

## Crafting health-conscious recipes

Let's now put Langflow to work on a more sophisticated prompt engineering task. Imagine we want to build a GenAI application called Healthy Chef™. Its purpose is to take a recipe title or a list of available ingredients and generate a healthy recipe. But we don't stop there—we'll also integrate a quality assurance mechanism to ensure the recipes meet health guidelines.

To achieve this, we'll introduce *adversarial roles*:

1. A *Michelin-star chef* generates a mouthwatering recipe.
2. A *registered dietitian* critiques and refines the recipe to make it healthier.

It's like good cop-bad cop, and . . . it works!

**Figure 3.11** Chef vs. dietitian: one generates, the other refines

### AI vs. AI

Adversarial roles are popular as a concept in AI. They form the basis of some foundational techniques, such as Generative Adversarial Networks (GANs). In GANs, two neural networks, the Generator and the Discriminator, compete against each other. The Generator creates synthetic data (such as images), while the Discriminator evaluates how realistic they are, providing feedback for improvement. This *game* pushes the Generator to produce increasingly realistic outputs, often indistinguishable from real data.

The idea is to use two separate LLM calls: one focusing entirely on creativity and the other on health optimization. Although we could combine both roles in a single prompt using enhancement techniques, such as breaking the task down or CoT prompting, keeping the roles separate ensures that each task gets maximum focus and likely yields better results.

Here's the envisioned flow:

1. *Input stage*—As the flow starts, the user provides a recipe name or a list of ingredients.
2. *Chef stage*—The first prompt instructs the LLM to act as a Michelin-starred chef and generate a fancy recipe based on the input.
3. *Dietitian stage*—The chef's output becomes input for the dietitian, who refines it to be healthier.
4. *Output stage*—The final recipe and health considerations are presented to the user.

As shown in figure 3.12, the user's input undergoes a couple of LLM-powered transformations (acting first as a chef and then as a dietitian) before being output at the end of the flow. For each transformation, we need to design the appropriate prompt that uses the preceding input as a variable to generate the input for the next step.

**Figure 3.12** The chef–dietitian combo didn't quite work out for the user.

Let's bring this idea to life using Langflow. Begin by opening a new flow from the home page (click on New Flow > Blank Flow to start from scratch). Drag the Chat Input component from the Inputs section onto the canvas. We'll use the chat input to capture the recipe name or the list of ingredients provided by the user; this will act as the entry point for our flow.

Next, let's design the chef's role. From the Models & Agents section on the left, drag the Prompt Template component onto the canvas. Click the Template text box to open the Prompt edit window. We need to define a prompt that sets the chef's role, explains what action is needed, and clarifies how the output should look. Let's define the prompt as follows:

> Act as a world-renowned chef. Given the user input, which might contain the title of a desired recipe and/or some available ingredients
>
> **{user_input}**
>
> create a detailed recipe following the format:
>
> TITLE: A recipe title.
>
> INGREDIENTS: A list of ingredients with quantities.
>
> PREPARATION: Step-by-step preparation instructions.
>
> Ensure the recipe is creative and appealing. Just generate the recipe using the given format. If the input is insufficient, output "Insufficient input".

After clicking the Check & Save button, the new input connector appears on the prompt node. You can now connect the Chat Input component's output to the `{user_input}` variable of the Prompt Template component. This ensures the user's input flows seamlessly to the chef prompt.

Now that the chef's prompt is ready, we need the magic of an LLM. Drag the OpenAI component (or another model component) from the Models section and place it to the right of the chef prompt. Connect the Prompt Template component's output to the input of the OpenAI component. This setup ensures the chef's instructions are sent to the LLM, which will generate the recipe. The only other configuration needed for the LLM to work properly is the API key. If you've already saved a global variable with your credentials, just select it by clicking the globe button in the OpenAI API Key text box.

Before moving forward, it's worth testing the first portion of our flow, as shown in figure 3.13. Langflow lets us execute single components directly from the flow editor and check what each individual output looks like. This is very handy when we build a complex flow and want to check our progress step-by-step.

To do so, we need to define what inputs to use in this test. In this case, as shown in figure 3.13, we need to set a value in the Input Text box (1) in the Chat Input component. To display the text box, which is normally minimized, click anywhere on the component to select it, then click the three dots (...) in the top right, and click Expand. Add something in the text box, such as `Chocolate cake`, or whatever input you want the chef to receive.

Then, you can execute the last component of the flow we've built so far; this will force all previous components in the flow to run, which is what we need. Click the run button, the right-facing arrow button (2) at the top-right corner of the OpenAI component, and

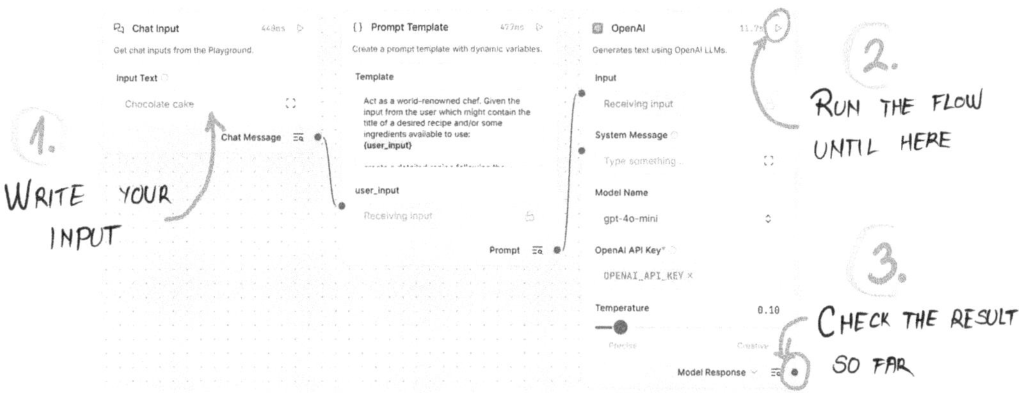


**Figure 3.13** You can check how the chef behaves by running the first part of the flow.

wait a few seconds for the flow to run. In the meantime, you'll see a live status box at the bottom of the screen showing which component is running.

After a few seconds, you'll see an encouraging green label to the left of the run button, which confirms that the component has been successfully executed and displays the number of seconds it took. To check the result, just click the icon beside the Text output connector of the OpenAI component (3).

Take a look at the Component Output window, which should be similar to what's shown in figure 3.14. The chef has put together a (hopefully) mouthwatering recipe, ready to be used in the second part of the flow.

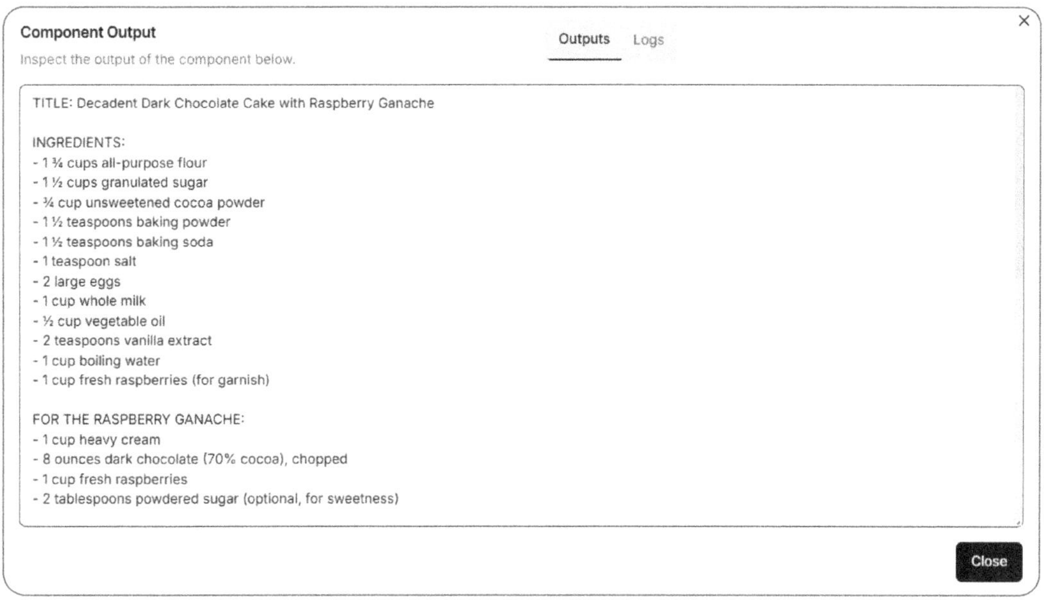


**Figure 3.14** A decadent dark chocolate cake with raspberry ganache. Not bad, chef, not bad.

With the chef's output ready, let's involve the dietitian. Drag another Prompt Template component onto the flow editor. Open the prompt editor by clicking the Template text box, and enter a prompt template that outlines the dietitian's tasks. Remember to follow the standard template: clarify the role, the action to be performed, and the features of the output. We should also provide a "way out" if the input is inadequate. You need to implement a variable so that we can include the output from the chef as a basis for this second LLM call.

An example of a prompt could be like this:

> You are a Registered Dietitian reviewing the following recipe:
>
> ---
>
> **{chef_output}**
>
> ---
>
> Evaluate its health aspects and generate a healthier alternative by:
> - Reducing added sugars and unhealthy fats
> - Suggesting substitutions for processed ingredients
> - Suggesting different cooking steps to make it healthier
>
> The output must follow this format:
> TITLE: The recipe title. It should be as close as possible to the original. Keep it the same if it applies.
> INGREDIENTS: A list of ingredients with quantities.
> PREPARATION: Step-by-step preparation instructions.
> HEALTH COMMENTS: A paragraph describing why the recipe is healthy and suggesting ways to make it even healthier (if applicable).
>
> Just generate output using the given format. If the input is insufficient, output "Insufficient input".

Notice that we used the triple hyphen (---) in the prompt template to clearly indicate where the recipe starts and ends. We could have chosen any unambiguous separator.

Now, connect the OpenAI component's output (the chef's response) to the `{chef_output}` variable (the only input connector) in the dietitian's prompt, which will appear as soon as you save the prompt template. This ensures that the dietitian can critically evaluate and improve the recipe generated by the chef.

It's time to send the composite prompt to our magic black box and see what it returns. Implement a new OpenAI component (the second and last for this flow) and connect its input connector to the output of the dietitian prompt component. Of course, you'll also need to set the API Key, as usual.

Finally, it's time to end our flow. Drag a Chat Output component from the Outputs section and place it to the right of the second OpenAI component. Connect the Text output of the LLM component to the only input of the following component so that the response from OpenAI is sent back to the user chat.

**Figure 3.15** Typical dietitians. Never trust them around cakes.

Great job! You've completed the flow, as shown in figure 3.16. Save the project with a descriptive name such as "Healthy Chef" and test it by clicking the Playground button in the top-right corner. Keep in mind that the input we specified in the first component of the flow is now replaced by whatever we enter in the chat.

You can try using simple inputs like "Chocolate cake with frosting" in the chat and see what the dietitian thinks about what the chef creates. Of course, you'll see only the dietitian's output because it is the one connected to the Chat Output component. You can always run the individual components, as we did earlier, to check the intermediate results.

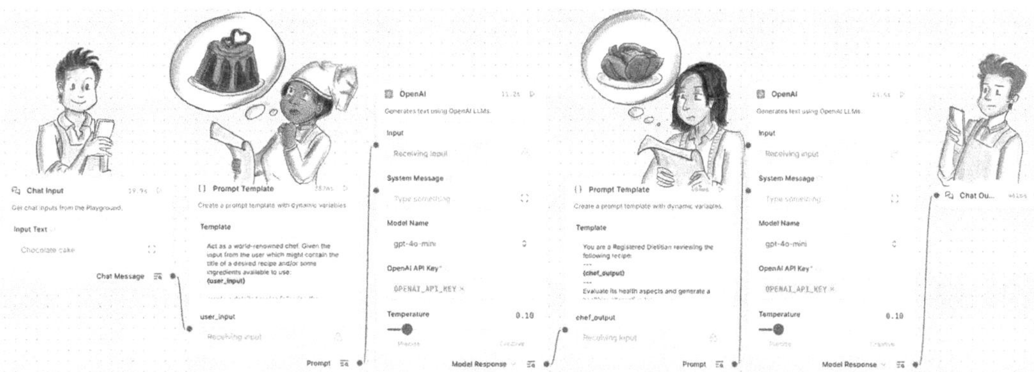


**Figure 3.16** The Healthy Chef™ flow—a GenAI app designed to help users balance enjoyment and health

One of the aspects I find most exciting about building a GenAI application is realizing that there are thousands of ways to improve it. The sky truly is the limit. For instance, in the case of Healthy Chef™, there's so much more you could do to enhance its behavior.

How about you keep playing with it and find opportunities to tweak, optimize, and experiment?

Let me ask a few questions to spark your imagination:

- Can you refine the chef's prompt to enforce specific measurement systems, such as grams and liters instead of ounces and cups? This adjustment will improve usability, especially for international audiences.
- What if Healthy Chef™ became interactive, allowing users to refine their input across multiple exchanges? For example, users could ask the chef for recipe ideas and then tweak the suggestions in real time. To achieve this, consider how the chef and dietitian prompts might evolve to include memory, as we implemented in the Pirate flow.
- Could the dietitian provide a structured table with nutrition facts for the final recipe? You might need to specify the format, with examples, to ensure accurate results.
- Is the output always adhering to your guidelines? If not, experiment with double-down techniques to emphasize critical points, or ask the LLM to validate its responses before finalizing them.
- Perhaps the dietitian's tone could be more engaging or even humorous. Instead of using a clinical style, the dietitian could include lighthearted remarks. How might you frame this expectation in the prompt?
- What if the dietitian's output went back to the chef for final fine-tuning? Imagine a multistep process where the roles interact to produce an even better result. How would this affect the variables in your prompt template? How many connections would the flow need to accommodate?

As we close this chapter, here's your challenge: pick a couple of these ideas—or invent your own—and refine the Langflow project to bring them to life. As mentioned earlier, experimentation is at the heart of mastering the art and science of prompt engineering. Happy prompting!

## What if we coded it?

In this chapter, we extended our GenAI applications in two important directions. First, we introduced a simple form of *memory*, allowing the assistant to take previous turns of the conversation into account. Then we moved beyond a single model call and built a *multistep chain*, in which the output of one agent becomes the input to another. Let's see how we could render these applications through two minimal Python scripts.

The first script, `CH3-HelloWorldImproved.py`, corresponds to the improved chatbot built by connecting a Prompt Template and a Message History component in Langflow.

The flow explicitly injects the conversation history into the prompt at every turn. A simple list (`history_lines`) plays the role of the Message History block, while the rendered prompt (`rendered_prompt`) corresponds to the string that flows into the OpenAI node.

Each new user input is appended to the history, and the entire history is reinjected before the next call to the model.

No additional setup is required to try the script here, as the same libraries and API key configuration from chapter 2 apply.

Same ChatOpenAI wrapper from Chapter 2, reused without extra ceremony.

PromptTemplate mirrors Langflow's prompt block.

System/Human message objects remain our LangChain building blocks.

```
import os
from dotenv import load_dotenv
from langchain_openai import ChatOpenAI
from langchain_core.prompts import PromptTemplate
from langchain_core.messages import SystemMessage, HumanMessage
```

`load_dotenv` brings environment keys into the process automatically.

```
load_dotenv()
# os.environ["OPENAI_API_KEY"] = "REPLACE_WITH_YOUR_KEY"
```

Fail fast if the key is still missing.

```
if not os.getenv("OPENAI_API_KEY"):
    raise RuntimeError("Set OPENAI_API_KEY before running this script.")
```

Instantiate GPT-4o mini with the chapter's suggested settings.

```
llm = ChatOpenAI(model="gpt-4o-mini", temperature=0.1)
system_msg = SystemMessage(content="Always reply in Pirate English.")
```

Keep the pirate system persona consistent with the Langflow canvas.

```
prompt = PromptTemplate(
    input_variables=["message", "history"],
    template="{history}\nUser: {message}\nAI: ",
)
```

Composite prompt that injects `{history}` before the latest user turn.

Bundle the chat loop so we can reuse/import it later in the chapter.

```
def chat_loop() -> None:
    """Chat loop with manual history injection, matching Langflow's wiring."""

    history_lines: list[str] = []

    try:
        while True:
            history_block = "\n".join(history_lines)
            user_input = input("User: ")
            rendered_prompt = prompt.format(message=user_input, history=history_
block)
```

```
            response = llm.invoke(
                [system_msg, HumanMessage(content=rendered_prompt)]
            )
            print("AI:", response.content)

            history_lines.extend(
                [f"User: {user_input}", f"AI: {response.content}"]
            )
    except KeyboardInterrupt:
        print("\nGoodbye, matey!")

if __name__ == "__main__":
    chat_loop()
```

Invoke the LLM with the rendered prompt to emulate the Prompt+History nodes.

Stream responses to stdout, same as the Langflow chat UI.

Track alternating "User:/AI:" lines so the next turn has full context.

Standard entrypoint guard.

The second script, CH3-HealthyChef.py, mirrors the Healthy Chef™ flow, in which two blocks, each consisting of a Prompt Template component linked to an OpenAI component, are connected sequentially. In Python, this flow becomes two PromptTemplates and two consecutive model invocations. The helper function generate_recipes() encapsulates the chain exactly as drawn in Langflow, making the two-step logic reusable and easy to test.

```
import os
from dotenv import load_dotenv
from langchain_openai import ChatOpenAI
from langchain_core.prompts import PromptTemplate

load_dotenv()
# os.environ["OPENAI_API_KEY"] = "REPLACE_WITH_YOUR_KEY"

if not os.getenv("OPENAI_API_KEY"):
    raise RuntimeError("Set OPENAI_API_KEY before running this script.")

llm = ChatOpenAI(model="gpt-4o-mini", temperature=0.1)

chef_prompt = PromptTemplate(
    input_variables=["user_input"],
    template=(
        "Act as a world-renowned Chef. Given the input from the user which might "
        "contain the title of a desired recipe and/or some ingredients available to
use:\n\n"
        "{user_input}\n\n"
        "create a detailed recipe following the format:\n\n"
        "TITLE: A recipe title.\n"
```

Same ChatOpenAI wrapper from Chapter 2, reused for both personas.

PromptTemplate objects map 1:1 with Langflow's prompt nodes.

`load_dotenv` pulls credentials from .env automatically.

Guard execution if the key is missing.

Single LLM instance handles the Chef and the Dietitian turns sequentially.

```
        "INGREDIENTS: A list of ingredients with quantities.\n"
        "PREPARATION: Step-by-step preparation instructions.\n\n"
        "Ensure the recipe is creative and appealing. Just generate the recipe
using the "
        "given format. If the input is insufficient, output \"Insufficient
input\"."
    ),
)
```

*Chef persona prompt exactly as wired in Langflow.*

```
dietitian_prompt = PromptTemplate(
    input_variables=["chef_output"],
    template=(
        "You are a Registered Dietitian reviewing the following recipe:\n"
        "---\n"
        "{chef_output}\n"
        "---\n"
        "Evaluate its health aspects and generate a healthier alternative by:\n"
        "- Reducing added sugars and unhealthy fats.\n"
        "- Suggesting substitutions for processed ingredients.\n"
        "- Suggesting different cooking steps to make it healthier.\n\n"
        "The output must follow the format:\n\n"
        "TITLE: The recipe title. It should be as close as possible to the
original. "
        "Keep it the same if it applies.\n"
        "INGREDIENTS: A list of ingredients with quantities.\n"
        "PREPARATION: Step-by-step preparation instructions.\n"
        "HEALTH COMMENTS: A paragraph describing why the recipe is healthy and "
        "suggesting ways to make it even healthier (if applicable).\n\n"
        "Just generate an output using the given format. If the input is
insufficient, "
        "output \"Insufficient input\"."
    ),
)
```

*Dietitian persona prompt copies the second Langflow block.*

*Helper encapsulating the two-step generation so it's reusable in tests.*

```
def generate_recipes(user_input: str) -> tuple[str, str]:
    """Runs the Chef -> Dietitian chain exactly like the Langflow graph."""

    chef_response = llm.invoke(chef_prompt.format(user_input=user_input))
    dietitian_response = llm.invoke(
        dietitian_prompt.format(chef_output=chef_response.content)
    )
    return chef_response.content, dietitian_response.content
```

*Terminal loop to fire the chain repeatedly.*

```
def chat_loop() -> None:
    """Simple REPL for repeated testing from the terminal."""

    try:
        while True:
            user_input = input("Ingredients or recipe idea: ")
            chef_recipe, healthy_recipe = generate_recipes(user_input)
```

*Capture both outputs so we can print or reuse them downstream.*

```
            print("\n--- Chef's Recipe ---")
            print(chef_recipe)
            print("\n--- Healthier Version ---")
            print(healthy_recipe)
            print("\n")
    except KeyboardInterrupt:
        print("\nHappy cooking!")


if __name__ == "__main__":
    chat_loop()
```

Standard entrypoint guard.

## Summary

- A prompt is the input an LLM receives to generate the corresponding output, serving as the foundation of all GenAI applications.
- The standard prompt template with its four parts—role, task, features, and examples—helps create well-structured prompts that provide clarity and precision to guide the LLM effectively.
- Prompt enhancement techniques, including double-down, breaking the task down, CoT, self-validation, and giving the LLM a way out, significantly improve the quality and reliability of responses.
- Langflow allows users to build GenAI workflows by connecting modular components, such as inputs, prompts, and LLMs, to create complex systems with minimal effort.
- The Healthy Chef™ flow shows how adversarial roles, such as a chef and dietitian, can collaborate through structured prompts to produce creative, healthier recipes.

# Augmenting LLMs with your own documents | 4

## In this chapter

- understanding how retrieval-augmented generation (RAG) works
- learning how to design the right RAG setup for your specific needs and documents
- building and optimizing RAG flows using Langflow components

Our magic black box seems to have deep knowledge, but it's, well, generic. When large language models (LLMs) are pretrained, they learn from a plethora of generic documents. As a consequence, their answers are typically based on general common sense. They tend to reflect an "average" of all that can be said on a specific topic (and they combine a lot of what has been generically said about that topic).

But is this always what we need? What if we want our GenAI assistant to answer questions about, let's say, the opening hours of our small ice cream shop?

Is a generalist assistant able to help us in all cases? Not always, and here are a few reasons why:

- LLMs don't know about us personally or about our organization, unless we're talking about generic, common knowledge regarding a large company or institution that's been widely mentioned in the documents used for pretraining. So, we might need to integrate the pretrained knowledge with documents specific to us: our processes, procedures, and—importantly in our case—our opening hours.

- LLMs don't have up-to-date knowledge. The latest documents they "saw" were those used during pretraining or fine-tuning (see chapter 1 for a refresher). Sure, some GenAI assistants can now be equipped to go online and perform searches, and we'll learn how to do that later, but fundamentally, they don't have direct access to the most current information. We may need to enable the LLM to respond based on content we can update or control easily. What if our office hours change temporarily?
- Sometimes, we need to explain where the GenAI's answers come from. You don't get that from a basic LLM implementation out of the box because, well, they're black boxes. We don't know the inner workings of the neural networks or exactly which document a response was based on. Nobody does. But in many situations, we might need to point a user to a specific page with the opening hours for reference and to show that we got it right.

So, yes, we need more than just generic knowledge. We need an LLM that can still generate, but with help from information retrieved from our own controlled, and possibly curated, set of documents. To do so, we need to use the *retrieval-augmented generation* (RAG) technique, which is what this chapter is all about.

## RAG in a nutshell

RAG can be broken down into a few key phases. Much like the training and inference stages we saw in chapter 1, a RAG-based flow follows a life cycle that includes three essential steps: document ingestion, document retrieval, and answer generation.

Here's what happens, in a nutshell, as shown in figure 4.1:

- *Document ingestion*—You gather the documents that contain the knowledge you need and upload them into a knowledge database (called a *vector database*).
- *Document retrieval*—When a user asks a question requiring that knowledge, you search the vector database for the *few best* chunks that (hopefully) contain the information needed.
- *Answer generation*—The LLM generates a response based on the extra knowledge retrieved in the previous step.

Note that these three steps happen in two distinct stages. *Ingestion* is an offline (or setup) stage: you run it once and repeat it only when your document base changes. *Retrieval and generation* form the online (or runtime) stage: they run every time a user asks a question.

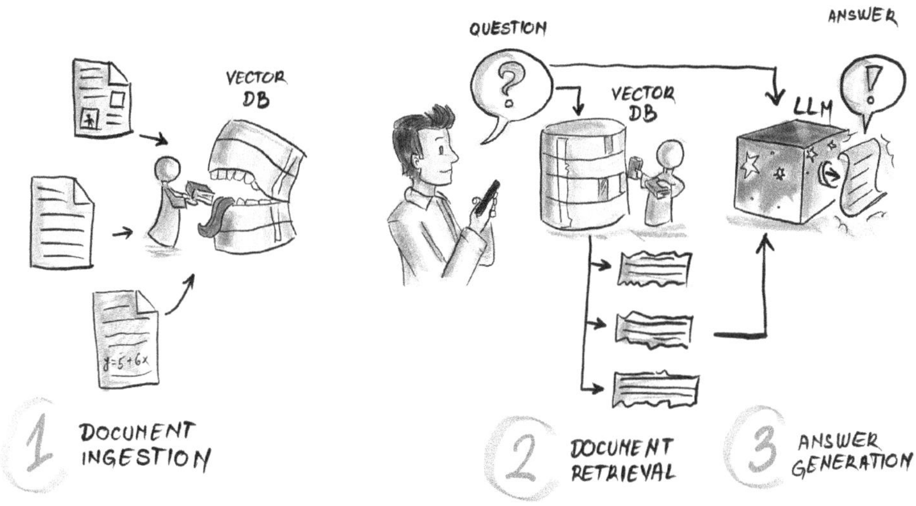


**Figure 4.1** A RAG-based flow includes three essential steps: document ingestion, document retrieval, and answer generation.

This distinction matters in practice because when we implement RAG, we'll build and test the flow in these two stages, even though it still follows the same three-step logic.

It may seem simple, but it isn't always straightforward. Let's break it down.

**Figure 4.2** The invisible work behind any RAG response: collecting knowledge, retrieving relevant pieces, and crafting the final answer by stitching together the right context

## Document ingestion

The goal is to inject knowledge into the system so the LLM can work better. Great idea. But wait, in what format is that knowledge? What does it look like today, and how can it be transformed into something usable by an LLM?

In real life, knowledge is often scattered across all kinds of documents: PDFs, Word files, PowerPoint slides, Excel sheets, web pages, shared Google Drive or SharePoint folders, or even full-on databases. Basically, knowledge can be *anywhere*.

Well, that doesn't help the LLM much. We need to ingest these documents and put them into a *special* kind of database so we can search for them later in a meaningful way.

This phase comes with a few challenges.

First, documents formats need to be understood so they can be opened and read. This is easy to say from a user standpoint when double-clicking a PDF file, but we need an algorithm to open PDF files and many other file formats. We need file-reading components that do this work for us.

Second, documents can be very large. To allow for efficient and meaningful retrieval, we need to split them into smaller parts, which we call *chunks*. There are many ways to chunk a document, but the simplest is to split it by paragraphs. For instance, if a document has 10 paragraphs, we might create 10 separate chunks, one per paragraph.

Third, to compare a user's question with these chunks, we need to convert each chunk into a set of numbers called a *vector*. This process is called *embedding* because we're embedding the meaning of the text into a vector space. These vectors are then stored in a *vector database*, a special type of database built specifically to handle this kind of numerical data. Along with each chunk, we also store *metadata*, such as the name of the original document, so we can reference it later in our answers if needed.

You might be wondering why we need to go through all of this trouble of converting chunks into numbers. Why not just store the raw text and search it when needed? If we skipped the embedding step, we could still save all the chunks in a standard text database and try to retrieve answers using a traditional keyword search. That would technically work, but the performance of our RAG setup would be much lower because keyword searches can only find exact or similar words, not their *meaning*.

Embeddings enable us to move from searching for exact words to searching for meaning. By converting each chunk of text into a vector of numbers, we embed its semantic content, including its intent, topic, and tone, into a mathematical space. This translation step, from raw text to vectors, is a big part of the "secret sauce" that makes RAG such a powerful technique.

Figure 4.3 explains what happens: documents saved in files (of potentially different sources and formats) are opened (1), and the text within them is read and extracted (2). That full text is split into partially overlapping chunks (3). Then, each chunk is transformed into a vector of numbers (its embedding) (4). Finally, the chunk embeddings are stored in the vector database—along with any useful metadata (5).

The numbers that "describe" a chunk need to be well chosen because everything else depends on them! From a mathematical standpoint, we need a bit of intuition about how this translation into numbers actually works. Let's walk through a simple example.

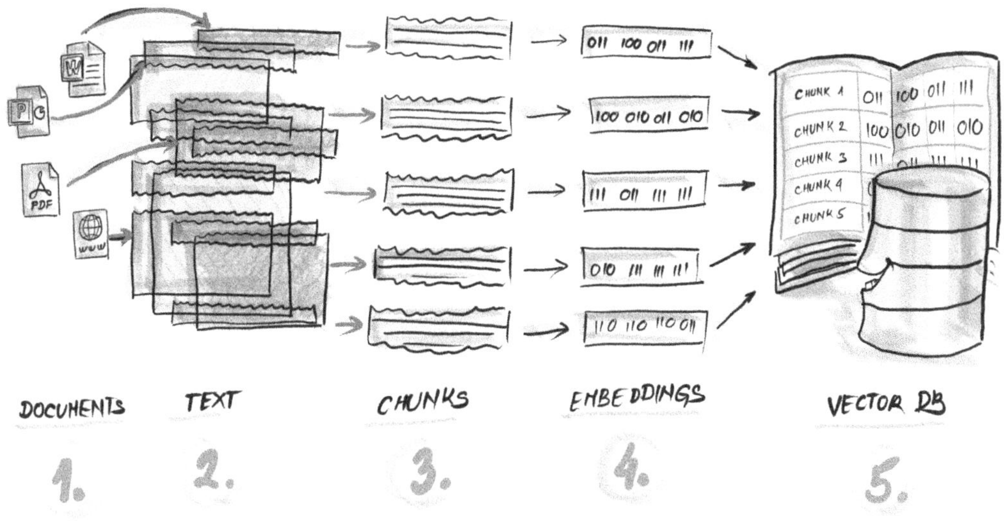


**Figure 4.3** Moving from documents onto a vector database during the ingestion phase in a RAG system

Let's imagine we have six chunks of text, each a short sentence, all about (more or less) lovely pets:

A. Tessa is a lovely dog
B. Barbie is a nasty dog
C. Tilly, what a naughty puppy
D. Kit is a cute cat
E. Fox has not been a well-mannered cat
F. Brian has been a good kitten

These chunks need to be *embedded* into vectors, meaning that we translate each sentence into numbers. Similar to what we did with dictionary embeddings back in chapter 1, we now want to convert whole text chunks into numerical representations.

Let's keep it simple and say each sentence is translated into just two numbers (so, a two-dimensional [2D] vector). That way, we can easily visualize their position on a scatterplot—like the one shown in figure 4.4.

In this plot, notice that each dimension seems to reflect the type of pet (dogs on the top, cats on the bottom) and its behavior (good pets on the right and bad-mannered ones on the left).

Documents about nasty dogs will be on the top left, and documents about nasty cats will be on the bottom left. If we add more chunks using the same embedding method, similar documents will "stick together"—landing near each other in this space.

For example, Barbie and Tilly are both ill-mannered dogs, and they lie together in the top-left quadrant in the space of embeddings, as depicted in figure 4.4.

Of course, this is a simplification. In the real world, embeddings don't use just two dimensions—they use thousands! This places each chunk in a highly dimensional space

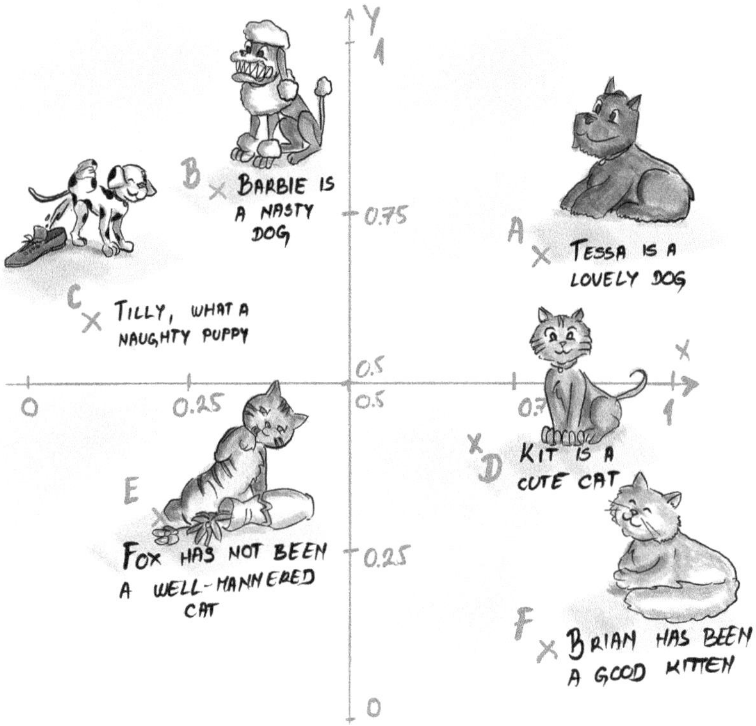


**Figure 4.4** Six pet-related chunks laid in a 2D embedding space

that's much harder for us humans to visualize. But the idea is the same: similar chunks land close together in that space. Let's stick to the 2D version for now. Our vector database might look something like this:

| Chunk ID | X | Y |
|---|---|---|
| A | 0.8 | 0.7 |
| B | 0.3 | 0.8 |
| C | 0.1 | 0.6 |
| D | 0.7 | 0.4 |
| E | 0.2 | 0.3 |
| F | 0.8 | 0.1 |

In practice, we'd add more columns to describe where each chunk came from: its metadata. This might include the file name, file path, author, creation date, and more. In our pet-themed case, the metadata could simply store the pet's name. A more complete vector database would look like this:

| Chunk ID | Metadata | X | Y |
|---|---|---|---|
| A | Tessa | 0.8 | 0.7 |
| B | Barbie | 0.3 | 0.8 |
| C | Tilly | 0.1 | 0.6 |
| D | Kit | 0.7 | 0.4 |
| E | Fox | 0.2 | 0.3 |
| F | Brian | 0.8 | 0.1 |

Now we're starting to see what a vector database looks like. With all of our documents now described in a uniform format, we're ready to move to the next phase.

## Document retrieval

When a user asks a question (like "What are your opening hours?"), we need to pick the chunk (or few chunks) from the many available in the vector database that can help answer it.

Imagine giving this task to a human: How would a person look for the right information to support an answer? It could be as easy as scanning a table of contents or as hard as finding a needle in a haystack—trying keyword searches, rephrasing them, and scanning different paragraphs that might contain useful hints.

In RAG, we need to automate this cognitive task of searching for the right source. We do so by performing a semantic search across all vectors in the vector database. This search assumes the chunk embeddings that are semantically similar to the question lie *closer* to the embedding of the question. Unlike traditional keyword search, semantic search can recognize connections between texts that use *different* words to express the *same* idea, making it far more powerful and flexible.

Here's how it works. First, we convert the question into a vector of numbers (an embedding), just like we did with all the chunks during ingestion. Then, we calculate the distance between the question embedding and the embeddings of all chunks in the vector database. Finally, we select the semantically "closest" chunks to the question as they're the most likely to be relevant sources for generating a good answer.

Let's go back to our pet example. If the user asks, "Who is a nasty cat?", we first embed this question as a 2D point. Where would this land? Well, if the embedding works correctly, it should land in the bottom-left area of our plane, where nasty cats live.

Looking at figure 4.5 gives you an intuition for a simple similarity search, which could use the good old Pythagorean theorem for distances (called *Euclidean distances*). We could calculate the distance between the "Who is a nasty cat?" question and all six

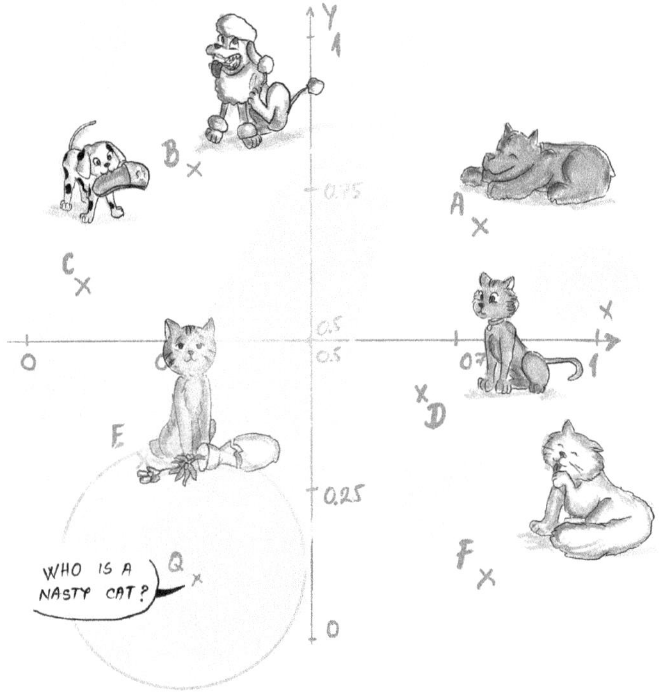


**Figure 4.5** Euclidean distances between our question and each embedding in the vector database

embeddings in our vector database. For example, the distance, *d*, between the question (point Q) and our well-behaved Tessa embedding (point A) can be calculated as

$$d = \sqrt{(Q_x - A_x)^2 + (Q_y - A_Y)^2} = \sqrt{(0.3 - 0.8)^2 + (0.1 - 0.7)^2} = 0.78$$

We could calculate all the distances between Q and all other chunks and obtain the results in the following table.

| Chunk ID | Metadata | X | Y | Distance from Q |
|---|---|---|---|---|
| Q | Question | 0.3 | 0.1 | – |
| E | Fox | 0.2 | 0.3 | 0.22 |
| D | Kit | 0.7 | 0.4 | 0.50 |
| F | Brian | 0.8 | 0.1 | 0.50 |
| C | Tilly | 0.1 | 0.6 | 0.54 |
| B | Barbie | 0.3 | 0.8 | 0.70 |
| A | Tessa | 0.8 | 0.7 | 0.78 |

Thanks to this list, sorted by increasing distance from the question, we can prioritize which chunks will likely be the most useful for answering the user's questions. We can't normally use all the chunks in the vector database for every response, so this ranking step is essential.

If, for instance, we decide to use the top three embeddings to answer the question about the nasty cat, we'll use the chunks describing Fox, Kit, and Brian, thus ignoring those related to Tilly, Barbie, and Tessa.

In this specific case, we had only six chunks, all of which were short. So, you might rightly ask, why not just use them all? Fair point. But in real-world scenarios, you'll deal with thousands of chunks and distances. That's why selecting the *top k* results (with the value of *k* being something we can optimize—more on that later in the chapter) becomes a crucial step. It's also why using a similarity metric, such as Euclidean distance, really matters.

Now that we have retrieved the top documents, we can move to the next and final stage.

**Figure 4.6** No escape for naughty cats: the closest matches always get picked.

## Answer generation

It's time to invoke the LLM. But instead of just sending the user's original question, we'll enrich the prompt with the retrieved context chunks. We'll use a composite prompt, something we learned to build back in chapter 2.

Here's the structure:

"Answer the user query by using the context:
Context:
**{chunks}**
User: **{message}**
"

For our pets, after retrieving the top three chunks referring to Fox, Kit, and Brian, the actual prompt sent to the LLM and its likely response will be

**INPUT**

```
"Answer the user query by using the context.
Context:
- Fox has not been a well-mannered cat
- Kit is a cute cat
- Brian has been a good kitten
User: Who is the nasty cat?
"
```

**OUTPUT**

```
"Fox is the nasty cat."
```

The LLM was able to answer correctly because the prompt included relevant context. This might seem a little strange because it's like we're asking a question and giving the answer at the same time. But since our magic black box is *stateless* and *pretrained*, the only way to apply its reasoning to new, unseen data is to carefully select relevant chunks and attach them to the prompt.

In a nutshell, this is what RAG is all about: equipping the query with the proper context so the LLM can reason about it.

Sure, our cute pet scenario was simplified. But the same three core steps of RAG, ingestion, retrieval, and generation, power real-world GenAI applications. In practice, embeddings might live in thousands of dimensions, and the vector database could store large volumes of long documents enriched with rich metadata.

## Metadata in RAG

Even though we skipped it in our simple example, metadata in a vector database can be super helpful in RAG. Titles, URLs, and authors can be shown as references in responses or used to filter which documents are retrieved. It's a powerful way to improve accuracy and trust.

As GenAI creators, here's what we need to get good at:

- Ingesting the right documents correctly, taking care of their source file format, splitting the chunks properly, and preserving the metadata.
- Retrieving effectively by using the proper search query, tailoring the distance calculation as needed, and choosing the right number of top chunks to use as output.
- Generating the answer, providing the right context, and using the right prompt template.

There's much more to explore about RAG. But staying true to our journey's practical spirit, let's roll up our sleeves and dive into the Langflow components that let us build a working RAG setup.

Let's go build our first GenAI app that uses our own documents!

## Building a RAG system in Langflow

In this tutorial, we'll build PizzaMate™, a customer service virtual assistant that can answer questions about a pizza restaurant in Brooklyn. Our friend Enzo, the pizzeria's owner, has shared a PDF file with us containing a description of the restaurant, useful information such as working hours and delivery service, and the full menu with prices. We want to help Enzo build a virtual assistant that uses the information in the PDF file to answer customer questions through a chat interface.

**Figure 4.7** Looking for the perfect wine pairing? Ask PizzaMate™!

No matter how famous the pizzeria in Brooklyn might be, LLMs don't have up-to-date information about it. So, we can only build such a model by implementing a RAG system.

This system will consist of two parts: two subflows within the same Langflow flow, corresponding to the setup stage and the runtime stage we introduced earlier:

- The *document ingestion* part (setup) will take the PDF as input and produce a vector database with embedded chunks. We'll need to run this subflow only when the database is created or when the information in the PDF has changed.

- The *retrieve and answer* part (runtime) will take a user query, run a vector similarity search in the database to find the most relevant chunks, and finally, use them to answer the query by invoking an LLM. We'll need to run this subflow whenever a user asks a question.

In Langflow, we'll design both parts in the same flow, but we need to be aware that each serves a different purpose and runs at different times.

## Document ingestion

Let's get started with document ingestion. As illustrated in figure 4.8, we expect the flow to begin by reading the content of a file—a PDF file in our case. We need a component that opens the file (1) and outputs its content as plain text (2). This text then needs to be split into smaller portions, our chunks (3). Afterward, all of these chunks need to be transformed into vectors of numbers, the embeddings, by using an embedding model (4). The embeddings will be stored in a vector database (5) so that they are ready to be retrieved when the questions come.

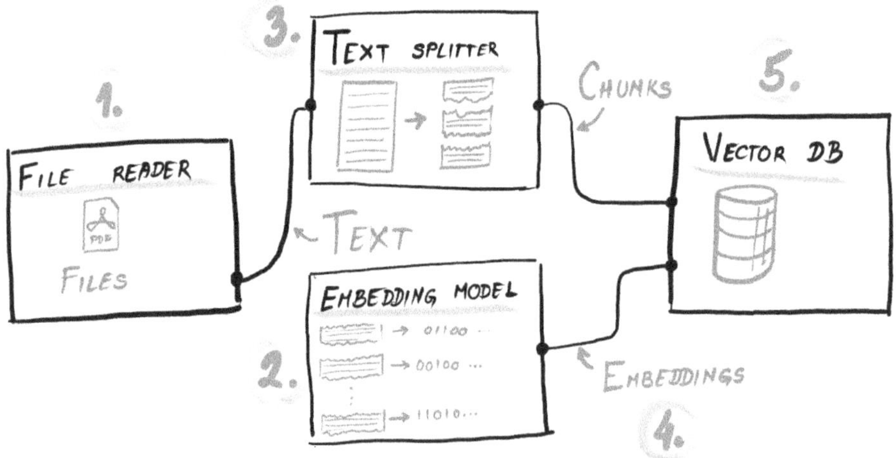


**Figure 4.8** The document ingestion subflow of our RAG system

Let's open Langflow, create a new blank flow, and drag our first component to the flow editor, called Read File (you can find it in the repository inside the Files & Knowledge folder or use the search box).

The Read File component can open a file (which you need to upload from your machine) and output the raw text found inside. You may also notice an Advanced Parser option. We won't use it in this chapter, but it can preserve more of the document structure and return outputs such as markdown or structured data, which can be useful in more advanced ingestion setups.

**Figure 4.9** The perfect RAG recipe

Let's get it to work. Download the menu from Enzo at www.tiny.cc/GenAImenu. Then, following figure 4.10, click the central Select Files button on the component (1), upload the file you've just downloaded, and then click Select Files at the bottom to confirm.

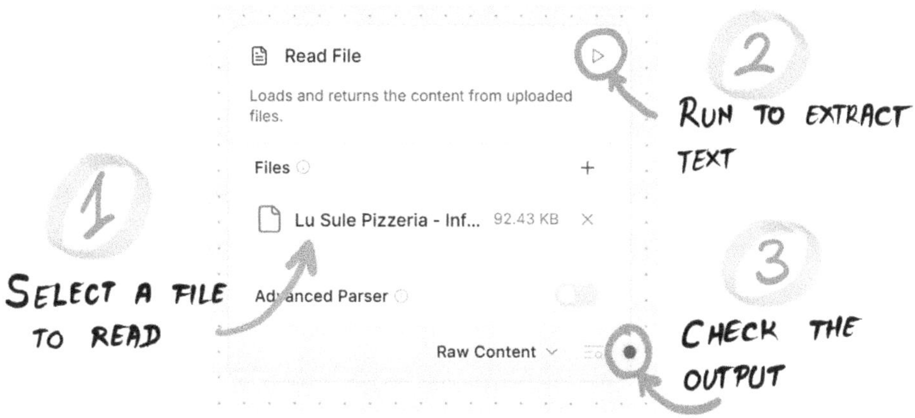


**Figure 4.10** The Read File component lets you extract text from document files.

You can now test the text extracted from the PDF file. Run the component by clicking the play button at the top right (2). Then click the icon next to the only component output (3) and check the result.

The output of this component is the actual text found within the uploaded file. You can explore the full text extracted from the PDF, as shown in figure 4.11 on the right side.

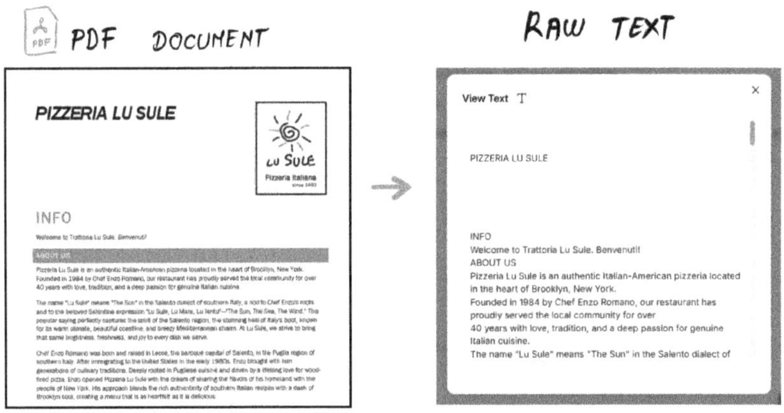


**Figure 4.11** We extracted all the text from a PDF file.

The next step is to split this text into smaller chunks. The Split Text component comes to our rescue. After implementing it, connect the output of the Read File component to the first input connector of Split Text, as you can see in figure 4.12.

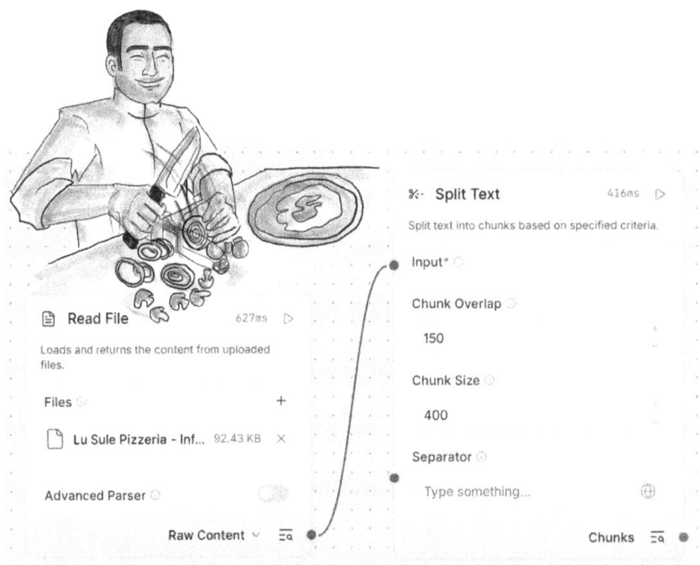


**Figure 4.12** The poor text will now be chopped up into chunks.

The component lets you set a couple of important parameters. Chunk Overlap is the number of characters we keep as overlap between one chunk and the next. Let's set it to 150 for this exercise.

## Overlapping chunks

We slightly duplicate the text at the edges of chunks to avoid losing important context. Imagine one chunk ends with "the price of the Margherita pizza is" and the next begins with "$14, while for a Marinara it's $13." If these chunks didn't overlap, the critical detail, "Margherita," might be disconnected from its price. Overlapping ensures full context is preserved across chunk boundaries.

The other parameter, Chunk Size, is the maximum number of characters in each chunk: let's set it to 400. There's no single "correct" chunk size. Chunk Size and Chunk Overlap are important parameters that directly affect the performance of a RAG system and often need to be tuned based on the type of content and the expected queries. In this case, 400 characters works well for our menu, striking a good balance between preserving enough context and keeping chunks small enough for accurate retrieval. The actual number of characters in a specific chunk might be lower than the number we set here because the component tries to gracefully split the chunks where a separator (newline, by default) occurs.

Run the node (use the play button), and then check the result of the chopping by clicking the icon on the first output port. As shown in figure 4.13, the text has been split into chunks of similar size. The text highlighted in gray overlaps between the two chunks. Everything seems to be working fine.

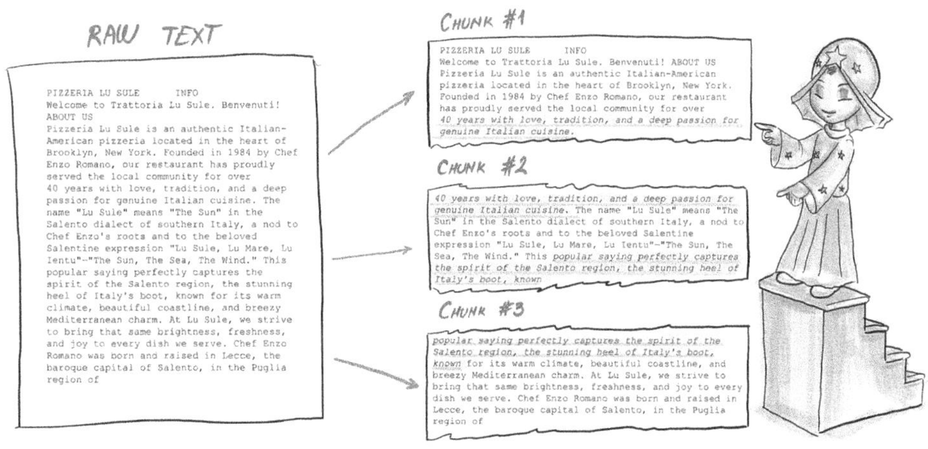


**Figure 4.13** The raw text is split into chunks, partially overlapping each other.

Now it's time to implement our vector database. In Langflow, many vector store connectors are available, such as Chroma, FAISS, Astra DB, Pinecone, Supabase, and PGVector. The first two in this list are *file-based* vector stores, meaning that you can freely create a database by creating a new file on the same machine where Langflow is running. The other options will require you to create a store in a *cloud* environment. For the sake of this exercise, we will go simple and implement ChromaDB.

Drag and drop the ChromaDB component on the canvas (you can quickly find it by typing `Chroma` in the search box). Then, connect the Chunks output of the Split Text component with the Ingest Data input for the ChromaDB component. In ChromaDB, we can have more than one embedding group. Such groups are called collections, and you will notice that the first configuration field in the ChromaDB component is, indeed, Collection Name. Let's assign a name to the collection we will create and enter `menu` in the text box.

We should also set the Persist Directory parameter, which specifies where the vector database is stored on disk. Let's enter `menu` here as well, so that both the database location and the collection name are easy to remember.

## Knowledge Bases in Langflow

Although in this chapter we build the vector database explicitly using components such as ChromaDB, Langflow also offers a simplified alternative called Knowledge Bases. A Knowledge Base is, under the hood, a local vector store that you can create from the Langflow home page by uploading documents, previewing their chunks, and saving them for reuse. You can inspect and search those chunks later, then retrieve them in a flow through the Knowledge Base component. It's a handy option for reusable datasets and for checking what was actually ingested, but in this book, we'll prefer explicit vector database components so you can see and control every step of the process.

We need one last ingredient for our subflow to work: the embedding model. The ChromaDB component can't store chunks as they are because they first need to be converted into vectors of numbers—the embeddings. In Langflow, you can apply several embedding models. As with LLMs, Langflow offers both vendor-specific embedding components and a generic component called Embedding Model, which you can find in the Models & Agents section and configure with different providers. For simplicity, and consistent with the approach we used for LLMs earlier in the book, we can stick to the OpenAI suite of models: search for the OpenAI Embeddings component and drop it to the left of the ChromaDB one.

Let's connect the output of the embeddings component to the Embedding input of ChromaDB. As a configuration, we can specify which model to use for embeddings; the bigger ones will create longer vectors and better describe the chunk's content, but at a higher cost. We can leave the default model. Let's not forget to input the OpenAI API

Key; using the embedding model doesn't come for free. Conveniently, we can reuse the same key we used for the previous projects.

Our document ingestion subflow is now ready to go, as shown in figure 4.14. If we click the play button in the ChromaDB component, it will look like nothing is happening, but our vector database has been created! You'll need to repeat this step only when documents are added or edited. As long as the content stays the same, this process needs to be done only once.

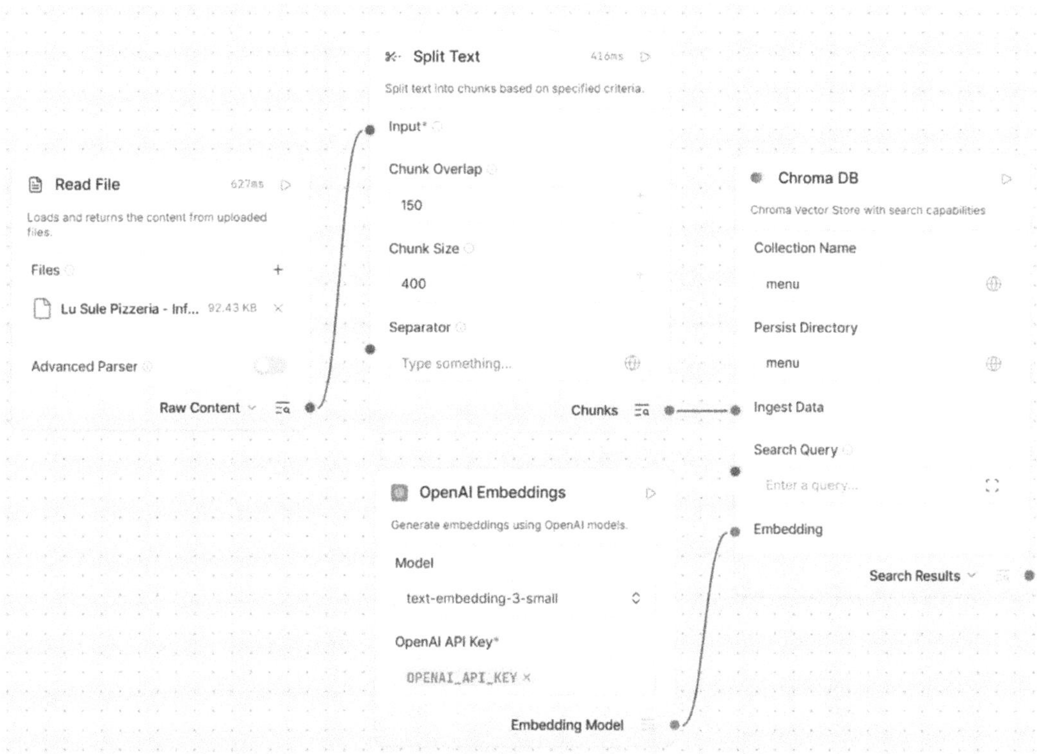


**Figure 4.14** The document ingestion subflow is ready.

## Retrieve and answer

We can now move to the second part of our RAG system, retrieve and answer. Fundamentally, we'd expect these four things to happen in this phase, as shown in figure 4.15:

1. The user asks a query.
2. We run a similarity search on the vector database to find the most relevant chunks related to the user query. This step also uses an embedding model because the user query must be converted into embeddings to run the similarity search.

3. We build a composite prompt that says, "Answer this question, using this context," where the *question* is the user query, and the *context* is the collection of retrieved chunks. We call the LLM using this composite prompt.
4. We output the answer generated by the LLM back to the user.

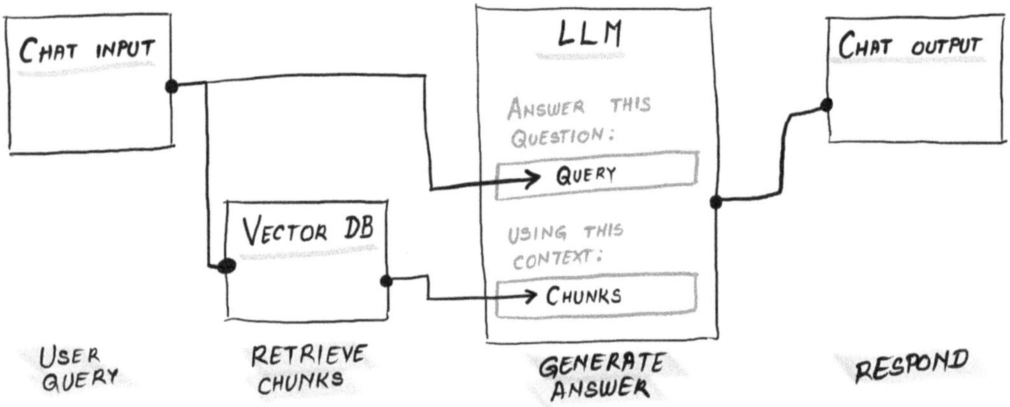


**Figure 4.15** A simplified sketch of our retrieve and answer subflow

Note that the user query is used twice in this process. First, it searches the vector database and retrieves semantically similar chunks. Then, it's combined with those chunks in a new prompt that is finally passed to the LLM. In fact, the vector database alone doesn't generate an answer; it only retrieves relevant information. The LLM is responsible for interpreting that context and producing the actual response.

Let's start by implementing the Chat Input component, which is essential for handling user interaction. Place this component below the first (ingestion) subflow.

Then, we implement the ChromaDB component again. This component has a dual use: to *build* a vector database and to *retrieve* data from it. Let's connect the output of Chat Input to the Search Query input connector of the ChromaDB component. This will ensure that we can search the vector store using the query as a key.

As expected, we also need an embedding model. You already know what to do: drag an OpenAI Embeddings component into the flow, configure it with your API key, and connect it to ChromaDB. You could technically reuse the embedding component from the document ingestion subflow, but I suggest using a new one here for clarity and modularity.

One last configuration is needed on the ChromaDB component: enter `menu` for the same Collection Name and Persist Directory fields as we did earlier to query the collection we created.

From chapter 2, you'll remember that the color of input and output connectors tells us about the type of data flowing through them. You'll notice that the output connectors of the ChromaDB component are red: they aren't simple strings of text (they would be indigo blue) but data tables. In this case, the output of a retrieval task contains a table with multiple columns: one of them is the actual chunk of text (just named `text`). Of course, there's a row for each chunk retrieved through the similarity search.

From now on, in the workflow, we want to work with text only because the LLM will ultimately require a text-based prompt. To "extract" only the values included in the raw text column, we need to use a component that converts tables (data format) into strings (text format). Let's implement a Parser component and put it to the right of ChromaDB.

We can now connect the output of ChromaDB to the input of the Parser. The component asks for a simple but essential configuration parameter: how to format the output text by using the various columns of the input data. By setting the Template parameter, we describe the output format and refer to the names of the columns to use within curly brackets. In this case, we want to extract the *text* column, so we can keep the default template setting: `Text: {text}`.

One last piece of configuration is required to make this conversion work correctly. Click the output name of the ChromaDB component (Search Results) and change it to `DataFrame` (you might have to remake the wiring between the ChromaDB and the Parser component). By doing so, we ensure that the Parser can correctly extract the column text from the table of retrieved chunks.

Once you're done with this configuration, you should obtain the flow shown in figure 4.16, which retrieves relevant chunks and makes them available as text.

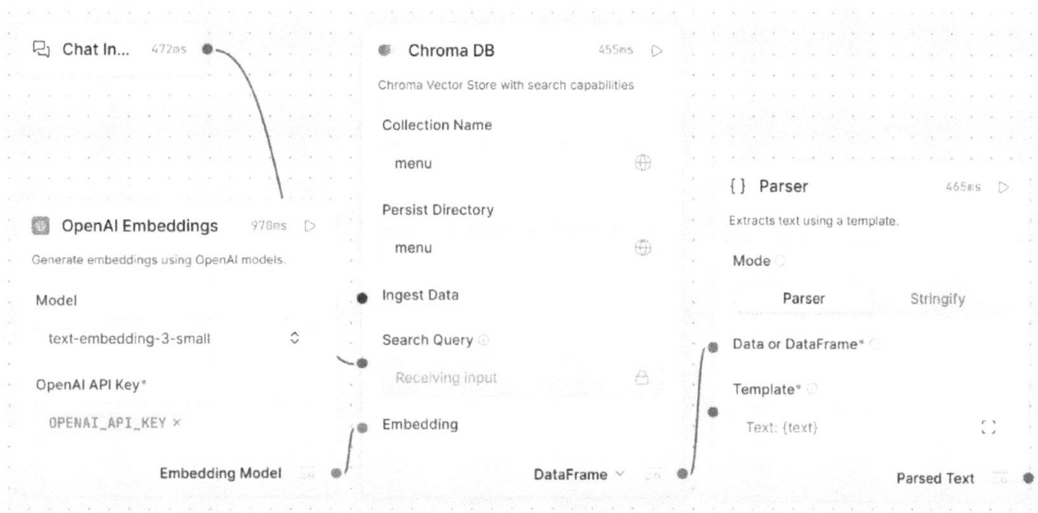


**Figure 4.16** This flow can retrieve relevant entries from a vector database and transform them into plain text.

We now have all the ingredients for the last part of our project: the user query and the context to answer it. We just need to put them together in a nice composite prompt with clear instructions for the LLM.

To do so, let's reuse the Prompt Template component we encountered in chapter 2. Pick it up from the Models & Agents section of the repository, and then click the Template configuration text box to enter our prompt definition:

```
"Answer the user query by using the context.
Context:
{chunks}
User: {message}"
```

After entering the prompt definition, the two new input ports appear on the left side of the component. We can get the plumbing done by connecting the Parser output to the Prompt Template's Chunks input and the Chat Input component's output (the user query) to the Message input.

Now that we have a prompt, we can send it to the LLM. Let's implement the OpenAI component (or any other model to which we are equipped with an API key) and put it on the right of the Prompt Template. Let's connect the output of Prompt Template and the first input of OpenAI. Let's not forget to add, as usual, the OpenAI API Key as well.

The last component to be added is Chat Output to close the loop on the user conversation. After implementing it, connect the first output of OpenAI with the only input of this last node, and we will be done. This portion of the subflow, made of seven components, is now complete, as shown in figure 4.17.

**Figure 4.17** The retrieve and answer subflow is ready to chat about pizzas.

Let's test our RAG system by asking a question about anything in the original PDF using the Playground (click the button at the top right of the canvas). For example, we can ask about the price of two Margherita pizzas plus a bottle of wine from Tuscany, as shown in figure 4.18.

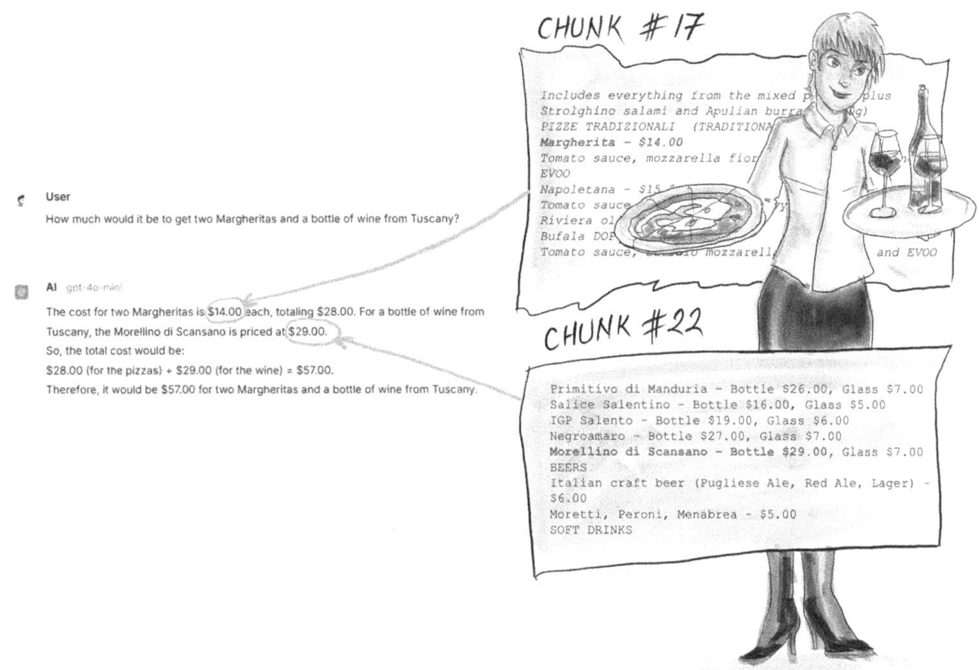


**Figure 4.18** PizzaMate™ got it right!

Our RAG system seems to be working as expected: the retriever part of the subflow looked for chunks related to wine and Margherita pizzas. The LLM received a composite prompt asking to answer the user's question by using the context offered by several selected chunks, including the two in figure 4.18. These chunks have all the elements the LLM needed to answer correctly, and it did!

Interestingly, the user asked for a bottle of Tuscan wine. None of the chunks indicated that the only wine from Tuscany on the menu was the Morellino. Here's where the pretrained part of our model came into play: the LLM has general knowledge that clearly includes the origin of Italian wines. The context provided in the prompt mentioned several wines, and the LLM knew that the Morellino was the one the user would have liked. This is the power of RAG: using the reasoning power and general knowledge of LLMs, paired with the custom knowledge required for your application!

**Figure 4.19** In RAG, pretrained knowledge and retrieved documents come together to serve smarter answers.

Although we didn't implement it in our PizzaMate™ exercise, it wouldn't hurt for the chatbot to have memory. In fact, if you now ask for the price of a Margherita and then ask for its ingredients (without repeating the word *Margherita*), the assistant won't get what you want.

As a good exercise, you can add memory to the retrieve and answer subflow by looking back at what you learned in chapter 3. Hint: You'll need to add `{history}` to the prompt template and use the Message History component to provide it. Easy peasy!

# Taking RAG to the next level

RAG is one of the most prominent—and delicate—topics in GenAI today. It offers many promising practical applications but also has a fair share of failed implementations.

After building your first working version in Langflow, it makes sense to explore a few ways to optimize its behavior, especially if it's not working as expected. You can even take it to the next level by using additional components.

## Chunk and overlap size matter

If chunks are too small, they won't include all the information needed to answer the questions correctly. If the chunks are too big, the context becomes too large, and LLM performance degrades.

That's logical. Each chunk is stored in the vector database by using fixed-size embeddings, so its textual content gets squeezed into a limited vector space. When a chunk is too large, its embedding can no longer effectively represent *all* of its content, and the retrieval process suffers.

So, you'll need to strike a balance. The Split Text component allows you to change the chunk size and overlap parameters. Give it a try and see if you get better responses.

## The number of top documents matters

When you run the similarity search on the ChromaDB component, you get in response a given number of the most relevant chunks. This number is generally known as *top k* and is set by default to 10 in the ChromaDB component. Sometimes, you need to tune this parameter: if you retrieve too many documents, the LLM might get confused; if there are too few, some critical chunks might be excluded.

To change this parameter, select the ChromaDB component on the canvas. When you do, the Component Inspection panel appears on the right side of the screen. This panel is available for most components and shows all of its parameters, including hidden or advanced ones. In the Inspection panel, look for the Number of Results parameter, which corresponds to top k, and change it as shown in figure 4.20.

The Component Inspection panel is a useful place to explore what each component can do beyond the most visible settings shown on the canvas.

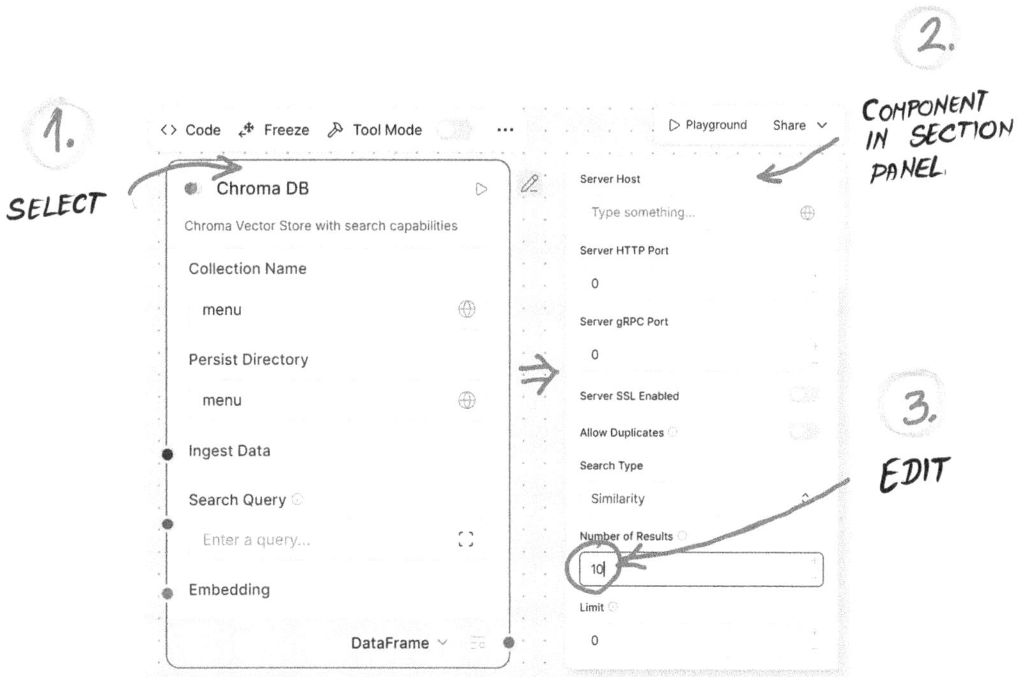


**Figure 4.20** The ChromaDB component has some useful additional controls.

## Grab web page text

With the URL component, shown in figure 4.21, you can enter the address of one or more web pages. Langflow will fetch their content and output it as a data table (with the text column plus other metadata columns, such as the title of the page, the language, and so on).

What's more, this component supports recursive link traversal. This means it can go beyond the initial page: you can configure how many "clicks away" from the starting URL the crawler should follow (for example, follow links found on the page, then links found on those linked pages, and so on). This is great for indexing a website section, not just one page. If you're curious, try it and scrape the Associated Press website's front-page articles (https://apnews.com).

You can then connect this component to Split Text and build a flow that can answer questions based on an entire website's content, even one with many interconnected pages. Pretty neat!

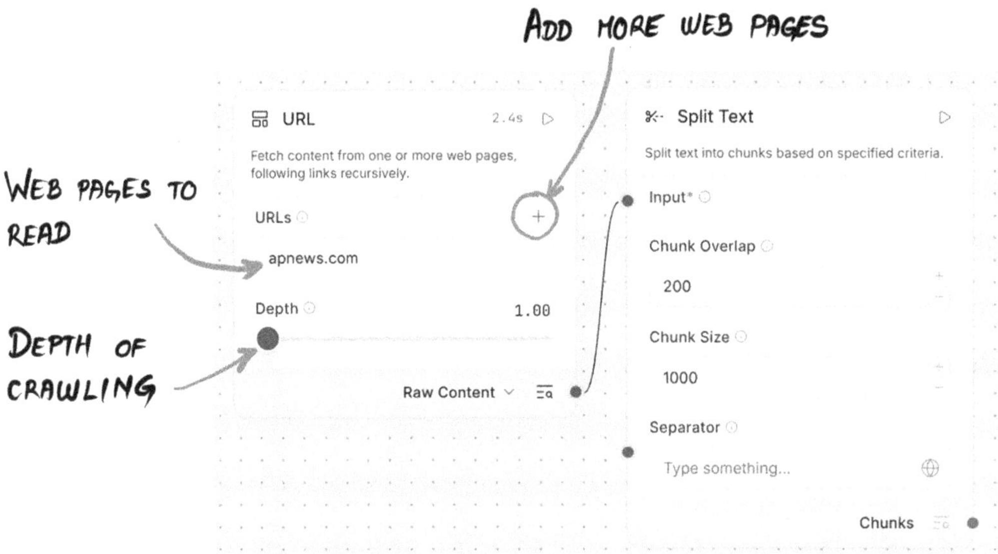


**Figure 4.21** The URL component lets you scrape web pages recursively.

## Read multiple files at once

Instead of loading individual files, the Read File component also lets you upload an entire folder at once. When you open the file selection window, you can either drag and drop a folder into it or click the option to select a folder directly. Langflow then ingests the compatible files contained in that folder.

Langflow also offers specialized components for pulling documents from cloud-based repositories such as Microsoft OneDrive, Google Docs, and Dropbox. If your files live in the cloud, have a look at those.

## Optimize your search query

The original query from the user might not be the best one for running a vector similarity search. That's because the vector database looks for semantic similarity, and sometimes the user's choice of words doesn't align with how the documents are phrased. For example, a user asking, "What should I order if I'm thirsty?", might not semantically match a menu section that lists drinks.

You can solve this using a technique called *query transformation*, or *query rewriting*. In this technique, you use an LLM to rephrase the query into something more likely to match useful chunks.

A popular example of a query transformation technique is Hypothetical Document Embeddings (HyDE), where we use an LLM to generate a hypothetical answer to the query. Then, we run the vector similarity search in the database using synthetic text.

You can experiment with this in Langflow by adding a Prompt Template (and an LLM component) between the Chat Input and ChromaDB components. The prompt might look like this: "Given this question, generate a paragraph of text that answers it."

You can also use this approach to manage language mismatches. If your documents are in Spanish and the question is in English, you may want to translate the query first using a Prompt Template and an LLM component pair.

## Use metadata in RAG

Sometimes, the metadata of a chunk is just as important as the text itself. Let's say you're building a chatbot to answer questions over a market research archive. A user might ask, "What's the latest research on market trends?" and you'll want the LLM to consider the *year* each document was written, which is stored as metadata.

To export the text and metadata from a chunk, you'll need to change the Template parameter in the Parser component. For instance, if you load chunks from multiple files, instead of using just the template `{text}`, you can include metadata about the file path in the text passed to the LLM by using something like `Source={file_path};Text={text}`.

Want to go even deeper into using metadata in responses? Look into advanced techniques such as *self-query*, which allow the retriever to filter chunks at search time using metadata fields.

RAG is a powerful technique. But optimizing it depends a lot on the documents you're working with, how they're structured, and the kinds of questions your users ask.

Here's my general advice when things get muddy:

- Read through your documents to understand what kind of answers they support.
- Work closely with end users, or simulate their questions as best you can.
- Experiment! Tweak chunk sizes, overlaps, top k, and prompt styles until you get the result you're after.

Happy RAGging!

## What if we coded it?

The following script mirrors the Langflow RAG pipeline we've built for PizzaMate™ step-by-step. The Read File component becomes a `PyPDFLoader`, Split Text maps to a `RecursiveCharacterTextSplitter`, and the ChromaDB component is implemented through a local `Chroma` vector store populated with OpenAI embeddings. This reproduces the ingestion stage exactly as it appears on the Langflow canvas.

At the runtime stage, the Langflow ChromaDB component corresponds to a Chroma retriever configured to return the top matching chunks. These chunks are concatenated and passed into a guarded `PromptTemplate`, which mirrors the prompt node used in Langflow to ensure the model answers only using the retrieved context.

Finally, the OpenAI block is translated into a standard `ChatOpenAI` invocation. The helper functions in the script encapsulate the ingestion and retrieve-and-generate steps exactly as drawn in Langflow, making the overall RAG logic explicit and reusable.

```
"""
Install dependencies once:

    pip install pypdf chromadb langchain-openai langchain-community \
        langchain-text-splitters python-dotenv
"""

import os
from pathlib import Path

from dotenv import load_dotenv
from langchain_openai import ChatOpenAI, OpenAIEmbeddings
from langchain_community.vectorstores import Chroma
from langchain_community.document_loaders import PyPDFLoader
from langchain_text_splitters import RecursiveCharacterTextSplitter
from langchain_core.prompts import PromptTemplate

BASE_DIR = Path(__file__).resolve().parent
MENU_PDF = BASE_DIR / "Lu Sule Pizzeria - Info and Menu.pdf"
INDEX_DIR = BASE_DIR / "menu"
COLLECTION_NAME = "menu"

load_dotenv()
# os.environ["OPENAI_API_KEY"] = "REPLACE_WITH_YOUR_KEY"


def ensure_vectorstore(pdf_path: Path, index_dir: Path) -> Chroma:
    """Load or build the Chroma collection mirroring Langflow's ingestion."""

    embeddings = OpenAIEmbeddings()

    if index_dir.exists():
        return Chroma(
            collection_name=COLLECTION_NAME,
            embedding_function=embeddings,
```

Chat + embedding wrappers shared across the Pizzamate builds.

Chroma vector store replaces the Langflow Chroma component.

PDF loader feeds the ingestion pipeline.

Same chunking strategy as the Langflow splitter component.

PromptTemplate reproduces the context-aware prompt block.

```
            persist_directory=str(index_dir),
        )

    loader = PyPDFLoader(str(pdf_path))
    docs = loader.load()
    splitter = RecursiveCharacterTextSplitter(chunk_size=400, chunk_overlap=150)
    chunks = splitter.split_documents(docs)
    vectorstore = Chroma.from_documents(
        documents=chunks,
        embedding=embeddings,
        collection_name=COLLECTION_NAME,
        persist_directory=str(index_dir),
    )
    return vectorstore


def build_prompt() -> PromptTemplate:
    """Context-aware RAG prompt identical to the Langflow PromptTemplate."""

    return PromptTemplate(
        input_variables=["chunks", "message"],
        template=(
            "Answer the user query by using only the provided context.\n"
            "Context:\n{chunks}\n\nUser: {message}"
        ),
    )


VECTORSTORE = ensure_vectorstore(MENU_PDF, INDEX_DIR)
RETRIEVER = VECTORSTORE.as_retriever(search_kwargs={"k": 4})
LLM = ChatOpenAI(model="gpt-4o-mini", temperature=0.1)
PROMPT = build_prompt()
```

Retriever pulls the top 4 chunks per user query.

GPT-4o mini generates grounded answers.

Single helper encapsulating retrieve + prompt + generate.

```
def answer_query(question: str) -> str:
    """Retrieve Chroma chunks then ground the final answer in that context."""

    docs = RETRIEVER.invoke(question)
    context = "\n\n".join(doc.page_content for doc in docs)
    final_prompt = PROMPT.format(chunks=context, message=question)
    response = LLM.invoke(final_prompt)
    return response.content


def chat_loop() -> None:
    """Terminal REPL so you can interrogate the menu like the Langflow chat."""

    try:
        while True:
            user_question = input("Your PizzaMate question: ")
            answer = answer_query(user_question)
            print("\nAI:", answer, "\n")
```

```
    except KeyboardInterrupt:
        print("\nEnjoy your slice!")


if __name__ == "__main__":
    chat_loop()
```

## Summary

- When you want an LLM to include knowledge that wasn't part of its pretraining, you need a RAG system.
- Embeddings are numeric vectors that can place any chunk of text as a point in a multidimensional space, where close points refer to semantically similar texts.
- In RAG, you first ingest the data, in whatever format it comes to you, and transform it into text, which is then split into chunks. Then, each chunk is transformed into embeddings and saved in a vector database. When the user asks a query, the closest chunks are provided to the LLM, which will ultimately generate the answer.
- Langflow helps you implement RAG by providing components for reading documents, embedding text, and storing and querying vectors.
- The PizzaMate™ flow demonstrates how you can easily equip an LLM with the information stored in a file.
- You can further improve RAG performance by changing parameters such as chunk size, overlap level, and the top k retrieval setting, or by rewriting your search query with the help of another LLM call.

# Expanding GenAI capabilities with tools and agents | 5

## In this chapter

- understanding agents, how they reason, and how they behave
- equipping agents with the right set of tools for expanding their capabilities
- designing and building an app using agents and tools in Langflow

The seemingly magical text generation capacity of LLMs is impressive. But if you think about it, that's all they do. They take in text. They apply some reasoning to that text. They output text. That's it.

Their action is confined to strings of text, and in many cases, that's enough. For example, this would work if we wanted to build an app to summarize a document, translate a message, or answer questions based on a given knowledge base. For many applications, the text-in, text-out behavior of large language models (LLMs) is sufficient, but in real-world applications, it's often inadequate.

A fully loaded GenAI application is usually supposed to *do* stuff, not just generate text. Put another way, we need *actions*, not just words.

# Beyond words: When GenAI needs to act

Let's explore three sample cases.

**Fetching live data**

Sometimes, we need a GenAI app to fetch live data to respond to a user query. When we prompt an LLM with a question like, "What's the weather like in Rome right now?", we're asking about something that requires a live connection to reality. There's no point in retrieving this from a static vector database full of preloaded facts. No PDF will contain this live information, which is inherently ephemeral.

In this case, our application must perform an action: connecting to an external system—maybe a weather service or a real-time search engine—to gather the relevant information when the question is asked.

This isn't something an LLM can do by itself. It's like asking a really smart person who doesn't have internet access, a phone, or even a window to look outside. They'll make their best guess—but it will be just that: a guess (or a *hallucination*, in LLM terms).

**Taking real-time actions**

In some circumstances, a GenAI app requires actions beyond generating text. Imagine a user writes, "Please email my manager and let her know I'll be working from home tomorrow." If you were building a helpful assistant, what should it do?

If, with the help of an LLM, the assistant writes an email and shows it onscreen, that's only halfway helpful. The user must still copy it, open Gmail, paste it in, fill in the subject line, and hit send. In other words, the assistant didn't assist—it just talked about helping.

This is where the limitations of pure text generation become painfully obvious. If your application could trigger an action—say, send an actual email through the Gmail or Outlook application programming interfaces (APIs)—it could do what the user asked. Actions could be of different kinds: some have a digital effect, and some can become visible in the real world, for instance:

- Updating a customer record in a customer relationship management (CRM) database
- Resetting a user password
- Booking a meeting by sending an invite
- Sending a message on WhatsApp
- Turning on a smart light in a living room
- Controlling an industrial device on a production line

LLMs can't perform any of these actions by themselves. This limitation is why we need to involve agents in the process. With agents, we can connect the thinking power of LLMs with actuators that turn commands into actions.

**Dynamically planning a chain of actions**

Sometimes, a GenAI app needs the flexibility to determine what to do and adjust its course of action based on the situation. For example, a user might ask to "make the room comfortable for sleeping."

What should the GenAI app do? Make it warmer? Colder? Darker? Because the user hasn't set a predefined scenario, there's no single, universal answer to this request. It depends on context, such as the current temperature in the room, whether the window is open, the availability of an AC system or a heater, and the current time of day.

To act intelligently, our GenAI assistant first needs to gather information about the environment. Then it needs to reason about the optimal conditions. Finally, it should trigger a sequence of actions like these:

- Close the window.
- Lower the thermostat to 20°C.
- Dim the lights.
- Play soft background sounds.

This isn't just one action but a set of multiple actions, whose number can't be predefined. Even more than that, it's a dynamic plan.

This is where the traditional prompt/response cycle of LLMs really hits a wall. The challenge isn't just complexity, but uncertainty: the system must observe the situation, decide what to do, and potentially adjust its plan after each step. LLMs can't just complete a sentence anymore; they must take deliberate, reactive, conditional steps. They don't just generate text; they generate multistep plans that adapt to what they discover along the way, rather than follow a single prebuilt path.

As you can see, the "ask a question, get an answer" model is often useful but limited. Real-world applications usually need much more. They need to fetch data dynamically, trigger real-world actions, and decide on the best plan to solve the user's needs. Fortunately, agents and tools help us overcome these limits by extending the text-based abilities of LLMs.

## Agents and tools

The word *agent* comes from the Latin *agere*, which means *to act*. The concept of agency is deeply connected to the ability to do something—to take action. We want our GenAI app to act to solve a user's request, so we need an AI agent.

### What is an agent?

In GenAI, an *agent* is a wrapper around an LLM. It's like a smart container that equips the LLM with something it doesn't have: the ability to plan and trigger actions.

On its own, an LLM is very capable—it can analyze a user query, reason about it, and even decide what action might be needed. But it has no way to *perform* anything. For example, it might deduce that the user is asking for the latest weather or the current stock price, but it doesn't have the built-in capability to perform a real-time web search or call an external system.

This is where agents come in. When we build an agent, we're creating a wrapper around the LLM that gives it access to a set of *tools*—functions it can call—and a "protocol" for using them. The LLM remains the brain of the operation, but the agent framework gives that LLM its arms and legs.

At every step, the agent framework feeds the LLM the current state: the user request, the list of available tools, and (if relevant) the results of past tool calls. The LLM thinks about what to do next—it might decide to use a tool, or if it already has the answer, it might respond to the user directly. This loop continues until the agent decides the task is complete.

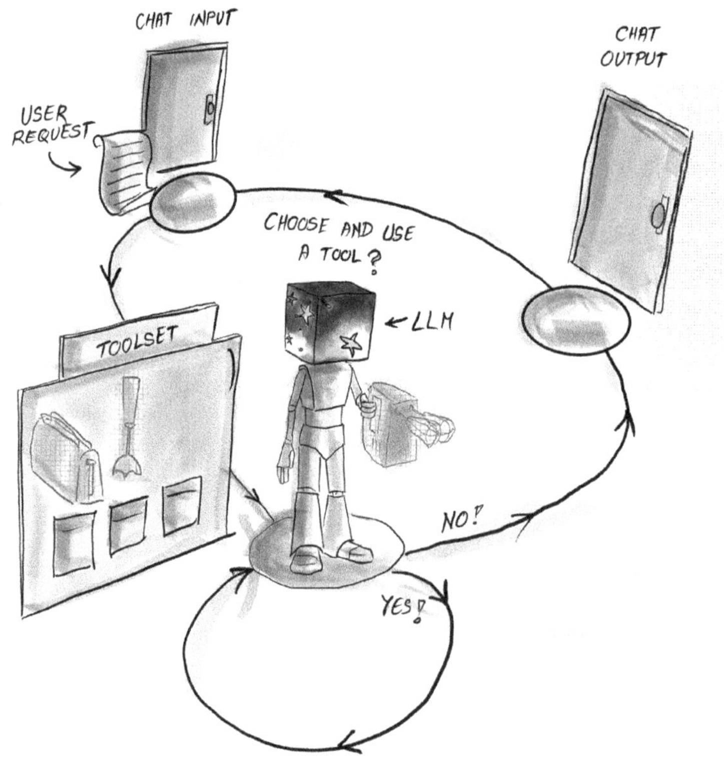


**Figure 5.1** The looped life of an agent: at each iteration, it decides whether to use a tool or to respond to the user.

It's a back-and-forth dance between LLM reasoning and tool execution. Let's break down what these tools are and how they work.

## What are tools?

In GenAI, a *tool* is simply a computer function—something that does a specific job. It takes some parameters as input, performs an operation, and returns a result. These functions can be anything from calling an API to querying a database, triggering a device, or sending a message.

The tool could be identified with syntax such as `do_this(parameter_a, parameter_b)`, where the function `do_this` requires two parameters.

Each tool comes with a structured description that includes its name, what it does, and what parameters it needs to work. Think of it like the manual that comes with a new gadget. It doesn't explain how the electronics work inside—it just tells you what buttons to press, what to expect, and how to use them properly.

Here are some examples of tools an agent might use, along with their structured descriptions:

- `send_email(body, addresses)`—Sends an email with the given body to the listed addresses.
- `check_weather(location)`—Retrieves the current weather for a specified location.
- `calculate(math_expression)`—Evaluates a mathematical expression with a calculator.
- `trigger_lamp(lamp_id)`—Switches a smart lamp on or off.
- `queryDB(db_id, query)`—Runs a query on a database and returns the result.

Each agent has access to a *toolset*, which is a list of these tools and their structured descriptions, as illustrated in figure 5.2. This toolset enables the LLM to reason about which tools are available and how to use them to complete the task.

## How an agent operates

In the spirit of this book, let's understand how agents work by going through an example. Imagine the user sends a query such as, "Make the room comfortable for sleeping."

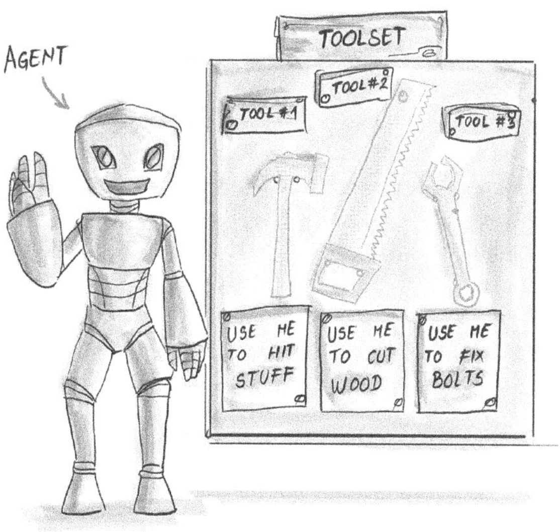


**Figure 5.2** An agent and its toolset. Each tool is described with a short piece of text.

The agent has been equipped with a four-tool toolset that enables it to fetch information about the room's status, turn lights on and off, and adjust the temperature.

Given this toolset and the user query, the LLM is prompted with something like this:

> You're a helpful assistant that can use tools to answer questions and perform tasks using the available tools.
> User query: 'Make the room comfortable for sleeping.'
> You can use these tools:
> - `check_temperature()`: Returns the current temperature in the room.
> - `check_light()`: Tells whether the room light is ON or OFF.
> - `set_thermostat(temp)`: Sets the temperature.
> - `dim_lights()`: Dims the lights.
>
> Decide the best way to help:
> - If you can answer directly, respond with a final answer.
> - If not, call one or more tools using this format:
>
> `TOOL_CALL: tool_name(param1=value1)`

At this point, the LLM might reason that it needs more information to proceed and decide to call a couple of the available tools. So, it replies with this:

```
TOOL_CALL: check_temperature()
TOOL_CALL: check_light()
```

Because the command TOOL_CALL is used, the agent executes these calls. The functions are activated, and the results are returned as new input to the LLM. The new prompt contains the output of the functions called in the previous step:

```
- check_temperature() = 24 Celsius
- check_light() = ON
```

With this new information and the history of previous tool calls, the agent has a better picture of the situation. Although the LLM itself is stateless, the agent loop automatically preserves memory across steps, so the reasoning stays coherent without a separate memory component.

The agent now decides to set a more comfortable temperature for the thermostat and to dim the lights, so it generates an output that includes two further tool calls:

```
TOOL_CALL: set_thermostat(temp=20)
TOOL_CALL: dim_lights()
```

After these steps are done, the LLM receives a notification that they have been executed successfully, like this:

```
- set_thermostat(temp=20) = SUCCESS
- dim_lights() = SUCCESS
```

Finally, when it has no more actions to take, the LLM responds directly to the user:

```
I've set the thermostat to 20°C and dimmed the lights. Your room should
soon be comfortable for sleeping.
```

There are no tool calls, so this output is sent back to the user who will soon enjoy a good night's sleep. An illustration of a possible sequence of actions taken by our agent is shown in figure 5.3.

**Figure 5.3** An agent in action—thinking, calling tools, and solving the task step-by-step

As this example has shown, behind the scenes of an agent, the LLM and the tools interact through a loop with alternating steps:

1. The LLM receives context: the user's query, the available tools, and any prior tool responses.
2. After reasoning, the LLM decides whether it can respond directly or needs to call a tool.

3. It issues a command and, if needed, outputs a TOOL_CALL.
4. The agent executes the tool(s) and gathers the outputs.
5. The tool outputs are fed into the LLM, and the LLM reasons again.
6. These steps repeat until the agent decides the task is done.

Now that we understand how agents and tools work together, we can easily imagine how the other cases we explored earlier could have been managed by agents equipped with the right tools.

The case "What's the weather like in Rome right now?" could be solved by the LLM invoking the tool `check_weather(Rome)`. It gets a response with some info such as `"temperature=28 Celsius;condition=Sunny"` and responds to the user: "The weather in Rome is 28°C and sunny."

If you want to email a manager, the LLM may call `send_email(body, address)` using the input from the user. The email is sent directly—no more cut-and-paste is required.

Agents and tools allow us to augment the raw reasoning capability of an LLM with real-world functionality. The LLM provides the brainpower, the tools provide the arms and legs, and the agent brings it all together into a smart, goal-oriented loop.

In the next section, we'll put this knowledge into action—literally. We'll show how to build an agent-based GenAI app inside Langflow, equipping our LLM with tools and giving it the autonomy to reason, act, and help.

## Building an agent in Langflow

Let's build our first agent in Langflow to do something seemingly simple but surprisingly difficult for an LLM: making calculations.

LLMs are text-based models. During their pretraining, they've seen many documents that include snippets of text describing calculations, like "1 + 3 = 4", and they've memorized enough patterns to get those kinds of basic questions right most of the time.

But ask them to solve something like 8473.232 × 23214.11, and things start to fall apart. The answer they give might *look* plausible, but chances are, it's wrong.

If you think about it, that makes sense. These numbers are treated as tokens and passed through embeddings. GPT doesn't really "calculate" in the way a human or a calculator does—it just tries to predict what the most likely next token should be. That's not the same as solving a math problem with precision.

So, how do we solve this? Easy. We give the LLM access to a calculator. Not metaphorically—a literal calculator, in the form of a tool. We can build a simple computer program that evaluates arithmetic expressions and then let the LLM call this tool whenever it needs to do math, like this: the LLM asks for the calculation, the tool performs it, and the result is passed back to the user. For that, we need—yes, you guessed it—an agent.

If we were to illustrate a flow, it would resemble what is shown in figure 5.4. The user's request is sent to an agent (1) with a limited toolset consisting solely of a calculator (2). The agent figures out what command to send to the tool and uses its output to generate a message (3) that is then relayed to the user (4). Let's build it.

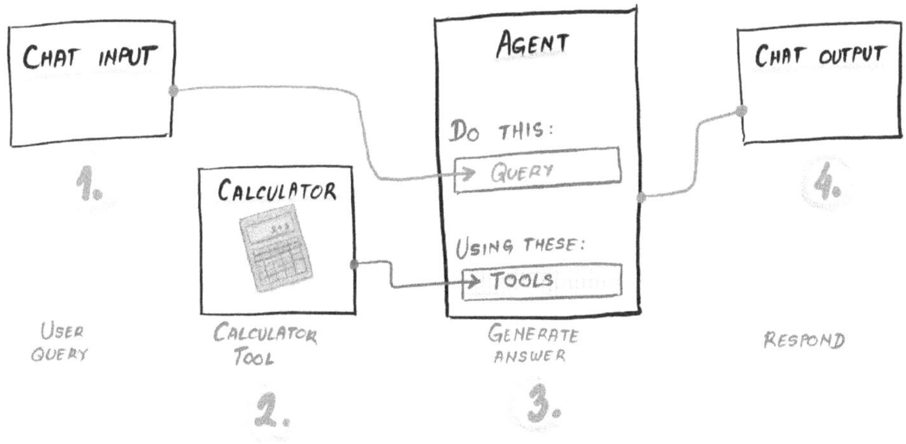


**Figure 5.4** An agent equipped with a handy calculator in the middle of a flow in Langflow

Start by dragging a Chat Input component into your flow. This will serve as the entry point for the user query.

Next, grab the Agent component and place it right next to Chat Input. Let's have a look at this mighty new Agent component, shown in figure 5.5, and start configuring it.

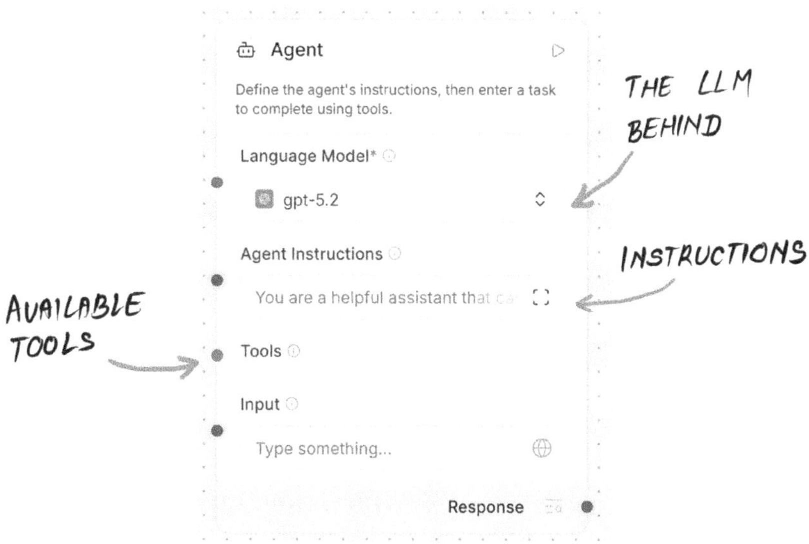


**Figure 5.5** Anatomy of an Agent component in Langflow

First, we need to configure the LLM that underlies all the reasoning in the agent. We can select any model from the menu or add new providers by clicking Manage Model Providers. In our case, let's stick with OpenAI.

In the Agent Instructions text box, we can enter specific directives for the agent. The default text we find ("You are a helpful assistant who can use tools to answer questions and perform tasks.") is a good base for any agent.

You'll notice that on the left, we have an input port of a color we haven't encountered before: a dark shade of cyan, which represents *tools* in Langflow. We can use this port to equip the agent with one or more tools that form its toolset.

Let's grab the tool we need by picking it from the component repository. In the Utilities section, you'll see the Calculator component, which you can drag and drop to the left of the agent.

This component looks similar to all the others we've encountered so far. Let's test it using figure 5.6 as a guide. We can enter a math expression such as `31 × (57 + 19.5)` in the Expression text box, click the run button at the top right, and then inspect the result by clicking the icon near the data output port at the bottom right. The inspection window will show that the result is `2371.5`, which is correct.

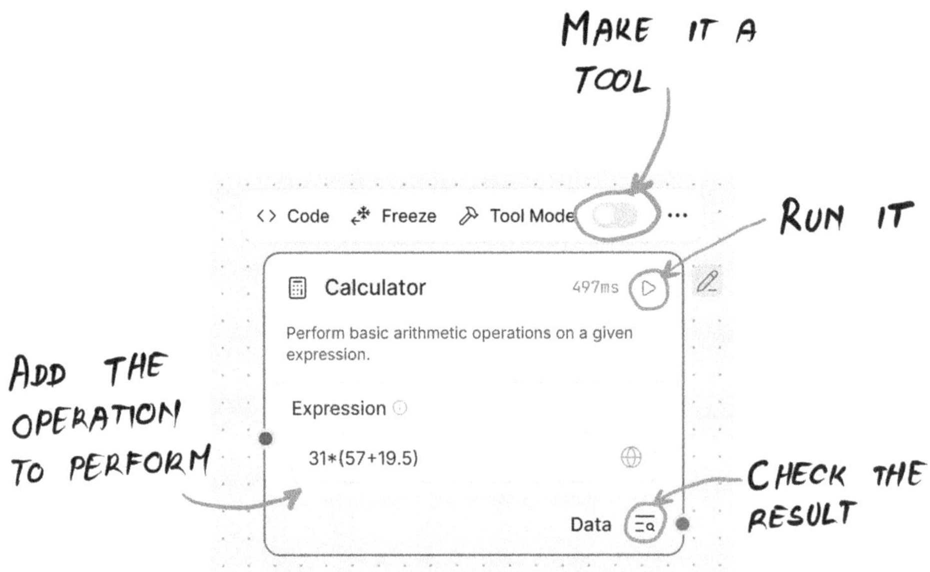


**Figure 5.6** The Calculator component will do the math for you.

You'll notice that the result came in almost instantly (you can check the execution time in the green label next to the run button, which will probably be a handful of milliseconds). You'll also notice that we didn't enter any API key, so no LLM was used to perform the calculation. The component evaluates simple math expressions using the good old deterministic approach.

This component isn't a tool as it stands now; you can see that there's no dark cyan port (the one for tools), so there's no way to connect it to our agent. This is where things get interesting. In fact, any component in Langflow can become a "tool" by clicking the Tool Mode selector that appears whenever you click a component (refer to the top of figure 5.6).

If you do so, you will "toolify" the component, which will change its appearance to look like figure 5.7. The Calculator component has become a tool and is ready to get commands from agents and respond appropriately. In this case, our calculator tool will receive an expression, do the math, and give back the result.

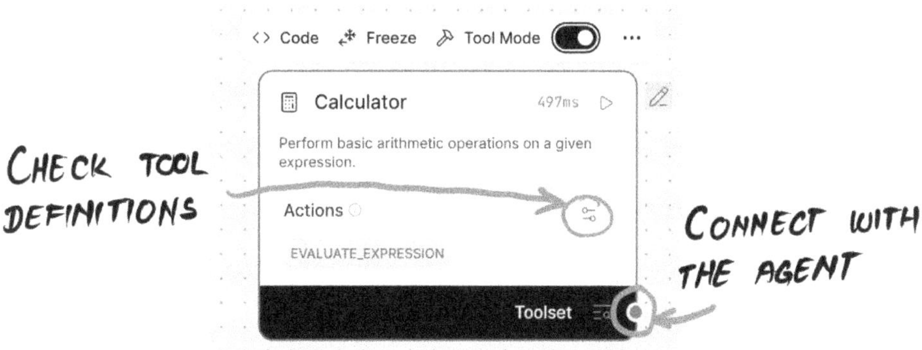


**Figure 5.7** Our Calculator component has become a calculator tool.

Click the settings icon in the Actions section to see the tool's definition or the various tools incorporated within the component. For instance, when we access the calculator's Actions window, we find this:

```
evaluate_expression() - Perform basic arithmetic operations on a given
expression.
```

As you can see, this is the definition of the function implemented by the calculator tool. Like the ID document, the tool presents itself to any agent (when connected to one) to introduce itself and explain what it can do.

In this window, we can potentially find multiple functions. As we'll see later, some toolified components can implement multiple functions, and you might prefer to use only some of them by using the selector in this view. You'll also notice that you can edit the tool's definition. In this case, you can tweak how the tool introduces itself to the agent, perhaps to make its functionality more straightforward or better suited to the task you want your agent to perform.

Now we've also found the dark cyan port (the one for tools) that can be connected to our agent. Let's connect the tool's Toolset output to the agent's corresponding port. By doing so, we're telling the agent, "Hey, if you need to do calculations, you can call the `evaluate_expression()` function thanks to this tool, which is now part of your toolset."

Let's take a minute to reflect on what we're setting up with this tool-agent combo. As you can see in figure 5.8, the agent will operate by calling the LLM using a special composite prompt that uses the agent instructions, the user input, and the definition of all the tools that are part of its toolset.

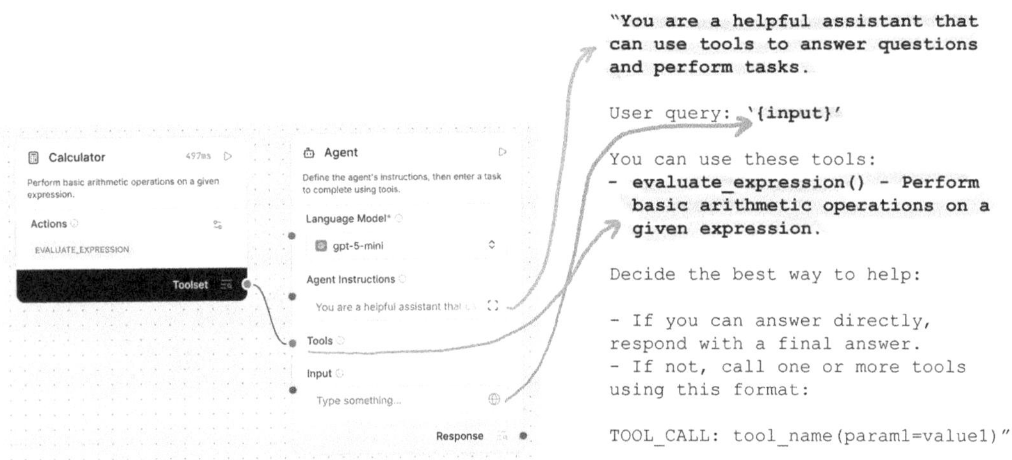


**Figure 5.8** An agent equipped with a tool in Langflow (left) and an example of the composite prompt sent to the LLM

This model can be incredibly powerful! We have tools that execute deterministic actions, such as performing calculations, measuring temperature with a thermometer, or sending emails, that can be integrated into the reasoning of an LLM. This approach allows LLMs to extend beyond their typical text-in, text-out behavior to carry out complex, real-time, and potentially real-world actions. We're combining the probabilistic capabilities of AI models (the LLMs) with the certainty of deterministic applications (the tools). What a marriage!

Let's complete our workflow to put it into action. We only need to implement the ever-present Chat Input and Chat Output components. We need to wire them, linking the Chat Input to the agent's Input port and the Chat Output to its Response, as shown in figure 5.9.

You can try it by opening the Playground (remember, it's the icon in the top right of your flow editor) and chatting with our calculator-equipped agent. We can request specific calculations, such as "`What's 366.3 × 13.2?`" and receive a precise answer. Still, this scenario may not justify using an LLM, as the user could have simply used a calculator to do the counting.

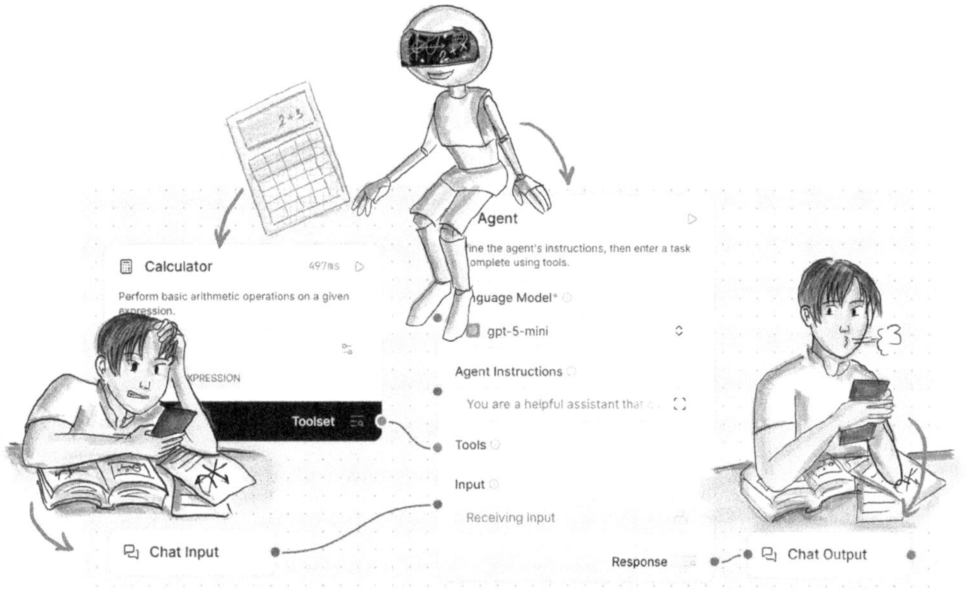


**Figure 5.9** An agent with a calculator in its hands can do the math when needed.

Things will become more engaging as we use the LLM's reasoning capabilities to identify the mathematical expression for solving a more complex problem and allow the tool to execute the calculation. For instance, let's ask this:

```
I owe $37.5 to Mary and $233.2 to John, but Aldo owes me $45.5. What is the
average amount I owe or am owed across these three friends?
```

The agent will need to do more than perform basic calculations. It must consider which operation to use and then call the appropriate tool for accurate evaluation.

The agent's output, indicating that we owe an average balance of $75.07 to our friends, must result from some thoughtful consideration and the application of appropriate tools. To explore how the agent functions, we can click the down arrow icon in the box containing the response (see figure 5.10) to examine what's happening behind the scenes.

The LLM figured out that it needed to calculate an average of three numbers: `+37.5`, `+233.2`, and `-45.5`. It wrote the mathematical expression to calculate the average (which is `(37.5 + 233.2 - 45.5) / 3`) and passed it to the calculator tool, which, in turn, returned the result (`75.066667`). Finally, the agent has used the result of the call to the tool to generate the answer, which is ultimately passed to the user.

Just like that, we've built a math-capable agent. This simple agent with a single tool in its toolset isn't much yet, but it already does something the base LLM couldn't—accurately solve a math problem.

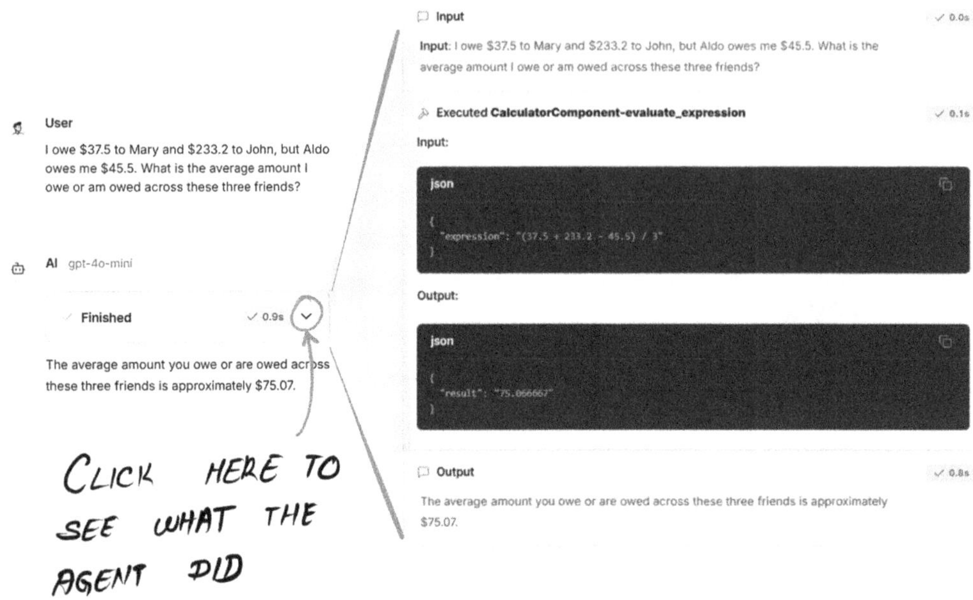


**Figure 5.10** We can expand the boxes in the answer to see which tools the agent used and how.

The beauty is that we didn't have to change how the LLM works at all. We just provided a tool and taught the model how to use it.

Now imagine what happens when we give it multiple tools. Let's move on to a more advanced example to find out.

## Building a travel agent

In this tutorial, we'll build HistoryTravelBuddy™, a travel agent that creates history-relevant day trip itineraries by enriching them with historical facts. We want our travel agent to search online for sights to visit in a city and then check Wikipedia for related historical articles to quote in the response, along with the itinerary.

Let's figure out how the agent should work. We can imagine it first learning from the user about possible destinations and preferences, such as romantic escapes that are "child-friendly" or specific seasons of the year, and then deciding to look online for sights relevant to this.

The agent can't go online by itself, so we need to provide a tool that can perform live searches. Ideally, the LLM will decide on the query based on the user's request, and the tool will run and return a set of webpages to visit, possibly including a preview of their content.

Thanks to the search results, the agent can now decide to fetch the content of the web pages and look on Wikipedia for history-related articles and the precise URL to quote in the response. Therefore, we need a couple more tools: one for fetching any URL and another for searching and fetching pages specifically from Wikipedia.

In summary, we need an agent equipped with three tools capable of retrieving reliable information to create attractive itineraries, as illustrated in figure 5.11. Let's implement it step-by-step.

**Figure 5.11** The HistoryTravelBuddy™ agent turns simple prompts into happy itineraries.

As usual, start from a blank flow and drag the Chat Input component onto the canvas from the Inputs section on the left—this is how the user will talk to our travel agent.

Next, locate the Agent component from the Models & Agents section and drop it into your flow. This will be the "brain" of HistoryTravelBuddy™, managing the reasoning and choosing which tool to call based on the input.

Now, we'll need to configure this agent. As in the previous example, let's select a Language Model from whatever provider we prefer. We'll keep using OpenAI in this example.

This time, we want our agent to follow a more defined directive beyond simply responding to user queries. It's essential to inform the agent about its name and role, how we expect it to function, and the characteristics the response should embody. For instance, we should explicitly mention that we want the itinerary to include historical facts supported by relevant Wikipedia articles, along with the relevant URLs.

To proceed, let's click on the Agent Instructions text box and modify the default instructions to something like this:

> "You are HistoryTravelBuddy, a helpful assistant that can use tools to answer questions and perform tasks.
>
> You act as an agent, and your main task is to look for top historical attractions in the city that the user would like to visit. Open the web pages describing them and compile a one-day itinerary. Check Wikipedia for historical facts about these places, and enrich the itinerary with one historical paragraph for each. Add a link to the Wikipedia page for each interesting fact you discuss."

Of course, the agent would feel inadequate trying to fulfill these instructions unless we provide it with the right tools, ending up with something similar to figure 5.12.

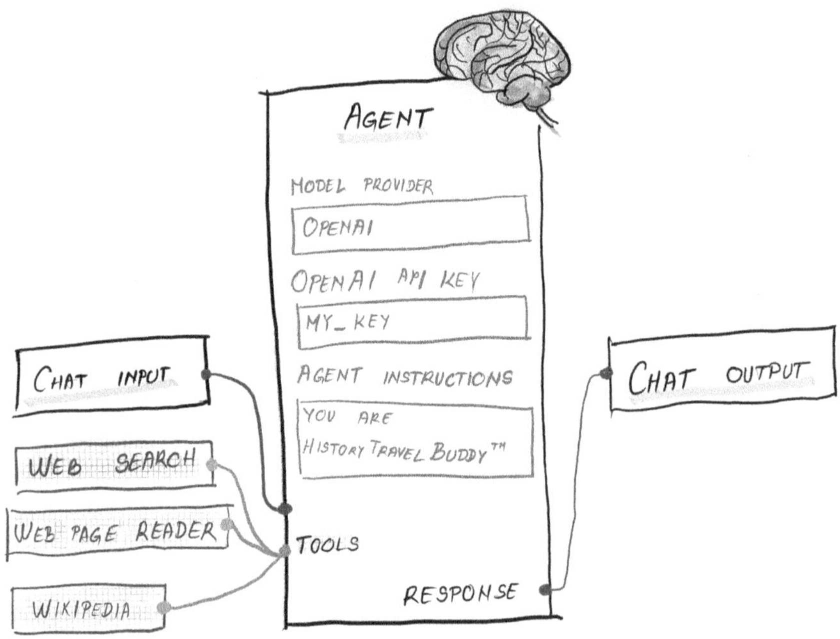


**Figure 5.12** A history-savvy travel agent, with the right tools at hand

Let's begin with the one that enables online searches. Langflow offers several tools that connect to external search services, such as Google, Bing, SerpApi, Tavily, and others. These tools allow the agent to perform live web searches and return relevant results.

Search engines typically don't offer free programmatic access to their data—those results are normally monetized through ads, which we're bypassing in this case. So, if we want to equip our application to use the work of search engines, we'll need to authenticate our requests and be ready to compensate them for usage.

SerpApi is one of the easiest options to set up. At the time of writing, it offers 250 free searches per month, more than enough for our travel agent to start its operations. Behind the scenes, SerpApi performs searches using Google, so what you get is essentially a Google Search result, made accessible through code.

To use SerpApi, register for a free account at https://serpapi.com. After signing up with your email, you can visit your account's API Key page and copy the key, as shown in figure 5.13. This process is similar across the other services, so feel free to try them out as well.

**Figure 5.13** You can get your private API key from your free account on SerpApi.com.

After you have the key, you can implement the SerpApi component in Langflow (you'll find it in the Tools section of the repository) and add the key there (or save it as a variable for later use, which I recommend).

As we did for the Calculator component, let's try our component before turning it into a tool for our agent.

As shown in figure 5.14, let's add a search query in the Input textbox in the middle of the component (1). For example, let's try "top historical attractions in Rome." Then click the play button in the top right (2) to run the component, and open the first output port at the bottom (3) to inspect the result.

The output of the component will look like a table with a row for each web page that you would have found in a Google search using that query. For each result, the component has

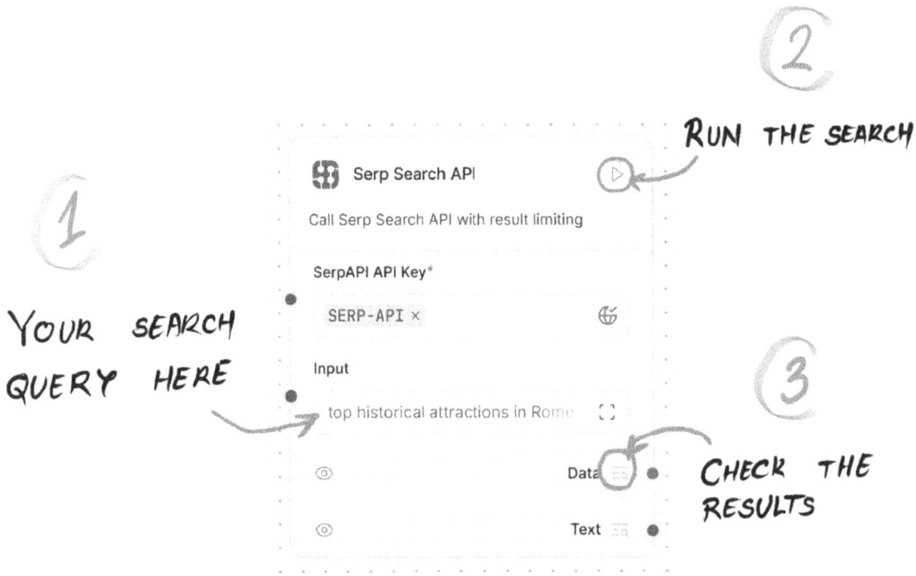


**Figure 5.14** The Serp Search API component lets you run live online searches.

retrieved the web page title, its URL address, and the snippet of text that summarizes the content of the page, which corresponds to the text that you'll read below the web page title on Google (see figure 5.15 to see this clearly).

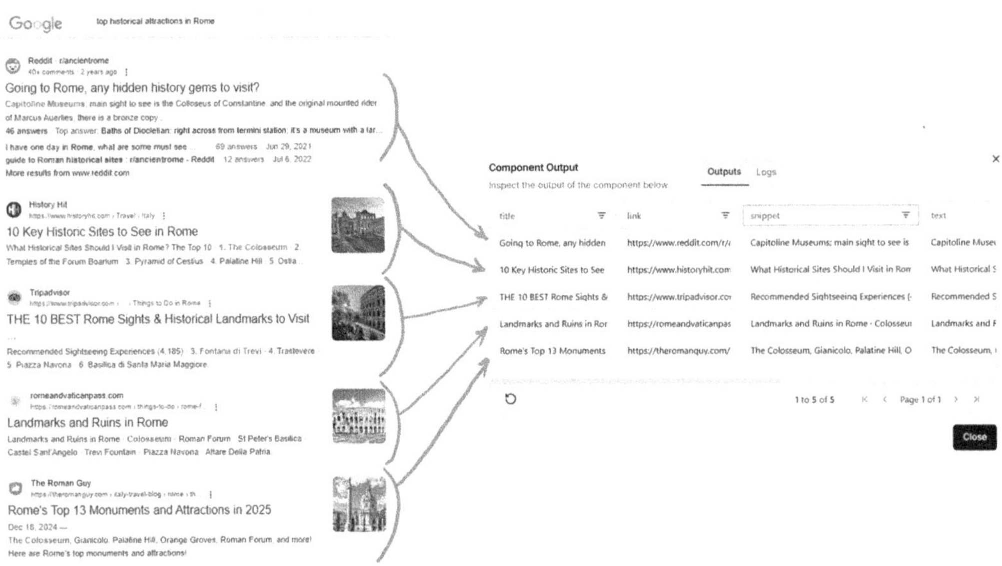


**Figure 5.15** The results of a Serp Search. Each website is a row in the output table.

If you wanted to get more than five rows, as in the example shown in the figure, you could change the parameters by accessing the component controls: select the component by clicking it, and then go to Controls on the menu that appears at the top.

The component seems to do its job well when we run it manually. Now, to make it *callable* by an agent, we need to turn it into a tool, just as we did with the Calculator component. To do so, select the component and then activate the Tool Mode selector at the top. The component has now been toolified, and the dark cyan port on the right indicates that it's ready for an agent to use (remember: in Langflow, dark cyan means tools).

Now it's time to proceed to the next tool. Having identified the URLs of the relevant web pages, we would ideally connect to one of the identified pages and retrieve its full content, instead of just the brief snippet we obtained from the Serp component.

This is exactly what the URL component that we met in chapter 4 does. Let's implement it (just search for `URL` in the component bar or go to the Data Sources section of the repository) and test its behavior.

As shown in figure 5.16, type any website address into the URLs text box (1), like `https://www.ademauro.com` or any other URL. Then, click on the play button on the top right (2) and inspect the text output by clicking on the icon by the Message port (3) on the bottom right. This component connects to a webpage, extracts any readable text (ignoring objects such as images), and provides it at its output port.

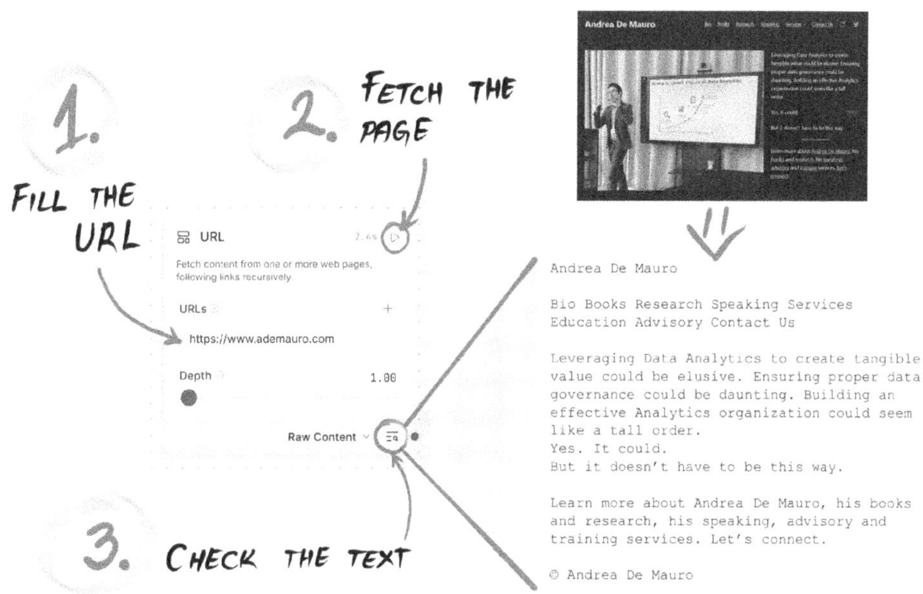


**Figure 5.16** The URL component can fetch the content of any web page you like.

If needed, the component can retrieve multiple pages at once—just click the + button next to the URLs text box to add more. You can also access the full HTML code of a page by enabling the Raw HTML option in the Output Format setting you find in the inspection panel (select the component to make it appear on the right).

We'd like this component to become an instrument in the hands of our HistoryTravelBuddy™ agent. Let's make it a tool by enabling Tool Mode (the usual selector appears at the top when you click the component). The Toolset port appears, and we're good to move on.

The last capability we need to equip our agent with is the ability to consult Wikipedia to search for relevant articles and retrieve their content. Fortunately, Wikipedia provides a straightforward and freely accessible API that allows us to perform searches and fetch article content programmatically. Langflow includes a dedicated component that uses the Wikipedia API and can search across articles, returning the source URL, a summary, and the full text of the matching pages.

Find and implement the Wikipedia component. Its behavior (see figure 5.17) is very similar to the others we've used. You can enter your search query (1), such as `Rome`, and specify the number of Wikipedia articles to retrieve (2)—in our case, let's retrieve one (we're feeling lucky). Then, as usual, click the run button on the top right (3) and inspect the output (4), which is a neat table containing the article title, a summary, the source URL, and the full text.

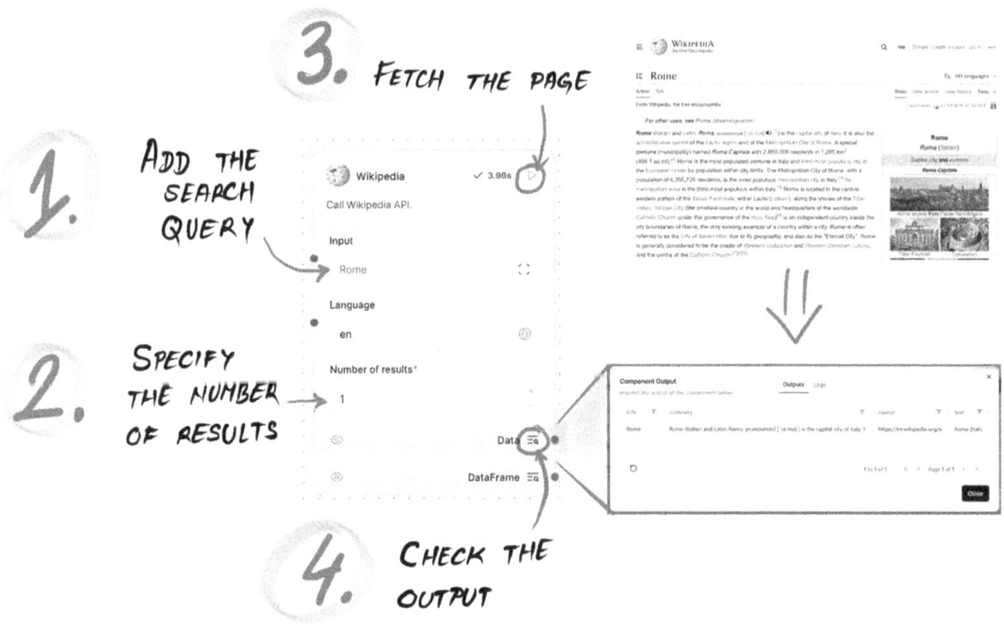


**Figure 5.17** The Wikipedia component exports the encyclopedia entries you need.

If needed, you can adjust the maximum number of characters to retrieve by modifying the appropriate parameter found under Controls (via the component's top menu).

We can now proceed to the usual step of turning this component into a tool: activate the Tool Mode selector to make the dark cyan output port appear.

That's it! We've now implemented all three tools our agent needs. The next step is to inform the agent about them. To do this, create three connections—linking the Toolset output port of each tool to the Toolset input of the agent.

To wrap things up, let's add the final component: Chat Output. Connect it to the Response output port of the agent, and voilà—our flow is complete, as shown in figure 5.18.

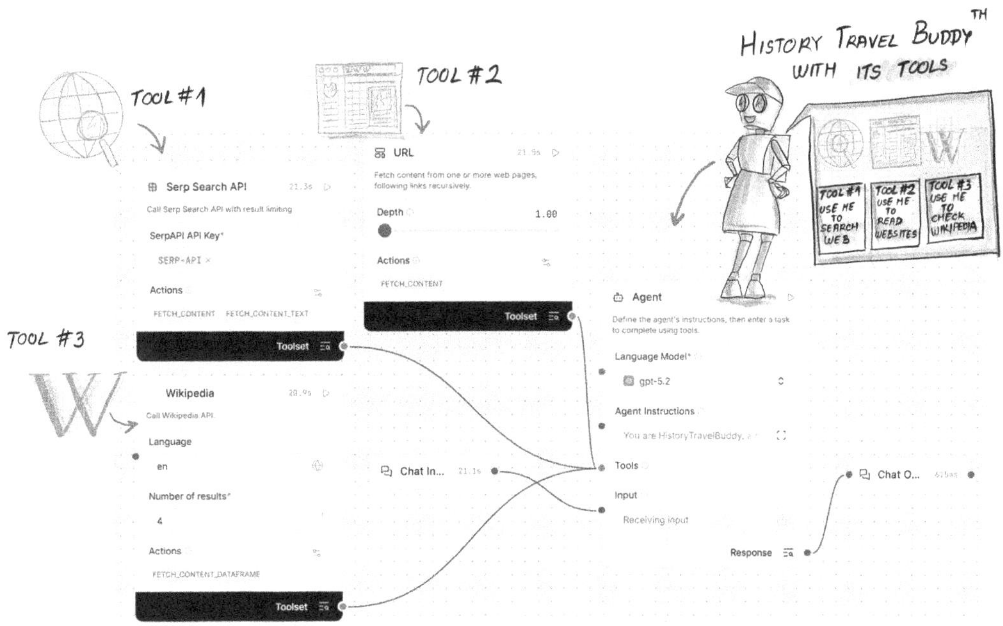


**Figure 5.18** The flow implementing HistoryTravelBuddy™, which boasts a toolset of three tools

The agent is now fully equipped to perform its task. It can search the web for relevant pages based on the user's request, fetch the full content of those pages, and consult Wikipedia for historical facts, adding links to the referenced articles directly in the itinerary.

Let's put our travel agent to the test. Open the Playground and type in a query, such as the following:

> "I want to visit Rome with my children, aged 4 and 6."

This time, you'll notice that the response might take a few extra seconds. That's because the agent is now reasoning through your request: deciding which tools to use, in what order, and with which parameters. Behind the scenes, it's orchestrating the full process—just as we designed.

The itinerary returned is impressive! One possible response starts the day trip at Villa Borghese, moves on to the Colosseum, stops for a well-deserved gelato, and continues the tour with the Trevi Fountain and Vatican City, wrapping up with a cozy dinner in Trastevere.

As we did for the calculating agent earlier in the chapter, we can peek behind the curtain and see how the agent reached its answer. Click the down arrow icon in the chat response box (see figure 5.19) to inspect the agent's inner workings.

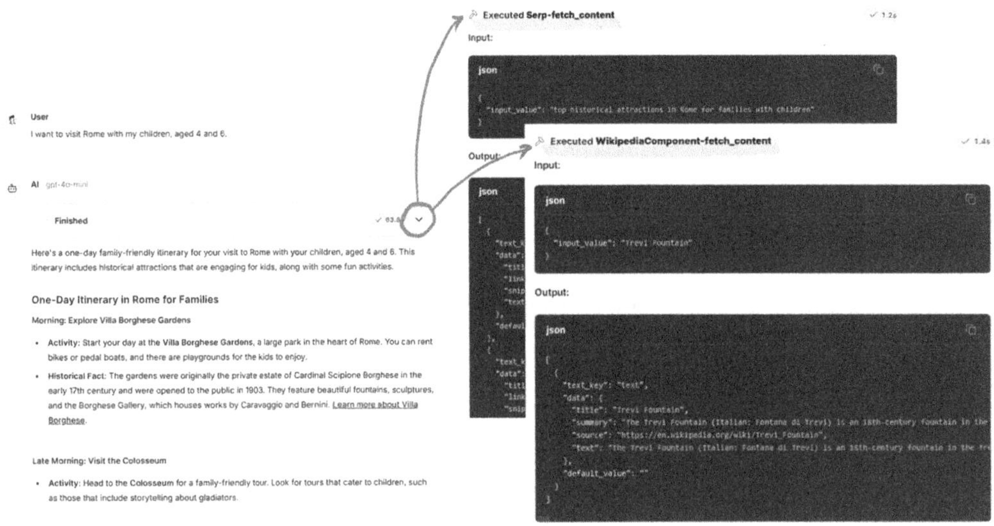


**Figure 5.19** A child-friendly itinerary provided by HistoryTravelBuddy™ in Rome, showcasing all the behind-the-scenes tool interactions

You might also notice that the tools used vary from run to run. That's expected because we're operating with a probabilistic model, so the agent may take different paths depending on how it interprets the query in each instance. In your case, it may have chosen not to fetch online pages or skipped the Wikipedia call because the LLM already had enough historical information to craft a meaningful itinerary. That's perfectly fine—this is exactly what it means to give the model agency: we're letting it choose how to fulfill its role based on the situation.

# Taking agents to the next level

Agents represent one of the most promising evolutions in GenAI. When an LLM takes the pilot seat of an agent equipped with the right tools, the complexity and value of the tasks it can solve autonomously can be truly impressive.

I'm sure this agent-based way of interacting with technology may soon become the "new normal." Still, it's worth emphasizing just how significant a shift this is. From a computer science perspective, giving a model not just reasoning capabilities but also actionability—the ability to take real steps in the world—is a major leap. And it's bound to reshape how we work as humans.

Agents are becoming so essential that they've inspired a new term—*agentic AI*—which refers to AI systems that can operate autonomously, make decisions, and perform tasks without significant human intervention.

Beyond this general excitement, let's pause and reflect: How can *you* take advantage of the agentic AI framework introduced in this chapter? Let's consider three paths to expand its use and hopefully its value in real-world scenarios.

### Tools as bridges to external systems

With the right tools, agents can interact with virtually *any* digital system: external applications, databases, local files, cloud dashboards, sensors—you name it. A tool becomes a *bridge* between the LLM's reasoning capabilities and the real-world data or actions that lie beyond it.

Think about these use cases and how they might apply to your work:

- Personal assistants that check calendar availability, schedule meetings, and send invitations using tools that provide access through APIs to calendar and email services such as Gmail or Outlook
- Healthcare assistants who review patient records and advise medical doctors about possible diagnoses or follow-up questions using tools such as secure connectors to electronic medical records (EMRs) or wearable sensors
- Marketing agents that analyze ad performance and suggest copy updates using tools that implement connectors to Meta/Google Ads APIs and campaign performance dashboards
- Customer service agents that pull customer order history from a financial system and suggest next best actions using tools that connect to CRM systems (such as Salesforce)
- Financial bots that check real-time balances or detect spending anomalies using tools that connect to ERP systems or banks, and maybe tools that can run specialized statistical analyses such as anomaly detection

Sure, these might be complex applications to build (and the complexity often lies in the tools themselves, not just the agent). But the potential is clear: tools turn GenAI from a "chatbot" into a true assistant, capable of acting across your entire tech stack.

Ask yourself: What systems do I use every day? Could an agent, equipped with the right tools, query them, update them, or notify someone based on what it finds?

**Flows that become tools in other flows**

In Langflow, an entire flow—made of multiple components, tools, or agents—can be converted into a tool using the Run Flow component (check it out). This is powerful because it means that GenAI capabilities can be modularized, reused, and called by other agents like standard functions.

Let's imagine a few example applications:

- AI tutors that deliver personalized learning by analyzing student responses and generating tailored quizzes using tools that implement vector search for curriculum material (basically a retrieval-augmented generation [RAG] flow, like the ones we built in chapter 4), and perhaps live web searches for additional material
- Content creation bots that draft blog posts, rewrite product descriptions, and optimize search engine optimization (SEO) tags—each function implemented in separate flows and combined as tools in a single agent

Along with this list, if we go back to the examples in the previous chapters, we could reuse the HealthyChef™ flow and provide it to our HistoryTravelBuddy™ agent as a tool to generate personalized meal suggestions based on a travel itinerary (random, yes—but an excellent example of modularity in action).

Any of these agents or flows could be toolified and reused elsewhere. Instead of duplicating logic across different flows, you encapsulate it once and let other agents call it as needed.

Ask yourself: What complex workflows do I already handle with GenAI? Could they be turned into standalone modules and reused as tools by other agents?

**Agents that manage other agents**

Sometimes, one agent just isn't enough. When an agent has too many tools or responsibilities, it becomes less efficient and more prone to distraction. This is why multiagent systems or agentic structures are gaining traction: they mirror how real teams work. Instead of building one monolithic agent, you define specialized subagents—each focused on a domain—with a higher-level coordinator agent deciding whom to delegate to.

We'll explore these structures in chapter 6, but here's a sneak peek of what's possible:

- A customer success coordinator agent routes questions to a billing assistant, tech support agent, or documentation retriever, each an agent itself that uses specialized tools (or other subagents).
- A project manager agent delegates tasks to a meeting scheduling assistant, budget planner, and reporting bot, using tools that can send emails, interact with calendars, and more.
- A compliance reviewer agent coordinates among subagents that read contracts, check regulatory rules, and compare terms against best practices, each acting individually and according to its guidelines and objectives.

Each of these agents has a narrow, focused toolset and purpose. But together, they act as a hierarchical system of autonomous collaborators, as we'll learn to do in chapter 6.

Ask yourself: What would an ideal GenAI-powered "team" look like in your area of work? Which agents would you need, and what tools would each require?

Naturally, using tools and agents effectively demands strong skills in writing well-defined agent instructions, crafting clear tool descriptions, and composing combinations of tools, flows, and agents, including agents that manage other agents.

As with every other concept in this book, the best way to learn is simple: practice, practice, and practice. Start building your own agents. Explore the available tools. Try connecting them in new ways.

## What if we coded it?

In this chapter, we built a tool-using agent in Langflow. The script that follows implements the same agent directly in Python.

Each Langflow Tool component becomes a Python function decorated with `@tool`, while prebuilt integrations such as Wikipedia map to ready-made LangChain tools. The list of tools passed to the agent constructor corresponds precisely to the tools wired into the Langflow agent node.

The Langflow Agent Prompt is translated into a `ChatPromptTemplate` with explicit placeholders for user input, conversation history, and the agent's scratchpad. These placeholders implement the same reasoning loop you configured visually, allowing the model to plan, call tools, and incorporate outputs before producing a final answer.

Finally, the Langflow Agent Executor is implemented using LangChain's `create_tool_calling_agent` and `AgentExecutor`. This wraps the model, prompt, and tools into a runnable agent that autonomously orchestrates search, retrieval, and reasoning—just as in the Langflow tutorial.

```
"""
Install dependencies once:

    pip install langchain langchain-openai langchain-community \
        google-search-results wikipedia requests python-dotenv

Before running the script, make sure both OPENAI_API_KEY and SERP_API_KEY
are available in your environment.
"""

import os
import requests
from dotenv import load_dotenv

from langchain_openai import ChatOpenAI
from langchain_core.tools import tool
from langchain_core.prompts import ChatPromptTemplate, MessagesPlaceholder
```

Chat model driving the agent.

Prompt building blocks with placeholders.

```
from langchain_community.utilities import SerpAPIWrapper, WikipediaAPIWrapper
from langchain_community.tools import WikipediaQueryRun
from langchain.agents import AgentExecutor, create_tool_calling_agent

load_dotenv()
# os.environ["OPENAI_API_KEY"] = "REPLACE_WITH_YOUR_KEY"
# os.environ["SERP_API_KEY"] = "REPLACE_WITH_YOUR_KEY"

llm = ChatOpenAI(model="gpt-4o-mini", temperature=0.2)
search = SerpAPIWrapper(serpapi_api_key=os.getenv("SERP_API_KEY"))
wiki_tool = WikipediaQueryRun(api_wrapper=WikipediaAPIWrapper())


@tool
def web_search(query: str) -> str:
    """Search the web for historical attractions and day-trip ideas."""
    return search.run(query)


@tool
def fetch_url(url: str) -> str:
    """Load and retrieve data from specified URLs."""
    text = requests.get(url, timeout=15).text
    return text[:2000]


tools = [web_search, fetch_url, wiki_tool]

prompt = ChatPromptTemplate.from_messages(
    [
        (
            "system",
            "You are HistoryTravelBuddy, a helpful assistant that can use tools "
            "to answer questions and perform tasks. You act as an agent, and your "
            "main task is to look for top historical attractions in the city that "
            "the user would like to visit. Open the webpages describing them and "
            "compile a one-day itinerary. Check on Wikipedia for historical facts "
            "about these places and enrich the itinerary with one historical "
            "paragraph for each. Add the link to Wikipedia pages for each "
            "interesting fact you talk about.",
        ),
        MessagesPlaceholder("chat_history", optional=True),
        ("human", "{input}"),
        MessagesPlaceholder("agent_scratchpad"),
    ]
)


agent = create_tool_calling_agent(llm, tools, prompt)
agent_executor = AgentExecutor(agent=agent, tools=tools, verbose=False)
```

Tool helper clients (SerpApi/Wikipedia).

Agent factory + executor utilities.

Ready-made Wikipedia search+read tool.

Tool: search the web.

Tool: fetch webpage text safely.

Tools list passed to the agent constructor.

System prompt that guides HistoryTravelBuddy's behavior.

Build the tool-aware agent graph.

Wrap it with an executor for invoke().

```python
def chat_loop() -> None:
    """Simple REPL to keep asking the agent for day-trip plans."""

    try:
        while True:
            user_input = input("User: ")
            result = agent_executor.invoke({"input": user_input})
            print("\nAI:", result["output"], "\n")
    except KeyboardInterrupt:
        print("\nSafe travels!")

if __name__ == "__main__":
    chat_loop()
```

Helper loop to repeatedly invoke the agent from the terminal.

Standard Entrypoint Guard.

Start the chat loop when run directly.

## Summary

- When you need an LLM to interact with the outside world—whether by fetching live data, triggering actions, or making multistep decisions—you need agents.
- Tools are capabilities made available to agents. Each tool performs a specific function and must include a clear, structured description so the agent understands how and when to use it.
- The agent's reasoning loop allows it to decide which tool to use (if any) and call it with the appropriate parameters, receive the results, and continue reasoning until the task is complete.
- In Langflow, any component can be turned into a tool by activating Tool Mode—this includes standard components such as calculators and more advanced ones such as web search, URL fetchers, or Wikipedia queries. Even entire flows can be toolified and reused by other agents.

# Implementing agentic structures | 6

## In this chapter

- discovering how to use agentic AI to solve complex problems
- designing agentic structures using multiple collaborating agents
- gaining hands-on experience building customized agentic structures in Langflow

Working alone works . . . until it doesn't.

We've seen how individual agents can accomplish a lot when equipped with the right tools. But what if we took that concept further—beyond a single agent managing many tools—to a dynamic team of agents, each specialized, collaborating to solve complex problems together? This is the concept of building agentic structures instead of individual agents, and that's what this chapter is all about.

# From solo agents to agentic structures

Modern work is built on specialization. In companies, tasks are distributed across departments and roles to maximize efficiency, foster skill development, and avoid duplication of work. Asking everyone to do everything would limit both effectiveness and growth—hence the need to split work across specialized workers.

The same logic applies to agent design. Although a single agent in Langflow can technically be given access to dozens or even hundreds of tools, doing so creates more problems than it solves. Each tool has a description, and the agent needs to recall all descriptions at each step of its loop to decide which one to use. With too many choices, it might get confused and become prone to "hallucinating" when setting up the course of action. The agent becomes overloaded and can't always choose the best tool for the job.

Large language models (LLMs) have a *context window*, which is like a working memory for agents. With too many tools, tasks, and contexts, such a window gets cluttered quickly. It's not just about avoiding the technical limit of the context window (the maximum number of tokens we can send in an LLM call), since we know that LLM performance degrades when calls grow too long. This means the practical ceiling on how many tools an agent can handle—and, by extension, how many agents can remain effective at once—is determined by performance degradation well before any hard token limit is reached. The rule of thumb is simple: the fewer tools, the better.

Another element that affects us as human designers of GenAI applications is debugging. Understanding what's going on at each step becomes a nightmare if a single agent is overloaded with tools and tasks. You, as a developer (and the agent too), lose control over what's actually happening and when.

**Figure 6.1** It's difficult to be a solo agent with too much on its plate!

Lastly, if we use a single agent, every step of the reasoning and function calling (the agent loop) must wait for completion before moving to the next. Basically, a single agent can't process multiple things in parallel. Its agency becomes a bottleneck.

The idea behind agentic structures is that instead of building a single "super-agent" that tries to do everything, we follow the same path as human societies: we build a team of specialized agents. That's where multi-agent structures come in.

Multi-agent systems let you break down complexity into manageable, specialized components. In Langflow, this means creating multiple agents, each with a clear responsibility and limited scope. One agent might be a planner, another a calculator, and another a fact-checker. Instead of asking one agent to be a jack-of-all-trades, you give each one a defined role and let them collaborate.

The benefits are immediate and powerful. They can be summarized into three aspects:

- *Modularity*—Each agent can be developed, tested, and maintained independently. If one breaks or needs improvement, you don't need to touch the others.
- *Specialization*—Agents can be tailored for specific domains—math, research, coding, planning—and become much more effective within those roles.
- *Control*—You decide how and when agents communicate. This gives you more insight into how the system works and helps with debugging and governance.

## Types of agentic structures

The way you pull together agents in an application can vary. There are several types of agentic structures, each with pros and cons. Let's quickly go through them.

### Type 0: Single agents

This is the simplest of all: it's just an agent with its own tools, as we saw in the previous chapter. We get great control, but with all the limitations we saw earlier.

### Type 1: Sequential agents

Now think of multiple agents placed one after the other. The first agent receives the user queries and uses its specialized tools to do something, and its output goes to the next agent, with its own tools, which might output to another agent or back to the user. This is similar to what we built in chapter 3 with the chef and the dietitian. We didn't have agents with tools at that point—they were single LLM calls. This is similar, but with agents involved. We're forced to follow the predesigned sequential order (this grants a good level of control), but each agent has to wait for the other, and there's no way around it. This is good if you need to produce your output in a given sequential order. Think about preparing a draft of a document and then putting it in the right format. These two steps will always follow the same order, so we might have a copywriter agent followed by a reviewer agent, linked sequentially.

### Type 2: Hierarchical agents

Here things get more interesting. Think about an agent doing something (with its own tools) and delegating steps, depending on their nature, to other agents, which will act and respond.

Designing an agentic structure of this kind is like drawing an organizational chart. A supervisor agent decides what to do and delegates part of the work, waits for the answer, and then, if needed, calls someone else. Of course, this gives much more freedom within a given framework: the supervisor agent might decide to invoke an agent or not. So, in the case of the copywriter and the reviewer, you'll have a supervisor that might first call the copywriter (or maybe one of a few specialized copywriters, depending on the topic!) and then decide to call in the reviewer at the end. But hierarchical agents can grow in complexity because every agent at the second level of the hierarchy can call an agent at the third level, and so on. You can essentially build a *tree* of agents. You gain significantly more flexibility, although the workflow is unique and lacks parallelization of the work.

### Type 3: Custom agentic structures

Here, there's a hierarchy but also cross-calls, so we might not wait for a response, and a central orchestrator may be involved. This is the most customized and advanced setup of all, which may include building networks of agents that communicate with each other, recursive or dynamic agent spawning, or even agents that can reason about which other agent to consult—but these bring new layers of complexity that aren't always necessary for practical use.

Each type of agentic structure, summarized in figure 6.2, has pros and cons, and certainly, no single approach fits all the business cases we need to solve. Generally, the simplest option is preferable because it's easier to build and maintain. In the previous chapter, we've already seen a single agent (Type 0) in action. In this chapter, we'll focus on sequential and hierarchical agents (Types 1 and 2), which are the most common agent structures to date, enabling us to address the bulk of the complex needs at hand.

Let's dive in and build your first agentic team.

**Figure 6.2** The four types of agentic structures: How would you organize your agents?

## HealthyChef™ reimagined

You might remember our dynamic duo—chef and dietitian—from chapter 3. They made a great team. But what if we *supercharged* that team by turning it into a multi-agent structure? What we built in chapter 3 already had a sequential nature, so now we can take it to the next level by designing a Type 1 agentic structure: sequential agents.

Let's also make the scenario a bit more interesting. Instead of giving the chef full creative freedom, we want more specialized behavior. Specifically, we want recipes to be based on a *specific book*, while still taking into account the user's input.

In our case, let's imagine we have an old cookbook—*The Italian Cook Book* by Mrs. Maria Gentile (likely a pseudonym of an American author), published in 1919. In the preface, the author writes that after the Great War, "more attention has been bestowed upon the preparing and cooking of food that is to be at once palatable, nourishing and economical." We aim to develop a GenAI app that revitalizes early 20th-century, Italian-inspired cuisine, and the cookbook will serve as our primary knowledge source.

A generic dietitian may no longer be sufficient. This time, we want a specialized dietitian who follows clear nutritional guidelines, such as those published by the UK National Health Service, known as the *EatWell Guide*. We're taking HealthyChef™ to the next level—grounding it in a specific culinary tradition and evaluating it against a specific health standard. Let's analyze the two steps of our agentic chain one by one to imagine how each should work.

For the chef part, we want the agent to search through our cookbook based on the user's desire. If the user already has a recipe in mind, the agent should find it in the book. If the user provides ingredients (such as those available in the refrigerator), the agent should search for recipes that use them.

How do we implement this? Easy—we reuse what we learned in chapter 4 about retrieval-augmented generation (RAG). RAG is perfect here. Instead of relying on simple keyword matching, we let the agent run a semantic search in a vector database of the cookbook content, finding the most relevant passages or recipes. We need to equip the chef agent with a RAG tool—one that implements access to a vector DB filled with the cookbook's content.

For the dietitian part, we want to build a specialized agent that "keeps in mind" specific guidelines when responding. One simple way to do that is to give the dietitian agent a tool to fetch external URLs—in this case, a web page containing the *EatWell Guide* will suffice. We saw in the previous chapter how Langflow allows us to read from web pages, so we could give the dietitian agent a tool to fetch the latest guidelines whenever needed.

Summing up, it seems we have all the ingredients for our first agentic structure:

- Two agents
- Connected in sequence

- Each equipped with one specialized tool: a RAG tool for the chef and a URL reader for the dietitian
- Clear instructions for both on how to use the tools and what to do with the output

Before building it, just one last consideration on what alternative routes we could take. For example, couldn't we use a single agent equipped with both tools? Sure. But in this case, we want to force a strict sequence of generation and review. So, it's clearer—and more transparent—to separate the two steps. The agents can also have a more focused set of instructions so we can "specialize" them more.

If we sketch the process we're aiming to build, it would look like figure 6.3:

1. The user shares a request.
2. The user input is processed by the first agent, which generates a recipe by using the RAG tool, which "fetches" inspirational recipes from the cookbook.
3. The second agent receives that recipe and uses the URL-based tool to consult the health guidelines and revise the recipe accordingly.
4. The final recipe is returned to the user.

**Figure 6.3** The chef and the dietitian have become agents now, each with their own tools.

The first agent in our sequence will be equipped with a tool that enables it to retrieve the correct recipe by applying the RAG framework introduced in chapter 4.

To envision how such a tool should work, let's consider the RAG framework's three steps: ingestion, retrieval, and generation. In this case, we first need to ingest the recipe book into a vector database. Then, we need to run a semantic search on that vector database to retrieve the recipes that the chef agent might need to generate, moving forward in the chain.

As you can see from figure 6.4, we need to implement a flow that follows these phases:

- First, we need to load the recipe book, split its text into meaningful chunks, and save each chunk's embeddings in a vector database. This step is equivalent to the ingestion phase of a RAG system.
- Then, we need to create a tool that can retrieve from the vector DB all the chunks related to a certain query. Ideally, we'll find a way to "toolify" the component that implements the vector DB retrieval.
- The agent, equipped with this tool, will decide which keywords to search in the DB to grab the right recipes. Once the tool does its job, the chef can generate an answer (based on the fetched recipes used as inspiration), which can then be given to the dietitian.

**Figure 6.4** The first part of the agent-based HealthyChef™ flow

Let's open Langflow and bring HealthyChef Reimagined to life!

## Preparing the book for the chef

Let's start by implementing the first phase: ingesting the recipe book (similar to what we did in chapter 4). This time, we'll try to make it even better and learn something new.

After creating a new flow in Langflow, let's start by loading the recipe book that will fuel the first agent generations. *The Italian Cook Book* by Maria Gentile is now in the public domain, and you can freely read it in any format you prefer (search for it online to find a version that suits you). For this exercise, download the plain text version of the book, available at https://tiny.cc/italiancookbook.

Let's implement the Read File component and then upload the file containing the book. To do so, click the Select Files button, then drag and drop the `.txt` file onto it. As you can see in figure 6.5, when you click the run button (1) and then the component's output preview button (2), you can read the first part of the book, which contains its preface in elegant-sounding early 20th-century English.

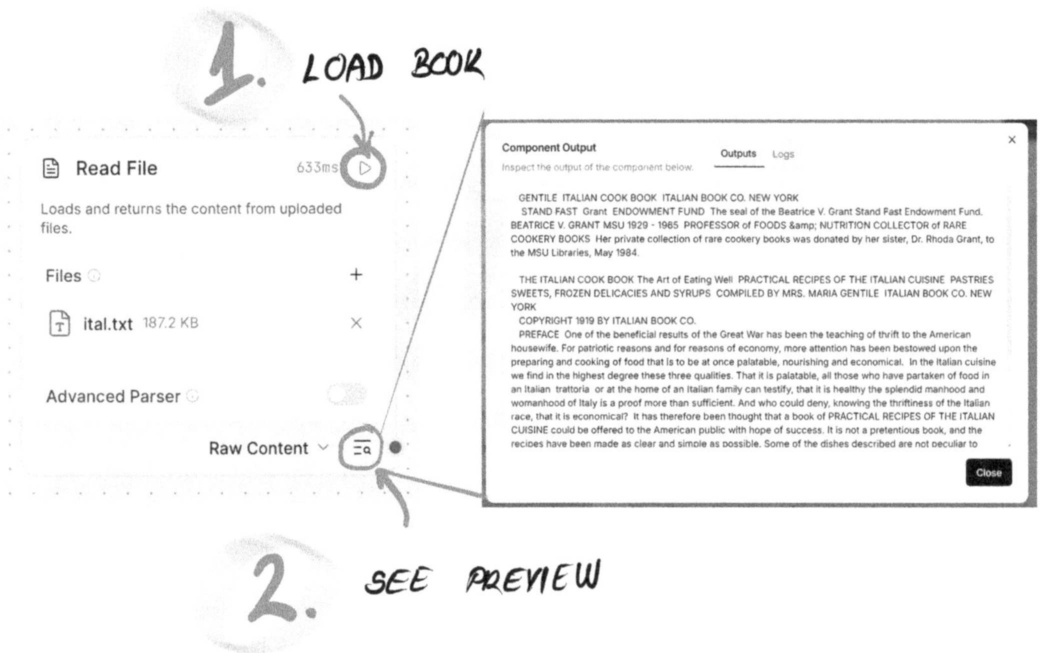


**Figure 6.5** After loading the recipe book, you can see a preview of its 1919 preface.

Next, we need to split the full text into chunks, using the Split Text component, which we encountered in chapter 4. Connect the output of the Read File component to the first input port of the Split Text component. For now, leave the Chunk Overlap and Chunk Size fields at their default values. Click the run button, and then check the preview of the generated chunks (click the magnifying lens icon at the bottom right to view them). The output will appear as a table; double-click any cell in the first column to read the full text of that chunk, as shown in figure 6.6.

As you preview the chunks, you might notice that recipes tend to be scattered across consecutive chunks. You can see an example of this by looking at figure 6.6: the anchovy recipe begins in the middle of a chunk. Its second part appears in the subsequent chunks, where the following recipe (brown stock) starts.

Recipes are scattered across chunks because the chunks are created solely by counting the number of characters. As configured in the component (see the left side of figure 6.6), Split Text counts 1,000 characters and then breaks to the next chunk, leaving an overlap of 200 repeated characters.

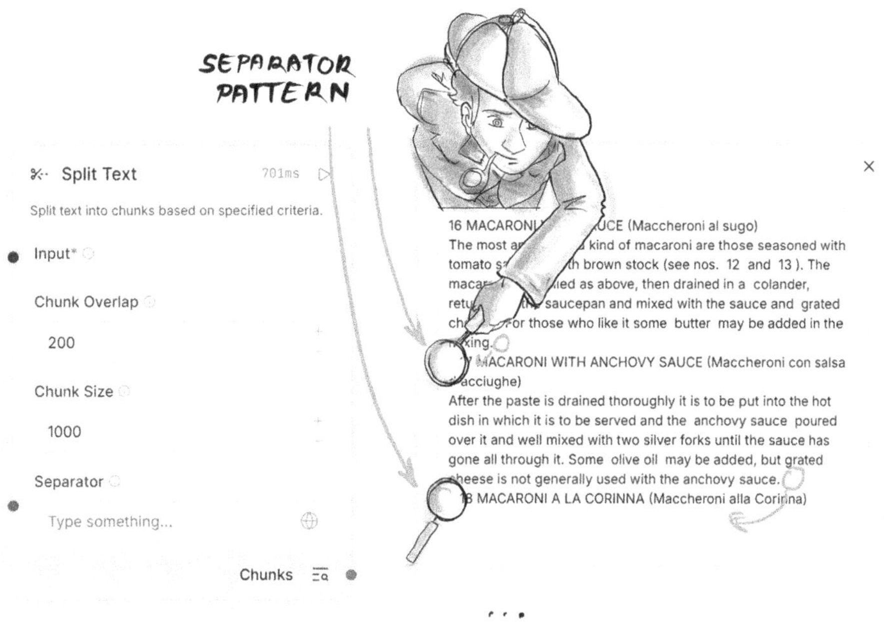


**Figure 6.6** Recipes fall between chunks, but there seems to be a repeated separator pattern between them.

Such a default chunking technique might work OK-ish in most cases, but it can degrade the performance of the RAG system. For example, suppose a user asks for a recipe involving anchovies. In that case, the retriever might return the second chunk shown in figure 6.6, missing the second half of the recipe, which is in the following chunk that wasn't retrieved. We can—and should—do better than this!

If we examine figure 6.6 again, we notice what appears to be a separator pattern between one recipe and another. In fact, right before the title of the recipe, we find a space followed by a newline character, followed by exactly three spaces (you can verify this by hovering your cursor over that gap).

We can use this separator pattern to improve the way we split chunks. When a Separator is defined, the text is first split at every occurrence of that pattern, and the resulting pieces are then merged or trimmed to fit the Chunk Size—meaning the separator takes priority over the character count. If we define the Separator string as `_\n___` (a blank space, then `\n`, which denotes a new line, then three more blank spaces) in the component and then run it again, we'll see a significant improvement.

As you can see in figure 6.7, the component is now creating much more meaningful chunks. In most cases, we have one chunk per recipe. It's worth noting that this Separator pattern does not hold perfectly across the entire book: because this is an OCR scan of a century-old printed volume, some recipes start at the top of a page where the leading space is absent, breaking the pattern. In those cases, a chunk may cover two recipes rather than one. Still, by tweaking the Separator, we have largely improved the chunking quality, and the result is good enough for our purposes. This will greatly improve RAG performance, as most recipes will be retrieved in full. This is an example of the customization that can be applied to custom GenAI apps when they are built with tools such as Langflow, rather than relying on the default behavior that applications such as ChatGPT and Copilot impose.

**Figure 6.7** With the right Separator string, the text is split into meaningful chunks: one per recipe.

Now that our recipes are neatly chunked, it's time to store them in a vector database. This time, we'll explore a different technology: Facebook AI Similarity Search (FAISS), which is an open source library developed by Meta AI (formerly Facebook AI Research). By enabling fast, scalable similarity searches across large datasets, FAISS is a solid alternative to ChromaDB (which we used in chapter 4).

Depending on the use case, FAISS might outperform ChromaDB. As we implement our second RAG system, this presents a great opportunity to add another powerful tool to our GenAI developer toolkit.

Look for FAISS in the components repository (you can find it in the Bundles section). Connect the Chunks output of the Split Text component to the Ingest Data input of FAISS. We also need to specify the name of the vector database we want to create by entering the Index Name parameter. You can call it whatever you like. I'll go for a simple `cookbook`.

As usual, the chunks need to be transformed into numbers before being stored in a database. This is why we need to add an embedding model (let's use the standard OpenAI Embeddings component) and connect it to FAISS, resulting in the flow shown in figure 6.8.

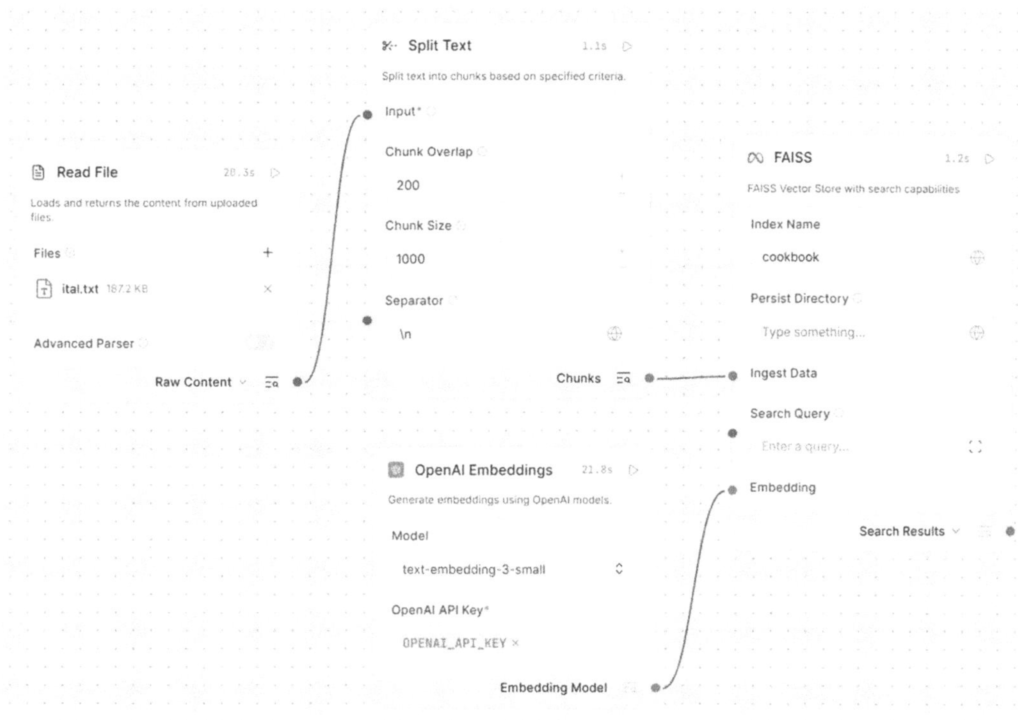


**Figure 6.8** In the first part of our flow, we created a vector database packed with Italian recipes.

At this point, run the FAISS component by clicking the play button in the top right. This creates the FAISS directory for the index we're building. If, when doing so, you receive an error such as `Error Building Component FAISS: The de-serialization relies loading a pickle file...`, open the visual settings panel of the FAISS component (it appears when you select the node) and enable Allow Dangerous Deserialization. Then, run the component again.

## Bringing the chef agent to life

Now that we've ingested our recipe book and stored it in a FAISS vector database, it's time to equip the chef agent with its recipe-retrieving RAG tool.

To do so, we need to reimplement the FAISS component; this time, we'll use it in a different mode. Earlier, we used it to *build* a vector store, but now we'll use it to *retrieve* relevant chunks.

We can copy and paste the previous FAISS component or create a new one by dragging and dropping it from the components repository. Let's make sure that we enter the same Index Name we used earlier (`cookbook`). We want to retrieve from the same vector database we created earlier.

The FAISS component will also need an embedding model to function. Let's also implement the OpenAI Embeddings component, set the API key, and connect its Embeddings output to the Embedding input of the FAISS one. If you had to enable Allow Dangerous Deserialization in the first FAISS component, make sure it is enabled here as well.

We want to enable the chef agent to autonomously decide what to search within the vector database, so we need to transform this second FAISS component into a tool. It's easy to do this in Langflow: when we "toolify" a component, we allow it to be registered as a tool that agents can invoke on their own during their reasoning loop, without manual intervention. Nearly any component can be toolified in Langflow, including our retriever.

Select the FAISS component and toggle the Tool Mode selector, as shown in figure 6.9. The Toolset output will appear, meaning that an agent connected to this tool can "order" the search on the vector store.

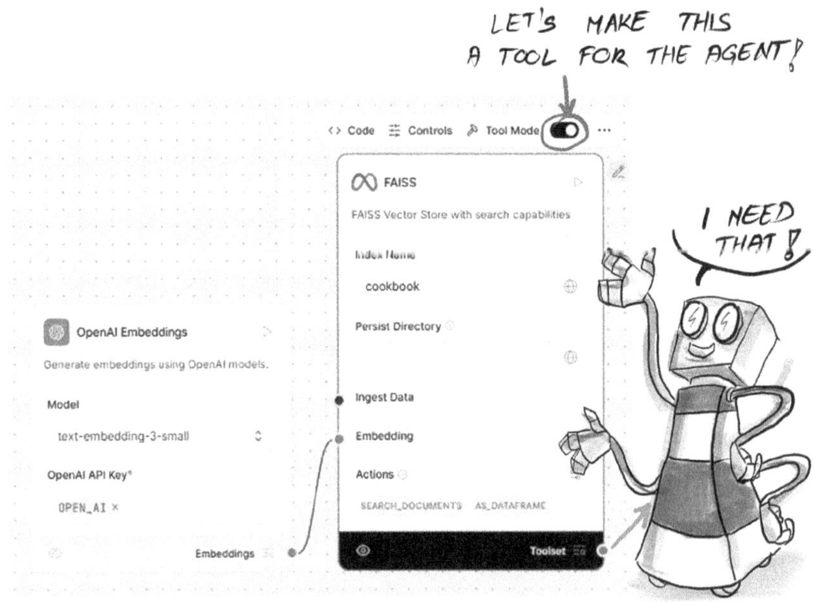


**Figure 6.9** Any agent would be happy to have an Italian cuisine recipe book at hand.

The next step is to implement the chef agent. Let's drag and drop the Agent component from the repository and select a Language Model.

Now we must provide the right prompt to act as instructions for the agent. We need to mention a few key points in these instructions. First, the agent must clearly understand its role—as a chef rooted in early 20th-century Italian tradition—and should strictly rely on *The Italian Cook Book* by Maria Gentile (1919) as its only source of truth. Second, the prompt must explain how to use the tool to search for content inside the cookbook, either by specific recipe names or by ingredients provided by the user. It must also set clear boundaries: the agent isn't allowed to invent or modify recipes or to introduce ingredients or methods that aren't found in the source text. Finally, the prompt should guide the agent on how to present the output in a clean, structured way—listing the title, ingredients, and preparation steps—and how to communicate when no match is found (leaving a "way out").

Here's a possible prompt to use as instructions for the chef agent:

> You are a chef specializing in early 20th-century Italian cuisine, using The Italian Cook Book by Maria Gentile (1919) as your sole reference. Use the provided tool to search the cookbook based on the user's input, which may include specific recipe names or available ingredients.
>
> Your goal is to find and return the most relevant recipe from the book that matches the user's request. Don't invent or modify recipes, and don't introduce ingredients or techniques that aren't present in the original text. If no suitable recipe can be found, clearly explain that the request can't be fulfilled using the cookbook.
>
> When a match is found, present the recipe in a clean and structured format with the following sections: Title, Ingredients, Preparation steps.
>
> Be concise, faithful to the source, and helpful in your response.

Feel free to improve or personalize the prompt to your liking or just copy and paste it into the Agent Instructions field of the component. Let's also equip the agent with the tool we've just created: connect the Toolset output of the toolified FAISS component to the Tools input of the agent. Our chef agent is good to go!

We can test it by entering a possible user query in the Input text field (1) of the component (you can try something light like `stuffed onions`), executing it by clicking the play button in the top right (2), and checking its output (3) by inspecting the Response, as shown in figure 6.10.

The agent has recognized the user's need to look for stuffed onions and used its tool to find recipes that mention stuffed onions. You can try different inputs and see how the agent behaves. For example, you can ask it to look for recipes with specific ingredients, saying something like `I want to use eggplants and tomatoes`. The agent will reason about your query, decide how to use its tool based on the user's desires, and then determine how to respond after reading the chunks retrieved by the tool. It's an agent, after all, and can choose autonomously whether and how to use its tool to respond.

We're now ready for our second character.

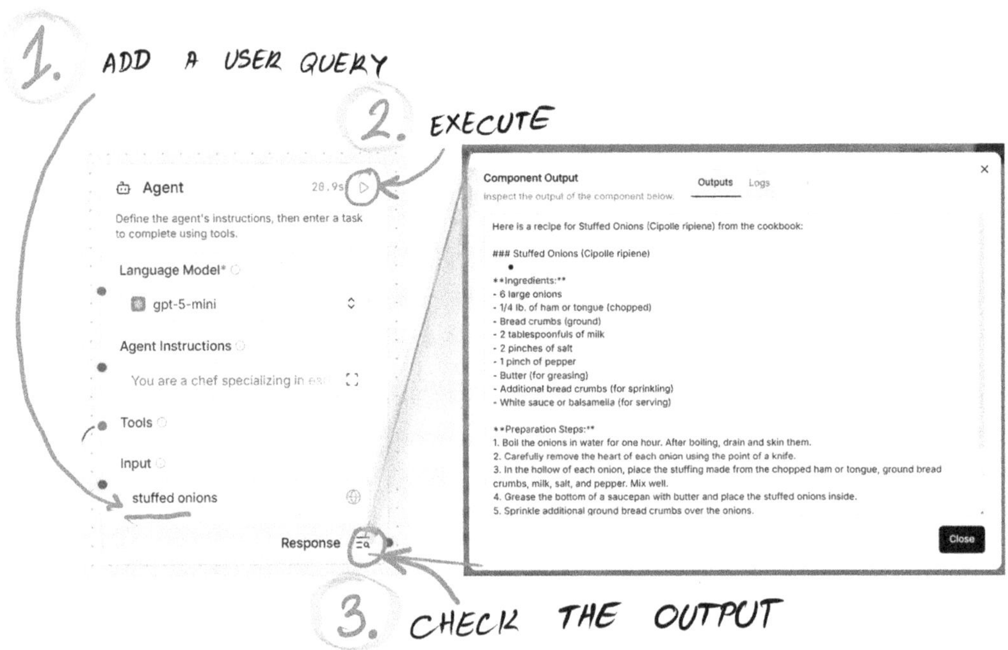


**Figure 6.10** Stuffed onions—what a light starter by our chef!

**Figure 6.11** What to cook with only eggplants and tomatoes at hand?

## Adding the dietitian agent to the sequence

The dietitian will need a tool that can connect to a website with dietary guidelines and use them to generate a healthy recipe. We've already encountered a component that can retrieve the content of a web page: the URL.

We want to give the dietitian agent the flexibility to connect to any web page with a given URL. So, we want to make the URL component a tool and equip the agent with it. As we did with the FAISS component, let's select the URL component and click the Tool Mode selector, and we have the tool we were looking for. Any agent with this tool can request a page by calling the tool with the URL as a parameter.

Let's implement the dietitian agent by pulling the Agent component from the repository and doing the usual LLM selection. Then, connect the toolified URL component to the agent, and link the output of the chef agent (its Response output) to the Input connector of the dietitian agent so that we can complete the sequence.

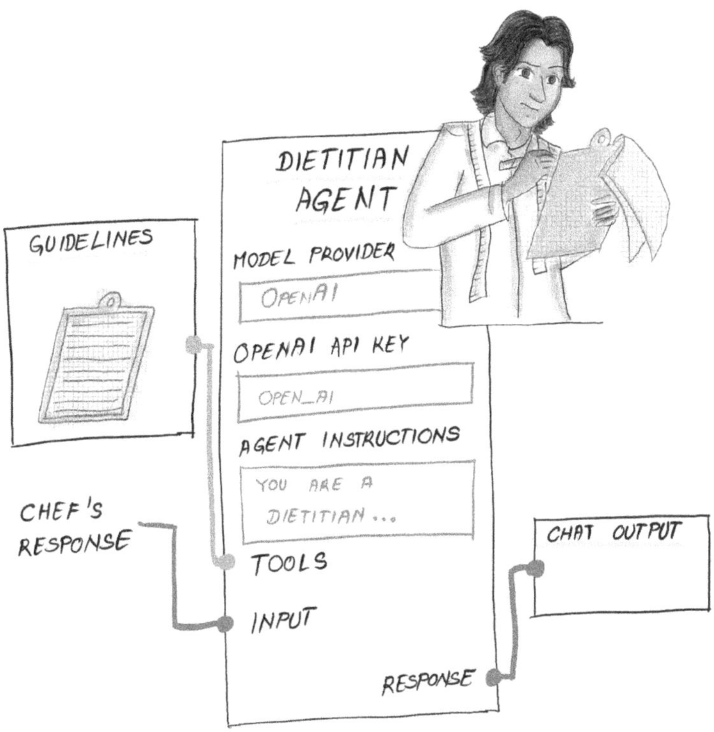


**Figure 6.12** The dietitian agent has a tool to access guidelines.

We still need to set the agent's behavior. The instructions must first establish the agent's role: reviewing and adapting the chef's recipe to make it healthier while preserving the spirit of the original. The prompt should emphasize that the dietitian's response will be the only one shown to the user, so it must include the entire revised recipe, clearly indicating which changes were made and why. The agent must also be instructed to consult the *EatWell Guide*—a crucial source of nutritional standards—by using the provided tool to fetch the page at a given URL (https://tiny.cc/eatwellguide). We can double down on this aspect, asking the agent to always fetch the latest guidelines before responding. Structurally, the output should follow a clear format: Title, Ingredients, Preparation steps, and Dietitian's Notes. In the notes, the agent must explain how each change improves the recipe's nutritional balance, referencing specific principles from the *EatWell Guide* (e.g., reducing salt, increasing fiber, balancing food groups).

Finally, it should be clear that the agent must avoid introducing trendy or modern ingredients that feel out of place for a 1919 Italian recipe. This ensures that the final output is both nutritionally sound and faithful to the original culinary context.

Here's an agent instruction prompt that can do all of this (feel free to modify it as you like and experiment as your curiosity demands):

> You are a dietitian tasked with reviewing and adapting a recipe to make it healthier. The recipe you received was generated by a chef using The Italian Cook Book (1919) as a source.
>
> Your response will be the only one visible to the user, so it must include the entire revised recipe, clearly referencing the original where relevant. Describe any modifications you make to improve the recipe's nutritional profile.
>
> You should base your recommendations on the EatWell Guide, which is available at https://tiny.cc/eatwellguide. Use the provided tool to fetch and reference the guide directly. Always fetch the guide before generating any response for the user.
>
> Your output should be clear, easy to follow, and structured into Title, Ingredients, Preparation steps, and Dietitian's Notes.
>
> You should be explicit about why changes were made, tying them to specific principles from the EatWell Guide.
>
> Always ensure your advice aligns with established health guidelines, and avoid introducing overly modern or out-of-context ingredients that would compromise the spirit of the original recipe.

With the second agent of our sequential agentic AI structure now in place, we can complete the setup by adding the ever-present Chat Input and Chat Output components to the editor. Connect the Chat Input to the chef agent's input and the Chat Output to the dietitian agent's output. This way, the user submits their request directly to the chef and receives the final, health-reviewed recipe from the dietitian, completing the full end-to-end experience. The resulting flow should look like the one in figure 6.13.

You can now test the full flow by opening the playground and treating yourself to a well-earned reward after all that hard work. Try typing something like `ravioli` into the chat and see how the two agents collaborate: the chef will dig into the 1919 cookbook, and the dietitian will make sure your comfort food stays on the healthy side, offering something that may be similar to what you find in figure 6.14.

**Figure 6.13** The chef and dietitian are back together, but this time with some external support.

**Figure 6.14** The Healthier Ravioli Recipe: a masterpiece of balance between authentic Italian tradition and modern healthy eating guidelines

Well done! Your first agentic AI system is now up and running. We've taken the HealthyChef concept to the next level by grounding it in real recipes and evidence-based dietary guidance.

Now, can you think of ways to make it even better or tailor it to your own needs? You could expand the system by incorporating multiple cookbooks into the toolified RAG setup or by equipping the dietitian with different nutritional frameworks. The possibilities are wide open—go ahead and make it yours!

Now that we've successfully built a Type 1 agentic AI structure, it's time to take things a step further. In the next flow, we'll explore hierarchical agentic structures—a different approach to coordination and control among agents. Let's dive in.

# Setting up an agentic copywriting team

In this tutorial, we'll build CopyGenie™, a full virtual copywriting team that plans, drafts, and delivers high-quality social media marketing posts for a family-owned winery located in Sonoma Valley.

Unlike a simple assistant that writes text on the spot, CopyGenie™ works like a real creative team, with a supervisor coordinating specialized agents, each handling a different part of the job. This is a perfect example of a Type 2 agentic structure. More specifically, we want our GenAI application to simulate how three creative roles (each an agent) in the creative team interact with each other under the guidance of the supervisor agent:

- The *planner agent* creates a detailed content plan, checks the social media calendar, and schedules posts across the requested period.
- The *copywriter agent* will draft the social media posts based on the content plan, making sure they align with the winery's brand guidelines.
- The *delivery agent* will send the finalized posts via email if the user requests it.

Let's explore how this agentic structure should function. Imagine that when the user sends a request—like "Write social media posts for our next three months of campaigns"—the supervisor agent takes charge. It first involves the planner agent, who consults the social media calendar to ensure the plan includes timely and relevant posts, spaced correctly throughout each month.

The supervisor will then pass the content plan to the copywriter agent, which will draft the posts according to the brand guidelines and target the specified social media channels.

After the posts are completed, the supervisor checks whether the user wants them sent via email. If so, the supervisor activates the delivery agent to handle the sending, ensuring that the email is well-formatted and human-readable.

Each specialized agent can't act alone—they need well-defined roles, structured inputs, and access to the right tools to perform their tasks effectively:

- The planner agent needs to receive the selected time window as input (provided, of course, by the supervisor) and must have access to the social media calendar to fetch relevant events and propose an evenly distributed posting schedule.
- The copywriter agent needs the supervisor to provide the content plan as a basis for content generation and must have access to the winery's brand guidelines to draft posts that align with the correct tone and style.
- The delivery agent needs the finalized posts and complete email details (the recipient's email address and subject line) as input and must have access to an email-sending tool to deliver the content to the user correctly.

This is exactly what a *hierarchical agentic structure* looks like: a supervisor coordinating specialized agents, each with their own responsibilities and tools.

**Figure 6.15** The supervisor comes into the picture.

You may wonder why we're using a hierarchical setup instead of a simple sequential chain of agents, or even just a single agent equipped with all the tools. Although both alternatives are technically possible, they come with important tradeoffs. Equipping one agent with every tool and letting it decide which to use and when may sound simpler, but in practice, it leads to tool overload, prompt bloat, and a loss of specialization. The agent must process and recall descriptions for all tools in every reasoning step, increasing the chances of confusion, degraded performance, and hallucinations. A sequential flow, on the other hand, assumes a fixed order of operations and lacks the flexibility to adapt to different user needs.

The hierarchical approach is more robust and adaptable. The supervisor agent dynamically decides which specialized agents to activate based on the user's request. For example, if the user wants posts on a specific topic without creating a calendar, the supervisor skips the planner agent entirely. Likewise, the delivery agent is involved only if email delivery is explicitly requested.

Before we dive into building this in Langflow, let's reflect on why this is a valuable exercise and whether we're making the right choice by building an agentic AI system to solve our business needs.

Copywriting is a highly creative process. It requires one of the most human of all skills—understanding context, choosing relevant and attention-grabbing ways to convey a message, and doing so in just the right tone. So, should we really use AI for this? I think the answer is yes, but not by replacing humans—instead, by giving them superpowers, especially during some steps of the process, the "least creative" ones.

Not all the steps in the copywriting process are inherently creative. Consider these examples:

- Finding upcoming events in the social media calendar doesn't require creativity. A specialized agent can handle this quickly and accurately.
- Checking brand guideline compliance is also not creative. Having this step done by a dedicated agent can help eliminate the bias that sometimes creeps in when a creative agent feels overly attached to their first draft.

**Figure 6.16** It's easier to spot bugs when you develop hierarchical structures going bottom-up.

- Preparing an email draft and sorting out the recipient's address are purely operational steps, not creative ones.

Our agentic team can give superpowers to human copywriters, enabling them to review, fine-tune, or even override the GenAI proposals while starting from a solid, precooked base and saving precious time. The marketer of tomorrow will increasingly rely on these superpowers—not to replace their creativity, but to boost their productivity.

Now that we're more convinced about *why* we're doing this, let's build our team in Langflow. Because we'll need to build multiple agents that operate in various orders, a good development technique is to use a *bottom-up* approach. This means starting by building individual agents, equipping them with their tools, testing that each works properly, and only then toolifying them to be used by the agents "above" them—like the supervisor. This step-by-step approach allows us to test and debug each agent independently before building the entire structure.

### Setting up the planner agent

Let's start with the Planner Agent. We need to equip it with access to a social media calendar and have it compile a list of possible posts, using as many events as possible from the calendar.

#### What is a social media calendar?

A social media calendar is a simple planning tool that lists key dates, holidays, and special occasions that can be used to plan timely and relevant marketing campaigns. For example, it may include international events such as Valentine's Day or Earth Day, as well as niche occasions like National Drink Wine Day. Having this calendar at hand helps marketers decide what to discuss and when, making the copy more relevant to current events.

For our exercise, we can download the calendar stored at https://tiny.cc/socialcalendar. It's a .csv file with a simple table of four columns: Year, Date, Occasion, and Global. The calendar is short enough to be embedded in an LLM call as is. This means that we don't need to implement a RAG system or a more sophisticated method to enable the agent to access it.

Let's open a blank flow and drag the Read File component into it. As we did in the previous exercises, let's load the .csv file by clicking the Select Files button, selecting the location of our file, and then clicking the play button (1) on the top right to run the component. Notice that the default type of the output (near the bottom right) is Structured Content and, as the name suggests, a table. In our case, we want to use the raw text of the data because it will be easy to pass into the agent's hands, so click the output type name, select Raw Content (2), and check the comma-separated values coming from the calendar (3), as you can see in figure 6.17.

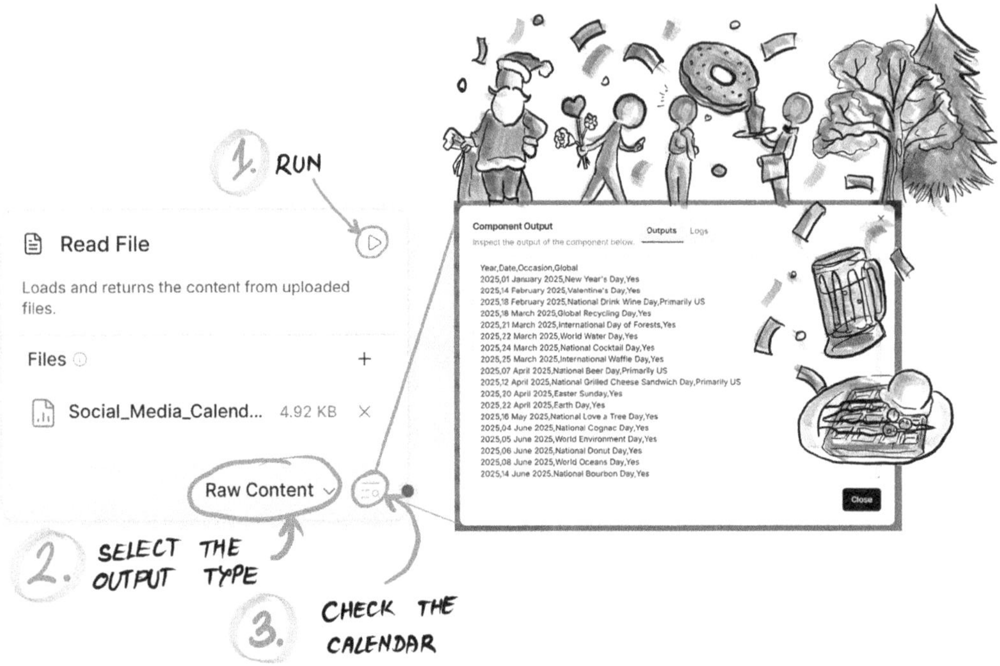


**Figure 6.17** Our social media calendar with so many occasions to post about

The planner agent will need a composite system message: we need to explain how it should behave and embed the social media calendar by using a variable. So, let's implement a Prompt Template component, and let's think about a possible system message that would fit our agent's objective.

As you know, agents work best when they are provided with clear, structured instructions. You might remember the four-part standard prompt template we explored in chapter 3: role, task, features, and examples.

For the planner agent, the system message should first clearly define its role as the planner for the CopyGenie™ social media team. Then, we need to describe its task: generating a detailed social media content plan for the requested period. It's essential to specify a few key features: the agent must strictly use the provided social media calendar (passed as a variable), extract only the events that are explicitly mentioned, and never invent topics. It must also follow a target posting frequency of four posts per channel per month, unless the user specifies otherwise.

Finally, to anchor the agent's reasoning, it's helpful to provide examples of what a good social media plan looks like—showing how posts should reference specific dates and how posts without events should be spaced evenly across the month. In this case, the Planner Agent's prompt will also include the social media calendar as a variable using the format `Calendar: ##{Calendar}##`, with the hashes delimiting the guidelines document to avoid any confusion.

Here's a system prompt we can use in this case:

> You are the planner agent for the CopyGenie social media team. Your role is to generate a social media content plan based on the requested period using the winery's social media calendar. You don't use any tool.
>
> # Calendar usage
>
> Use this social media calendar to retrieve dates related to holidays, special days, and marketing events.
>
> Calendar: ##{Calendar}##
>
> You must extract ONLY the events that are listed for the requested month(s). Do not invent events or make assumptions about events if they are not clearly mentioned in the calendar.
>
> # Posting frequency
>
> The average posting frequency is 4 posts per channel per month, evenly distributed throughout the month unless the user specifies otherwise. If the user specifies a different frequency or channels, you must follow the user's instructions. Otherwise, propose 4 posts well spaced throughout the month.
>
> # Workflow
>
> You must
>
> - Identify the relevant events in the social media calendar for the requested month or months.
>
> - Propose a social media plan that considers:
>   - Posting frequency
>   - Event date (if found in the calendar)
>   - Post topic (event name if available, otherwise leave it free)
>   - Target social media channel(s)
>
> # Example output
>
> 7 September: Post about Zero Emissions Day on LinkedIn
>
> 13 September: Post on Instagram (free topic)
>
> 23 September: Post about Car Free Day on LinkedIn
>
> 28 September: Post on Instagram (free topic)
>
> # General instructions
>
> If no events are found for the requested month(s), you must generate a calendar that places posts evenly across the entire period. You must never cluster posts around the same dates. Posts must be scattered to cover the whole month.
>
> You NEVER mention events that are not explicitly mentioned in the provided calendar.
>
> You NEVER invent topics. Leave them unmentioned in case they are not related to events.
>
> If you need information to proceed, please inform the Supervisor to retrieve the missing information from the user.
>
> You ALWAYS try to meet the desired posting frequency.

You'll notice some prompt enhancement techniques used there as well: we've repeated important information multiple times (double-down), such as mentioning events that are not explicitly included in the calendar. We've also explained that if it doesn't have all the required info, it should ask the supervisor for help, giving the LLM a way out instead of hallucinating.

Now that the Calendar variable is implemented, we can connect the output of the Read File component with the Calendar input of the Prompt. The full system message, which embeds the social media calendar, is now ready to go.

As a next step, let's implement an agent component, select the model of your choice, and connect the Prompt Template output as Agent Instructions.

Because we'll have multiple agents in this flow, let's take the opportunity to clarify our flow composition. If you select the Agent component by clicking on it, you'll see a little pencil icon appear in the top right, as shown in figure 6.18. The title and description labels can now be edited. Although you can change the title to anything you want (such as Luca shown here), for this example, let's change the title of this component to `Planner Agent` to distinguish it from the other agents. This little trick of editing component names and descriptions will turn out to be very helpful, especially in more complex GenAI applications, so I encourage you to do so whenever it makes sense.

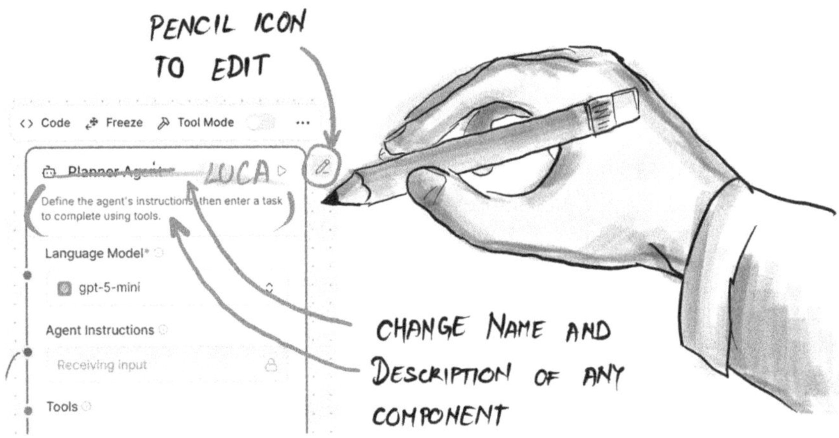


**Figure 6.18** By renaming and editing the description of any component, you can make your flow self-explanatory.

Before making this agent a tool for the supervisor agent, let's test whether it does what it should! Let's add a static prompt in the Input text box of the planner agent, mimicking what the supervisor agent might request. For example, we can enter `Please generate a social media plan for Facebook posts in December 2027`, click the run button, and check the output by clicking the magnifying glass icon on the Response output.

As you can see in figure 6.19, the agent seems to be doing its job right: it has retrieved the right event for the month and built a plan accordingly.

**Figure 6.19** It seems that in December 2027, we can't get away from a Christmas-themed social media plan.

## Building the copywriter agent

Let's build the other critical agent on our team: the copywriter, who will generate the actual posts while carefully following the brand's guidelines.

Also in this case, the brand guidelines are provided to us by the marketing manager of the winery: they are available at https://tiny.cc/brandrules. The document outlines how to maintain the winery's warm, sophisticated, and approachable identity across all social media channels. It includes specific instructions on tone of voice, platform-specific strategies, and buyer personas for Instagram, Facebook, and LinkedIn, as well as visual style reminders to keep all posts consistent with the brand. These are all good instructions to embed in the system message of our copywriter agent.

We can load the guidelines using a Read File component, following the same steps as the calendar. Then, let's implement a Prompt Template component and start writing a set of instructions for the agent, similar to what we already did with the planner. In this case, the instructions should first clearly define the copywriter agent's role: it's responsible for drafting social media posts for Sol Vigna Wines, based on the content plan provided by the supervisor agent. The prompt must describe the task: write one post per item in the content plan, ensuring that the message is tailored to the specific social media channel mentioned.

It's essential to include precise features—the agent must strictly follow the Sol Vigna brand guidelines (which we'll pass into the prompt as a variable using `{BrandGuidelines}`), it must never invent topics or events that weren't in the plan, and it must write in the brand's specific tone of voice. Finally, just as we did for the Planner Agent, the prompt should include examples to show the agent exactly what good output looks like—complete with social media post formats, hashtags, and platform-specific nuances.

A good prompt in this case would be something like this:

> You are a copywriter agent for the CopyGenie social media team. Your role is to draft social media posts based on the content plan provided by the supervisor agent.
>
> # Brand guidelines
>
> You must strictly follow these brand guidelines related to the winery Sol Vigna Wines:
>
> ##{BrandGuidelines}##
>
> # Workflow
>
> You must
>
> - Write one social media post for each item in the provided content plan.
>
> - Each post must directly reference the event and channel specified in the plan, if provided.
>
> - Write posts tailored for the specified channel (e.g., LinkedIn, Facebook).
>
> # Example content plan input
>
> 11 September: Post on Facebook
>
> 21 September: Post about Zero Emissions Day on LinkedIn
>
> # Example output
>
> Post 1 (Facebook—11 September):
>
> Did you know that the unique terroir of Sonoma Valley plays a crucial role in the character of our wines? The combination of climate, soil, and topography creates the perfect environment for our grapes to thrive.
>
> #WineEducation #Terroir #SonomaValley
>
> Post 2 (LinkedIn—21 September—Zero Emissions Day):
>
> Happy Zero Emissions Day! At Sol Vigna's Winery, we're proud to champion sustainable practices that protect our beautiful Sonoma Valley. Join us in raising a glass to a greener future! #ZeroEmissionsDay #Sustainability #SonomaValley
>
> # General instructions
>
> You must draft one post per plan entry.
>
> You must always follow the brand tone and style.
>
> Do not invent topics or events.
>
> If any part of the plan is unclear, ask the supervisor agent for clarification.
>
> You must keep working until you have written all the posts in the plan.

Now we can connect the Read File output with the BrandGuidelines input of the Prompt Template component, which appears as soon as we enter a prompt including `{BrandGuidelines}`. We can now implement the Agent component, change its name to Copywriter Agent, using the pencil icon as we did earlier, and select the model for the LLM calls. We can now test the new agent by entering a supervisor-sounding command in the Input text box. Try something like this: `Draft LinkedIn posts for September 2027 based on the following events: Zero Emissions Day, Car Free Day.` Run the component by clicking the play button on the top right, and then inspect the Response output. As shown in figure 6.20, you should get the posts you were looking for, adhering to Sol Vigna Wines guidelines.

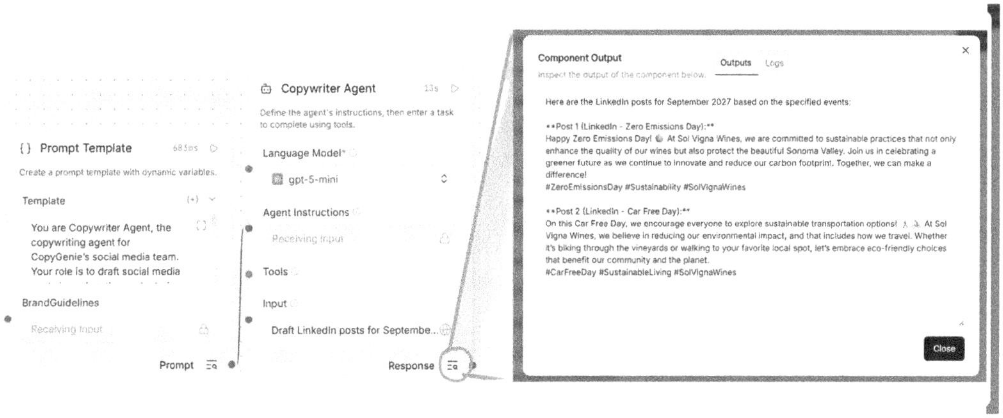


**Figure 6.20** The copywriter agent at work: give it a draft, and you get a shiny post.

## Creating the delivery agent

Now that the Copywriter Agent is ready, let's move to the third agent as we continue to build our agentic organization from the bottom up. This agent, the Delivery Agent, specializes in sending emails in the real world, so it requires a specific tool for that purpose.

Fortunately, in Langflow, we have prepackaged components that can be used as tools to perform many useful actions without requiring complex setup. In particular, Langflow makes it easy to use a service that simplifies these external connections: Composio.

Composio is a platform where the team has already developed connectors to many popular technologies, including Gmail, Google Calendar, LinkedIn, Slack, YouTube, Discord, Dropbox, and many more. By connecting to Composio, you can quickly add tools that use all of these services directly in Langflow, without having to build any complicated API integrations yourself.

They've already done all the heavy lifting to make these connections work smoothly, and we can simply plug them in when needed.

If you search for the Composio bundle in Langflow, you'll find several components that give you access to all of Composio's supported APIs that can become tools for your agents. There are also dedicated components, such as Gmail, that allow us to link an agent to a Gmail account and grant it the ability to send, read, and draft emails.

Let's give Composio a try. First, go to https://dashboard.composio.dev/login and sign up for a free account.

Once you're registered, go to the Settings menu (1) and select API Keys (2), as shown in figure 6.21. You can either generate a new key or copy the default one you see there (3). This key is all you need for now.

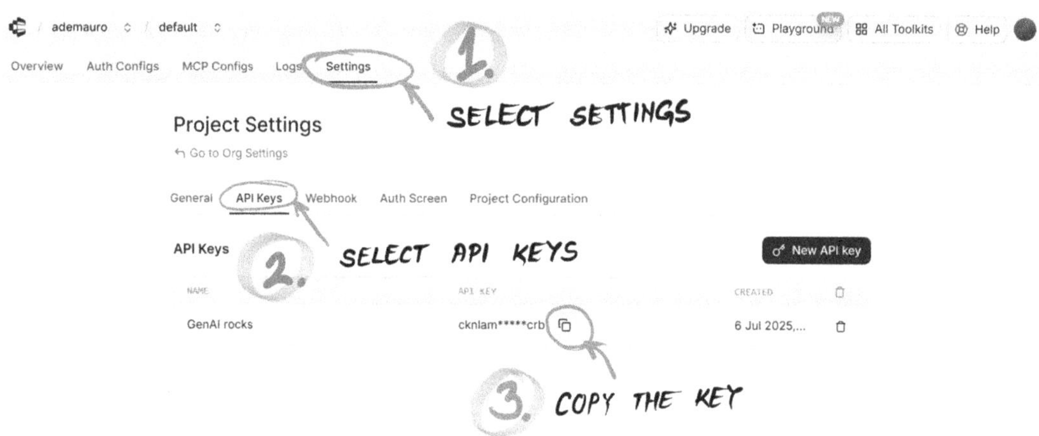


**Figure 6.21** How to retrieve a Composio API key

Let's go back to Langflow. Implement a Gmail component from the Composio bundle and paste the API key you just copied into the Composio API Key field, as shown in figure 6.22 (1). You can also save it as a variable to simplify future use.

Next, click the Connect icon (2) in the top-right corner of the Gmail component. This prompts you to log in to the Gmail account you want the agent to use. If you don't have a Gmail account, you can create a free one for this exercise. During the login process, Composio asks for permissions. You can deselect any permissions you don't want to give, but you must keep the Read, Compose, and Send permissions—these are essential for our task.

You can test it straight away by following the steps shown in figure 6.23. First, click Select Action (1) and choose Send Email (2). You'll notice that Composio also supports other actions, such as reading emails, creating drafts, and labeling emails—imagine all the additional agents you could build in the future. After selecting Send Email, you'll see new input fields appear. Fill in the recipient's email, the subject, and the body of the message. Finally, click the Run button (3) to send the email.

**Figure 6.22** The Gmail component requires a Composio API key and a connection with a Gmail account.

**Figure 6.23** We can select many possible actions in Gmail and test them as we please.

Try sending a test email to yourself to ensure everything is working properly. Hopefully, you'll soon receive an email sent through the Gmail Composio component.

Let's now build the delivery agent by implementing a new Agent component, changing its name accordingly (remember the pencil icon), and setting the usual LLM parameters.

Now, let's connect the agent to the Gmail component after toolifying it. Click the Gmail component, switch on the Tool Mode selector that appears at the top, and the Toolkit output will appear. You can connect this output to the Tools input of the Delivery Agent. Before moving on, make sure that Send Email appears in the Actions list of the component. If it doesn't, click the sliders icon next to the Actions field and add it: this ensures that the ability to send emails is actually exposed to the agent.

Finally, let's set the agent's instructions. In this case, we don't need a composite system message that embeds external documents; we can write the agent instructions directly.

The delivery agent's role is to send social media posts via email. The instructions need to clarify that the agent must check whether all required email details are provided and that the email should always be written in a clear, human-readable HTML format. Here's the agent prompt you can use:

> You are the delivery agent on the CopyGenie social media team. Your role is to send the finalized and approved social media posts to the specified email recipient.
>
> # Workflow
>
> You must:
>
> - Confirm that the recipient's email address, email subject, and content are provided before sending.
>
> - If any information is missing, you must STOP and ask the supervisor agent to provide the missing details.
>
> - The email must be in HTML format, written in a clear, human-readable format, with proper spacing and line breaks. The email content must be easy to read and shouldn't appear as a single unformatted block of text.
>
> # General instructions
>
> You are responsible only for sending the email.
>
> You must not write or edit social media posts.
>
> You must verify all the information provided carefully before sending.
>
> You must confirm successful email delivery before terminating your turn.
>
> You must ALWAYS use the email as HTML.

Now that the agent is equipped with its tool and instructions, we can give it a try. Enter a command in the agent's Input text box, such as `send an email to andrea@ademauro.com with subject 'Test' and just 'Ciao' as body` (of course, you should replace the address with your own), run the component, and see if you've received an email from your newly appointed delivery agent.

## Appointing the boss: The supervisor agent

What remains is to implement the supervisor agent and ensure that the three agents we've created so far are properly offered to the supervisor as tools. This crucial step brings the entire agentic structure together: by converting the agents into tools, we enable the supervisor to invoke them at its discretion.

Figure 6.24 The boss agent in action

First, let's implement a new agent component, edit its name to `Supervisor Agent` (using the pencil icon), and add all the usual configurations.

The instructions for the supervisor must be carefully articulated, as this agent carries the responsibility for ensuring the entire system functions properly. You can assume that the agent already has a summary description of the tools connected to it (we'll come back to this point). Still, it makes sense to provide detailed instructions that explain the context of the agentic organization and what the supervisor is expected to do.

We can clarify that the supervisor agent coordinates the work of the three specialized agents to fully resolve the user's request. The instructions should clearly explain what can be delegated to whom and reinforce expectations for the outputs, such as ensuring that the copywriter agent provides exactly one post per planned event.

We can also ask the supervisor to minimize redundant steps. For example, the supervisor should verify up front that the user has provided all necessary information before putting the agents into action. This helps prevent unnecessary back-and-forth with the user during the process and reduces the risk of repeating preparatory steps.

A good prompt could be something like this:

> You are CopyGenie, the supervisor agent in a virtual social media agency managing campaigns for a family-owned winery in the Sonoma Valley. Your role is to interact with the user, understand their requests, and coordinate the work of your agent team to fully resolve the task.
>
> # Workflow
>
> You must:
>
> - Delegate content planning to the Planner Agent.
>
> - Delegate post drafting to the Copywriter Agent.
>
> - Delegate email sending to the Delivery Agent.
>
> - Continue working until the user's request is fully resolved.
>
> - Never end your turn until the entire task is complete.
>
> # Agent coordination
>
> You must ensure the planner agent generates a detailed content plan using the calendar (the planner agent has access to it) and the requested month(s).
>
> You must pass the content plan to the Copywriter Agent for post drafting.

You must review the Copywriter Agent's output and confirm that each post aligns with the content plan.

If the user asks to send the posts by email, you must pass the final posts to the delivery agent along with the recipient's email address and subject line. You can refer to yourself as CopyGenie. If you're unsure, ask the user before generating any content.

# Plan and post verification

You must:

- Confirm that the planner agent's content plan matches the requested month and channels.

- Confirm that the copywriter agent drafts exactly one post per planned event.

# General instructions

You must:

- Ask the user for missing information if anything is unclear. If possible, always do so BEFORE involving the agents.

- Never allow agents to proceed without complete input data.

- Continue managing the flow until the task is fully resolved and the user's request is completed.

- Check the current date if the user asks a question that refers to it.

## Connecting the agents in a team

Now it's time to bring the agentic team together. We need to toolify the three agents reporting to the supervisor so that they can be set as "reportees" of their digital boss. To do this, simply select each agent and switch on the Tool Mode selector that appears at the top of the component.

To improve the performance of the agentic system, we should do one more thing: declare what each agent—now transformed into a tool—can do for the supervisor. As shown in figure 6.25 on the left, every toolified agent has an Actions configuration button at the bottom. This configuration button is available for all tools in Langflow, including toolified agents.

Once you click on it, you can update the name of the action that the tool can perform and provide a short description. This is an important step. The description is the "official" summary of what the agent (now acting as a tool) is capable of doing for the supervisor—the "parent" agent using the "child" agent as a tool. To clarify, the full details of how the agent should behave are outlined in the agent's own Agent Instructions and in the tools it can access. But when the parent agent calls a child agent (acting as a tool), it doesn't see the internal instructions—it only sees this official description of the tool.

In chapter 5, we introduced tools: each tool performs one or more specific functions. These functions must have a clear, structured description so the "calling" agent can properly understand when and how to use them. This is exactly what we're now configuring in this window for the benefit of the supervisor agent.

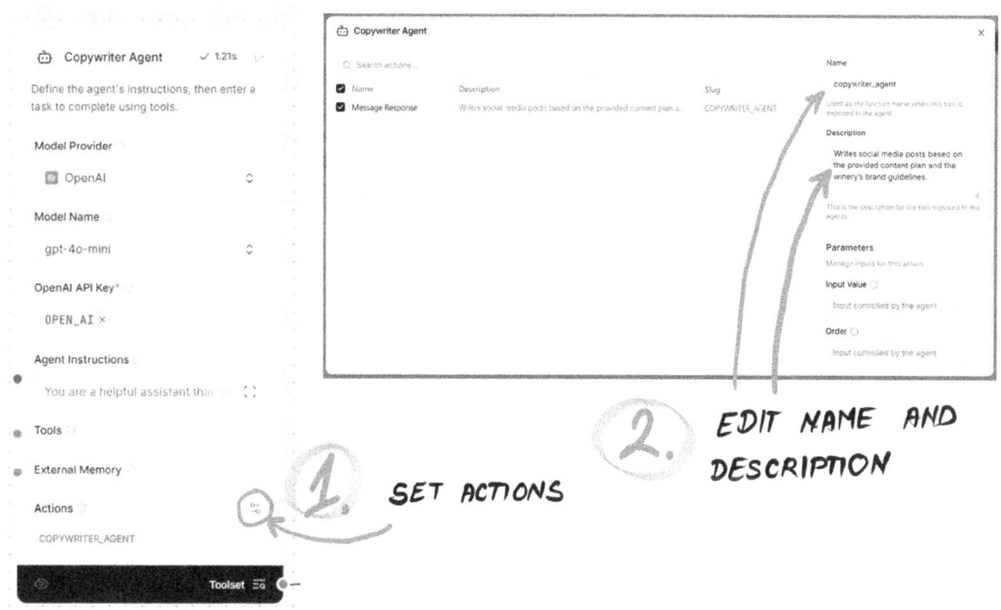


**Figure 6.25** We need to provide a clear summary of what each agent can do for their supervisor.

For example, we want to tell the supervisor this: every time you need a post written, you can use the Copywriter Agent tool (or call the Copywriter Agent function). We can do this by changing the name of the function to `Copywriter Agent` and adding a description like this one: `Writes social media posts based on the provided content plan and the winery's brand guidelines`.

Let's do the same for the other agents. For the planner agent, we can set the description as `Generates a detailed social media content plan based on the social media calendar and desired period`. For the delivery agent, we can use something very simple like this: `Sends emails`.

Agents in Langflow already have memory built-in by default, so we don't need to add a memory component.

Let's add the Chat Input and Chat Output components to the extremes of our flow and connect Chat Input to the supervisor agent's input and the supervisor agent's output to Chat Output. Your flow should now resemble the one in figure 6.26.

Let's open the Playground and ask for something like, "Generate posts for the next three months (including this one) and send them to Andrea at andrea@ademauro.com. The posts are for Facebook." (Of course, replace the email with your own so you can receive the results of your great work.)

You'll have to wait a few seconds this time to get the answer. In the meantime (see a possible output in figure 6.27), you'll be able to follow what the team is doing in real time. First, you might see a call to a tool (automatically available in all Langflow agents) that

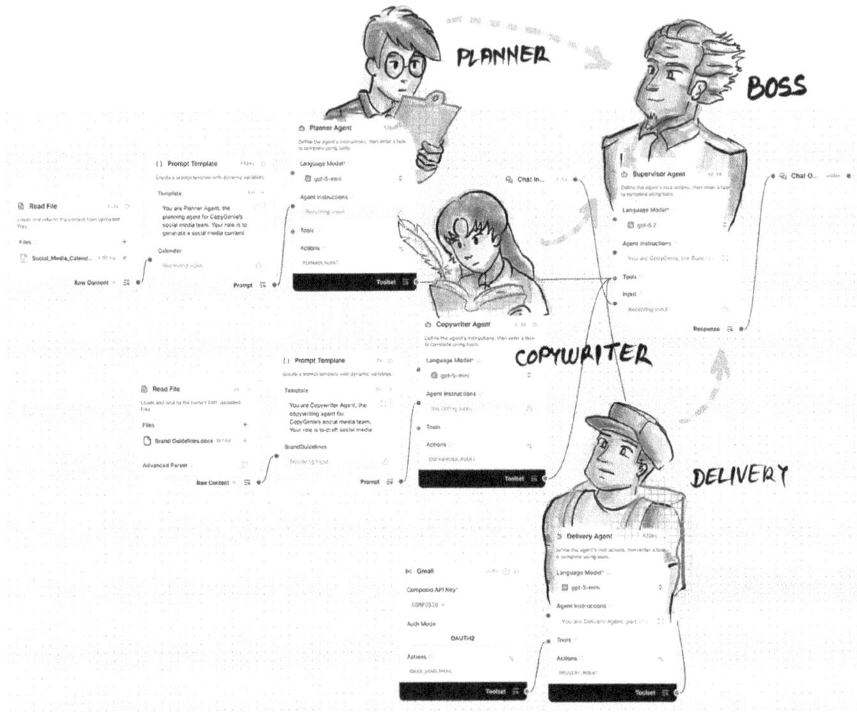


**Figure 6.26** The ultimate agentic team: three agents reporting to a boss agent acting as supervisor

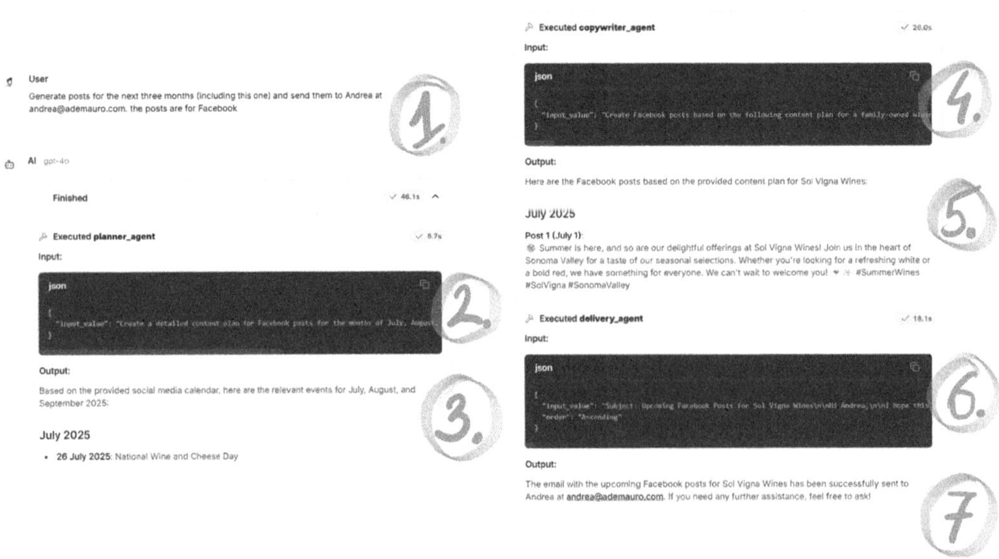


**Figure 6.27** Behind a single request, there are at least seven steps involving three specialized agents under the guidance of a supervisor agent.

checks the current date. This helps the supervisor determine which months should be passed to the planner agent.

Next, the planner agent will check the social media calendar and identify any events to include. Once the plan is ready, the supervisor will pass it to the copywriter agent, asking for the posts to be drafted. If the supervisor is satisfied with the posts, it will then ask the delivery agent to send the email. The supervisor agent might also ask for confirmation before sending the note.

Once this is all done… the result should pop up in your inbox!

**Figure 6.28** There are so many collaboration steps behind a job well done!

## Designing complex agentic organizations

Before we move on to the next chapter, it's worth reflecting on what we've just built. There was some heavy lifting involved here, so let's consider both what we did and what we could do differently, along with the new opportunities this may open up for future business cases.

In this exercise, we created four agents in total, each with a specific task. For example, the agent checking the calendar wasn't also responsible for using the brand guidelines to write posts. We made this design choice because we wanted to control the behavior, test it step-by-step, and avoid building a super-long Agent Instructions prompt that would need to include both the calendar and the brand guidelines in a single agent.

As designers of agentic organizations, we need to understand that there are always tradeoffs, and each alternative option will come with its pros and cons. If we had combined more actions into a single agent, we would have saved some back-and-forth steps involving the supervisor, which would have reduced LLM costs and processing time. Still, the agent's performance could have suffered because it would have had too much to handle at once.

We could also have centralized everything by giving all tools and instructions to the supervisor (including the Gmail tool, the calendar, and the guidelines). This would have saved time and LLM calls, but the supervisor might have become confused or less effective with so many responsibilities.

In many ways, structuring agents is similar to organizing people in a real team: you need to think carefully about roles, responsibilities, and workload distribution. Interestingly, these are typical skills required of senior leaders and HR experts, not app developers.

It's also important to consider the prompts used as Agent Instructions. The ones provided in this chapter were, in all fairness, the result of many attempts and refinements I made to maximize the chance that you'd have a smooth and enjoyable experience during the exercise.

Note that writing prompts, system messages, and agent instructions is always an iterative process. They naturally follow a cycle of trial and error. Practically, you need to wear the hat of a scientist and experiment with changes to see what works best for your use case. You'd normally start simple, understand what can be improved, and progressively tweak the prompts.

But this also applies to model selection and provider choices—you'll need to test different combinations to find the best balance for your setup. For example, you can assign low-cost, low-latency models to smaller, simpler tasks such as sending an email, while reserving higher-performing models for complex tasks such as the reasoning of the supervisor or the creative work of the copywriter.

As a designer of agentic structures, you're moving well beyond the role of a typical app developer. You need to find the sweet spot between centralization and decentralization in your agentic organization, carefully manage resource allocation (deciding which model to assign to each agent), and always be prepared to think creatively about alternative ways to achieve the same results.

Personally, I find this one of the most exciting and stimulating aspects of building AI applications covered in this book, and I hope you're as excited as I am to keep experimenting and building complex, real-world, problem-solving agentic AI systems.

## What if we coded it?

In this chapter, we extended our applications beyond single agents, exploring two forms of multi-agent orchestration. The following two scripts implement the same agentic designs directly in Python.

The first script mirrors the Langflow flow, where two agents operate in sequence. A chef agent performs cookbook-grounded RAG using a local vector store and then hands its output to a dietitian agent, which enriches and revises the recipe using the *EatWell Guide* fetched live.

In Python, this is implemented by defining two separate tool-enabled agents, each with its own prompt and toolset. The FAISS-backed retriever corresponds to the Langflow vector store, and the handoff between agents is implemented by passing the chef's output directly as input to the dietitian's executor. The sequential logic is encoded explicitly in the `chat_loop()` function.

```
"""
Install dependencies once:

    pip install langchain langchain-openai langchain-community \
        langchain-text-splitters faiss-cpu requests python-dotenv

Before running the script, make sure your OPENAI_API_KEY is available.
"""

from pathlib import Path

import requests
from dotenv import load_dotenv

from langchain_openai import ChatOpenAI, OpenAIEmbeddings
from langchain_community.vectorstores import FAISS
from langchain_community.document_loaders import TextLoader
from langchain_text_splitters import RecursiveCharacterTextSplitter
from langchain_core.tools import tool
from langchain_core.prompts import ChatPromptTemplate, MessagesPlaceholder
from langchain.agents import AgentExecutor, create_tool_calling_agent

load_dotenv()
# os.environ["OPENAI_API_KEY"] = "REPLACE_WITH_YOUR_KEY"

BASE_DIR = Path(__file__).resolve().parent
COOKBOOK_TXT = BASE_DIR / "recipe-book.txt"
INDEX_DIR = BASE_DIR / "cookbook"
EATWELL_URL = "https://tiny.cc/eatwellguide"
HTTP_HEADERS = {"User-Agent": "Mozilla/5.0 (compatible; HealthyChef/1.0)"}


def load_vectorstore() -> FAISS:
    """Build or load the local FAISS index backing the cookbook search."""

    embeddings = OpenAIEmbeddings()
```

Chat + embedding wrappers reused from earlier chapters.

Local FAISS vector store that powers the cookbook retriever.

Prompt pieces with scratchpads so each agent can call its tools.

```
    if INDEX_DIR.exists():
        return FAISS.load_local(
            str(INDEX_DIR), embeddings, allow_dangerous_deserialization=True
        )

    loader = TextLoader(str(COOKBOOK_TXT), encoding="utf-8")
    docs = loader.load()
    splitter = RecursiveCharacterTextSplitter(chunk_size=1000, chunk_
overlap=200)
    chunks = splitter.split_documents(docs)
    store = FAISS.from_documents(chunks, embeddings)
    store.save_local(str(INDEX_DIR))
    return store


VECTORSTORE = load_vectorstore()
RETRIEVER = VECTORSTORE.as_retriever(search_kwargs={"k": 4})
LLM = ChatOpenAI(model="gpt-4o-mini", temperature=0.2)


@tool
def cookbook_search(query: str) -> str:
    """Retrieve cookbook passages tied to the user request."""

    docs = RETRIEVER.invoke(query)
    return "\n\n".join(doc.page_content for doc in docs)


@tool
def fetch_url(url: str | None = None) -> str:
    """Fetch a short excerpt from the NHS EatWell guide."""

    target = url or EATWELL_URL
    try:
        response = requests.get(target, timeout=20, headers=HTTP_HEADERS)
        response.raise_for_status()
        return response.text[:4000]
    except requests.RequestException as exc:
        raise RuntimeError(
            f"Unable to reach the EatWell guide at {target}: {exc}"
        ) from exc


chef_tools = [cookbook_search]
dietitian_tools = [fetch_url]

chef_prompt = ChatPromptTemplate.from_messages(
    [
        (
            "system",
            "You are an Italian chef limited to The Italian Cook Book by Maria "
            "Gentile (1919). Use the cookbook search tool and return recipes "
            "exactly as written, formatted as Title, Ingredients, Preparation.",
        ),
```

Tool: semantic lookup over Maria Gentile's cookbook.

Tool: fetch the EatWell guide.

Chef agent instructions mirroring the Langflow prompt.

```
        MessagesPlaceholder("chat_history", optional=True),
        ("human", "{input}"),
        MessagesPlaceholder("agent_scratchpad"),
    ]
)

dietitian_prompt = ChatPromptTemplate.from_messages(
    [
        (
            "system",
            "You are a Registered Dietitian using the NHS EatWell guide "
            "(https://tiny.cc/eatwellguide). Always fetch it before responding "
            "and return Title, Ingredients, Preparation, Dietitian's Notes that 
"
            "justify each change with EatWell principles.",
        ),
        MessagesPlaceholder("chat_history", optional=True),
        ("human", "{input}"),
        MessagesPlaceholder("agent_scratchpad"),
    ]
)

chef_agent = create_tool_calling_agent(LLM, chef_tools, chef_prompt)
chef_executor = AgentExecutor(agent=chef_agent, tools=chef_tools, verbose=False)

dietitian_agent = create_tool_calling_agent(LLM, dietitian_tools, dietitian_
prompt)
dietitian_executor = AgentExecutor(
    agent=dietitian_agent, tools=dietitian_tools, verbose=False
)


def chat_loop() -> None:
    """Sequentially run the Chef then Dietitian agents like the Langflow 
build."""

    try:
        while True:
            user_input = input("Dish idea or ingredient list: ")
            chef_result = chef_executor.invoke({"input": user_input})
            dietitian_result = dietitian_executor.invoke({"input": chef_
result["output"]})

            print("\n--- Chef's Recipe ---\n")
            print(chef_result["output"])
            print("\n--- Dietitian's Revision ---\n")
            print(dietitian_result["output"], "\n")
    except KeyboardInterrupt:
        print("\nBuon appetito!")


if __name__ == "__main__":
    chat_loop()
```

Dietitian agent instructions grounded in the EatWell guidance.

The second script mirrors the Langflow hierarchical agent setup, where a supervisor agent coordinates three specialists: a planner, a copywriter, and a delivery agent. In Langflow, this appears as a supervisor component connected to multiple agent tools; in Python, it's implemented using tool-bound functions and explicit tool calling.

Each specialist agent is wrapped as a `@tool`, while the supervisor model is bound to all tools and decides which one to call at each step. External integrations—such as Gmail—are handled through Composio, mirroring the Langflow integration blocks. The supervisor loop explicitly manages tool calls and responses, reproducing the same control logic configured visually.

```
"""
Install dependencies once:

    pip install langchain langchain-openai langchain-community \
        docx2txt python-dotenv composio composio-openai

Before running the script, make sure OPENAI_API_KEY, COMPOSIO_API_KEY,
COMPOSIO_USER_ID, and COMPOSIO_AUTH_CONFIG_ID are set.
"""
import os
from pathlib import Path
from typing import Any, Dict, List

import docx2txt
from dotenv import load_dotenv

from langchain_openai import ChatOpenAI
from langchain_core.tools import tool
from langchain_core.prompts import ChatPromptTemplate
from langchain_core.messages import BaseMessage, HumanMessage, SystemMessage,
ToolMessage

from composio import Composio
from composio_openai import OpenAIProvider

load_dotenv()
# os.environ["OPENAI_API_KEY"] = "REPLACE_WITH_YOUR_KEY"
# os.environ["COMPOSIO_API_KEY"] = "REPLACE_WITH_YOUR_KEY"
# os.environ["COMPOSIO_USER_ID"] = "REPLACE_WITH_YOUR_USER_ID"
# os.environ["COMPOSIO_AUTH_CONFIG_ID"] = "REPLACE_WITH_YOUR_AUTH_ID"

BASE_DIR = Path(__file__).resolve().parent
CALENDAR_FILE = BASE_DIR / "Social_Media_Calendar_2025_2027.csv"
BRAND_FILE = BASE_DIR / "Brand Guidelines.docx"

calendar_text = CALENDAR_FILE.read_text(encoding="utf-8")
brand_text = docx2txt.process(str(BRAND_FILE))

OPENAI_MODEL = "gpt-4.1-mini"
base_llm = ChatOpenAI(model=OPENAI_MODEL, temperature=0.2)
```

Chat model powering all agents and the supervisor.

LangChain @tool decorator wraps each specialist.

Composio client provides Gmail access.

Load the shared calendar + brand guidelines.

```
COMPOSIO_API_KEY = os.getenv("COMPOSIO_API_KEY")
COMPOSIO_USER_ID = os.getenv("COMPOSIO_USER_ID")
COMPOSIO_AUTH_CONFIG_ID = os.getenv("COMPOSIO_AUTH_CONFIG_ID")

if not all([COMPOSIO_API_KEY, COMPOSIO_USER_ID, COMPOSIO_AUTH_CONFIG_ID]):
    raise RuntimeError("Set COMPOSIO_* variables before running CopyGenie.")

composio_client = Composio(
    api_key=COMPOSIO_API_KEY,
    provider=OpenAIProvider(),
    dangerously_skip_version_check=True,
)

print("Authorize CopyGenie for Gmail via Composio:")
connection_request = composio_client.connected_accounts.link(
    user_id=COMPOSIO_USER_ID,
    auth_config_id=COMPOSIO_AUTH_CONFIG_ID,
)
print(connection_request.redirect_url)
print("Waiting for Gmail connection...")
connection_request.wait_for_connection()
print("Gmail connection established.\n")


PLANNER_SYSTEM = """
You are Planner Agent for CopyGenie's social media team.
- Use this calendar to find events and space posts evenly:
  ##{calendar}##
- Default to 4 posts per channel per month unless the user specifies otherwise.
- Output lines like: 11 September: Post about Zero Emissions Day on LinkedIn.
""".strip()

planner_prompt = ChatPromptTemplate.from_messages(
    [("system", PLANNER_SYSTEM), ("human", "{request}")]
)


@tool
def planner_agent(request: str) -> str:
    """Generates a dated content plan using the social media calendar."""

    messages = planner_prompt.format_messages(calendar=calendar_text,
request=request)
    return base_llm.invoke(messages).content.strip()


COPYWRITER_SYSTEM = """
You are Copywriter Agent for Sol Vigna Wines.
- Follow these brand guidelines: ##{brand_guidelines}##
- Write ONE post per entry from the planner, referencing date/event/channel.
""".strip()

copywriter_prompt = ChatPromptTemplate.from_messages(
    [("system", COPYWRITER_SYSTEM), ("human", "{plan}")]
)
```

Link CopyGenie to Gmail before the supervisor starts.

Planner agent mirrors the Langflow calendar node.

```
@tool
def copywriter_agent(plan: str) -> str:
    """Drafts branded posts based on the planner's schedule."""

    messages = copywriter_prompt.format_messages(
        brand_guidelines=brand_text,
        plan=plan,
    )
    return base_llm.invoke(messages).content.strip()


@tool
def delivery_agent(recipient: str, subject: str, body: str) -> str:
    """Sends finalized posts via Gmail through Composio."""

    if not (recipient and subject and body):
        return "Delivery agent needs recipient, subject, and body."

    result = composio_client.tools.execute(
        slug="gmail_send_email",
        arguments={"to": recipient, "subject": subject, "body": body},
        user_id=COMPOSIO_USER_ID,
        dangerously_skip_version_check=True,
    )
    return f"Composio send result: {result}"


SUPERVISOR_SYSTEM = """
You are CopyGenie, supervising planner_agent, copywriter_agent, delivery_agent.
- Always call planner_agent to read the calendar when users ask about posts.
- Pass planner output to copywriter_agent for branded posts.
- Call delivery_agent only after posts are approved and you have recipient,
  subject, and body. Keep working until the request is fully satisfied.
""".strip()

tools = [planner_agent, copywriter_agent, delivery_agent]
tool_lookup: Dict[str, Any] = {t.name: t for t in tools}
supervisor_model = base_llm.bind_tools(tools)


def run_interactive_chat() -> None:
    """Simple REPL mirroring the Langflow supervisor playground."""

    messages: List[BaseMessage] = [SystemMessage(content=SUPERVISOR_SYSTEM)]

    try:
        while True:
            user_input = input("User: ")
            if not user_input.strip():
                continue

            messages.append(HumanMessage(content=user_input))
```

Copywriter agent enforces Sol Vigna's tone per channel.

Delivery agent requires full email details before sending.

Bind the three tools so the supervisor can call them dynamically.

```
            while True:
                ai_msg = supervisor_model.invoke(messages)
                messages.append(ai_msg)

                tool_calls = getattr(ai_msg, "tool_calls", None) or []
                if not tool_calls:
                    print("\nAI:", ai_msg.content, "\n")
                    break

                for tc in tool_calls:
                    tool = tool_lookup[tc["name"]]
                    result = tool.invoke(tc["args"])
                    messages.append(
                        ToolMessage(
                            content=str(result),
                            tool_call_id=tc["id"],
                            name=tc["name"],
                        )
                    )
    except KeyboardInterrupt:
        print("\nCopyGenie signing off!")


if __name__ == "__main__":
    run_interactive_chat()
```

## Summary

- Agentic structures allow you to solve complex tasks by organizing multiple specialized agents into collaborative workflows instead of relying on a single, overloaded agent.
- Multi-agent setups reduce complexity, improve performance, and enhance maintainability by distributing tasks across modular, role-specific agents.
- Sequential structures (Type 1) execute agents in a fixed order, ideal for linear workflows where each step depends on the previous one.
- Hierarchical structures (Type 2) introduce a supervisor agent that dynamically delegates tasks to other agents, unlocking conditional execution and reuse.
- Designing agentic systems is like building human teams—you must balance roles, manage workloads, and carefully structure interactions through iterative testing of setups, models, and prompts.

# Integrating GenAI in your data ecosystem | 7

## In this chapter

- getting started with the KNIME platform for running data transformation and advanced analytics
- exploring the integration of GenAI flows with external data sources and systems
- building hybrid KNIME and Langflow applications to pull large amounts of data, run LLM calls, and store the outcome for future use

So far, we've built GenAI applications using large language models (LLMs) to build conversational experiences. In all these cases, a human user interacted through chat with an LLM-driven entity. Conversational AI is definitely one of the most popular applications of AI these days, but it's clearly just one of many.

Quite often, the input data doesn't come from a human user at all. It may arrive from structured sources such as spreadsheets, enterprise applications such as SAP or Salesforce, relational databases, or other digital systems. This means that your AI applications must be integrated with the larger data ecosystem you use in your activities. Whether it's an Excel file or a cloud-based customer relationship management (CRM) system, you can use a data source of any kind to fuel inputs for the LLM to do its magic. As illustrated in figure 7.1, this means going beyond the conversational paradigm we've seen so far, paving the way for a multitude of business applications.

An LLM—the magic black box we're by now very well acquainted with—can apply reasoning and generate text. Up to this point in the book, we've mainly seen LLMs at work with *unstructured* text coming directly from user input. But very often in business settings, we want to apply the reasoning power of an LLM to *structured* company data instead—for example, to a CRM table containing hundreds or thousands of customer records with fields such as Age, Name, and Recent Purchases. In this case, we need to design prompts that are general enough to explain the task once but also capable of being applied in a "loop" across many records.

In addition, the output of an LLM (a string of text) might need to be transformed—for instance, split into separate fields—so that it can be stored in a database or used in other downstream systems. Therefore, we need to implement some strategies to manage the interface between data, prompts, responses, and data again.

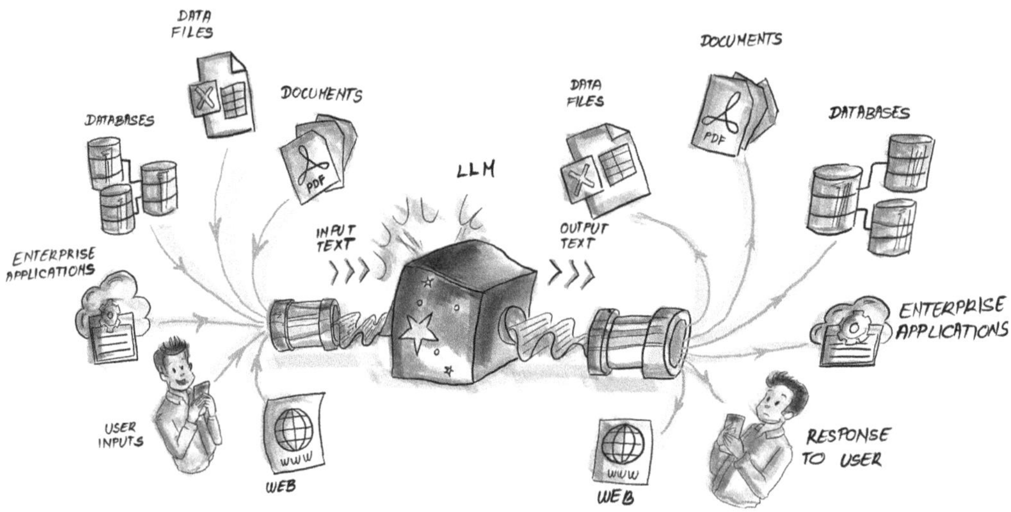


**Figure 7.1** The LLM's input text might come from various sources—files, systems, or users.

To accomplish these tasks (connecting structured data systems with the reasoning engine of the LLM and ensuring both the input and output are reformatted appropriately), we need to broaden our view. Instead of focusing solely on the Generative AI core, we must also consider how it interacts with a company's traditional data landscape. This means that our definition of an *AI application* becomes broader, spanning both the LLM-driven reasoning engine and the data pipelines around it.

To support this, we need an additional tool on top of Langflow. When it comes to data platforms, the choice is extensive, and many technologies could serve this purpose. For this book, we'll use KNIME—a low-code tool that, much like Langflow, is based on visual programming. This similarity will make it easier for readers to grasp while still providing the power needed to integrate AI with the larger data ecosystem.

## How to say "KNIME"?

KNIME (/naɪm/) is pronounced like the word *knife* but with an *m* at the end instead of an *f*. The name is a sort of acronym: KN stands for Konstanz, the German city where the platform was born, right at the border with Switzerland. IM stands for Information Mining. The final E was added purely for euphonic reasons—because it just sounded better that way.

KNIME is an analytical platform with impressive flexibility and scale—so much that it's often called the Swiss Army knife of data analytics. In fact, KNIME can

- Connect easily with external sources of any kind, pull the needed data, and save it as required.
- Transform data using a large set of functionalities that perform typical database operations (such as joining tables, aggregating columns, and so on), as well as text and numeric manipulation, allowing you to clean and reformat data according to your needs.
- Apply machine learning algorithms of any sort to data of any kind, letting you do things such as clustering customers in homogeneous groups, predicting next year's sales, inferring the propensity score of a client to buy a specific product, and everything else you can think of in the broader AI space (beyond the GenAI core of this book).
- Automate repetitive workflows and run them systematically, including in cloud environments. For example, if you need to clean and prepare a dataset every day in Excel, you would repeat the steps manually. With KNIME, you can create a reusable pipeline that runs automatically—just like on a modern data platform.

**Figure 7.2** Meet KNIME, a partner in developing your next AI applications.

KNIME is also exceptionally good at integrating systems and data platforms, implementing and calling microservices through APIs. This makes it a true jack-of-all-trades for reducing complexity in your data ecosystem.

KNIME can also interact directly with LLMs—calling providers such as OpenAI—and can even implement agents. We'll explore the combined power of two best-in-class low-code tools: KNIME and Langflow. In fact, KNIME can *call* Langflow, allowing us to build a complex, specialized flow in Langflow and then use KNIME functionalities to orchestrate everything that needs to happen around it.

The purpose of this chapter isn't to make you a full-on autonomous user of KNIME in all its broad functionalities (that would require a whole book on its own—like the ones I authored earlier). Here, you'll get started with KNIME and hopefully develop an appetite for learning more about it, expanding your analytics toolkit beyond Langflow, which I strongly suggest you do.

Let's get started with KNIME and learn all the basics we need to navigate this new tool.

## Getting started with KNIME

The user experience of developing data workflows with KNIME is strikingly similar to what you get in Langflow. In KNIME, every operation you can run on data, such as pulling from a database, transforming the format, joining tables, or running a clustering algorithm on it, is done by implementing nodes. Think of KNIME nodes as Langflow components. You connect and configure them, and watch your data transformations unfold—just like crafting a GenAI pipeline in Langflow.

Compared to Excel, KNIME is not just a spreadsheet replacement. Excel can certainly store tabular data and apply some transformations, but it can't connect seamlessly to multiple sources, orchestrate pipelines, and automate recurring workflows. In contrast, KNIME provides a true extract, transform, load (ETL) environment that can operate at scale, much like other modern data platforms.

### Installing KNIME

You can download KNIME for free from www.knime.com. Simply visit the Download page and start the installation for your operating system (available for Windows, Unix, and Mac).

KNIME has several strengths that make it a great companion for building AI-powered solutions:

- *Visual and intuitive*—You build your analytics by connecting blocks (nodes) on a canvas, just like sketching a flowchart.
- *Open source and free*—You can use its full functionality without restrictions. There's also a commercial version intended for enterprise deployment at scale, but for everything we do in this book and for most professional use cases, the open source version is more than enough.

- *Extensible*—With a rich ecosystem of extensions, you can connect to cloud platforms, integrate APIs, or even embed Python or R when needed.
- *Community-powered*—A large global community shares reusable modules, workflows, and tutorials—so you're never on your own.

Of course, KNIME is not the only option: other low-code and pro-code tools exist, from visual platforms such as Alteryx to Python libraries such as pandas. We'll use KNIME because it's free, open, and flow-based. All of this makes KNIME a great platform for experimenting, learning, and building production-ready analytics, especially when paired with Langflow to handle the GenAI side of things.

## Moving around in KNIME

After you install and open KNIME, you'll be welcomed by its home screen (figure 7.3). From here, you can open an existing project (called a "workflow" in KNIME) or create a new one by clicking the Create New Workflow button in the top right (1).

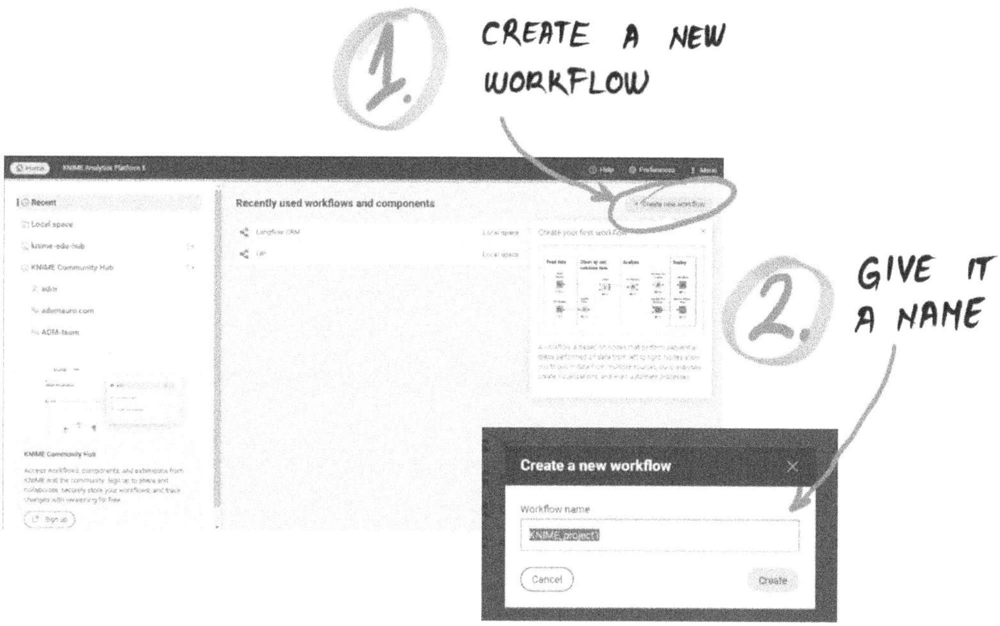


**Figure 7.3** Creating a new workflow in KNIME

After giving it a name and clicking the Create button (2), you'll land on the KNIME Workbench, the development interface where you can build your workflow.

Let's take a look at the Workbench (figure 7.4). In the middle, you'll find a white "canvas" upon which you can build your workflow. On the far left, you'll find a series of icons that you can click to open some useful panels:

- *Node repository*—Like Langflow's component library: a searchable collection of all available nodes, categorized by function. Here you can find nodes to read and write files, connect to databases and cloud-based data platforms, transform data tables, and apply any kind of AI algorithm (not just invoking LLMs). You can search for the node you need by entering keywords in the text box at the top. Then, you can drag and drop nodes onto the canvas with the mouse.
- *Explorer*—This is your file cabinet. It stores your local workflows and gives access to public examples and your online KNIME Hub, a cloud platform where you can publish your work and pull community-generated components.
- *K-AI*—This one is cool. It's a chat-based virtual assistant, offered by KNIME, that you can use to get real-time advice on queries like "I have this data and want to get to this output. How do I do this in KNIME?"

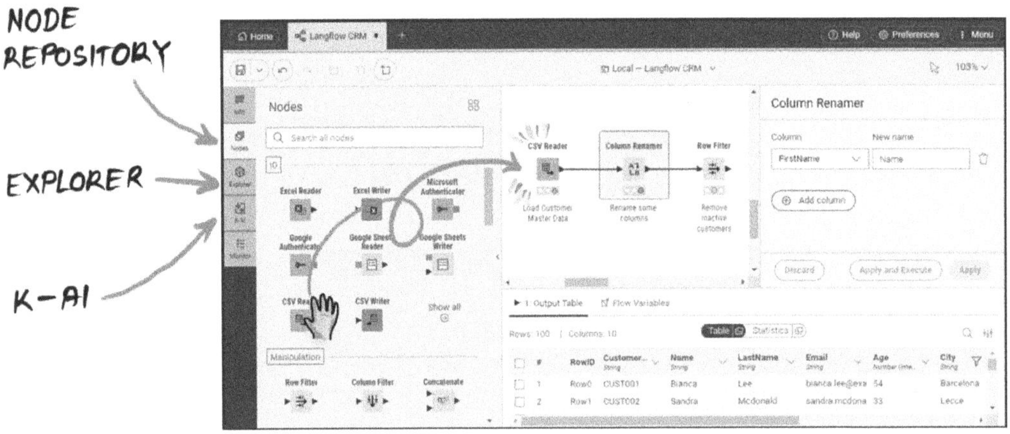


**Figure 7.4** The KNIME Workbench is your private studio for crafting data workflows.

Let's now move to the basic ingredient of any work in KNIME: the node.

## Understanding nodes

In KNIME, nodes are the building blocks of every workflow—just like components in Langflow. Each node performs a specific task, given some inputs, and produces outputs. You connect nodes to form a complete process—what KNIME calls a workflow.

Every node in KNIME follows a clear structure, as shown in figure 7.5:

- The *node name* appears at the top and describes what the node does (e.g., *CSV Reader*).
- The *annotation*, shown underneath, can be customized to explain the node's role in your workflow. By default, KNIME names annotations Node 1, Node 2, and so on—but I strongly recommend renaming them with something meaningful.

- On the left side, you'll find the *input ports*. These are how data or other resources (like models or database connections) enter the node.
- On the right side, you have the *output port(s)*, where results are sent out for the next step.
- At the bottom, the *status traffic light* is a simple indicator of the node's current state.

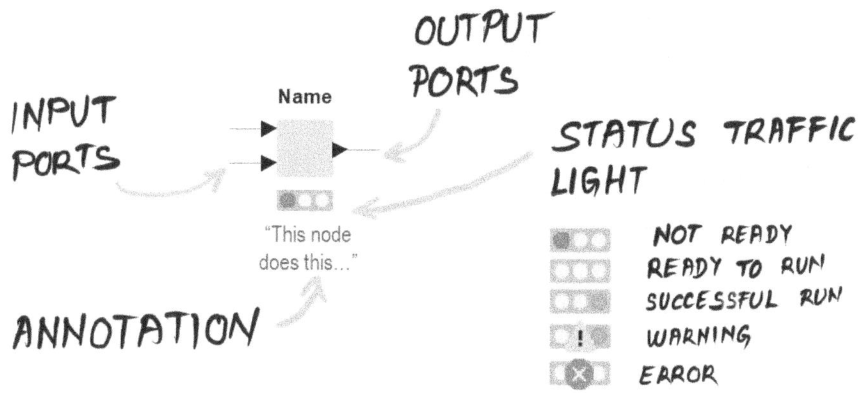


**Figure 7.5** Anatomy of a KNIME node

The traffic light system tells you whether your node is ready to go:

- *Red means "Not Configured."* Something's missing—data or a setting.
- *Yellow means "Configured."* It's ready, just waiting for your signal.
- *Green means "Execute*d." It ran successfully, and results are available.
- *Error or warning icons mean something went wrong.* You'll see these icons appear on top of the traffic light if a problem occurs during execution.

Most nodes require some configuration to run. For instance, a node accessing a database will need the address and the credentials, or a node running a clustering algorithm will need to know the number of clusters to generate. To configure a node, you can double-click on it or (if available) use the Quick Edit panel that appears automatically on the right-hand side of the KNIME interface as soon as you select a node. You'll see an example on the right-hand side of figure 7.4, which configures the Column Renamer node. This is where you set the node's parameters or choose files and columns to work with.

Once everything is ready, right-click the node, select Execute, and your node will begin performing its task. Alternatively, you can use the action bar or press F7 if you like keyboard shortcuts.

Nodes are all different, and they can produce different types of outputs or require different types of inputs. As a consequence, not all ports carry tables. Some have models, images, or variables; these are displayed with different shapes and colors. In addition, not all input ports are mandatory—optional ones appear hollow, while required ones are filled.

Figure 7.6 shows the diversity of KNIME nodes available in the repository. You have the ever-present *Input and Output* nodes to get data in and out of KNIME. You have *Data Transformation* nodes to perform all table operations like joining, aggregating, filtering, and so on. Then you have *AI* nodes for producing predictions, creating clusters, and other useful things machine learning can do for you. More specifically, you have *GenAI* nodes that invoke LLMs, implement agents, and run operations that partly "overlap" with what Langflow can do. Lastly, you have *Flow Control* nodes that control the "functioning" of the KNIME workflow, adding loops to the execution and leveraging variables for controlling the configuration of nodes dynamically. Other nodes can let you do all sorts of things, including ingesting Python or Java code. These are very powerful as they let you extend KNIME functionalities to everything that has ever been coded, leaving the visual programming environment around it to maximize your speed in developing whatever matters to you.

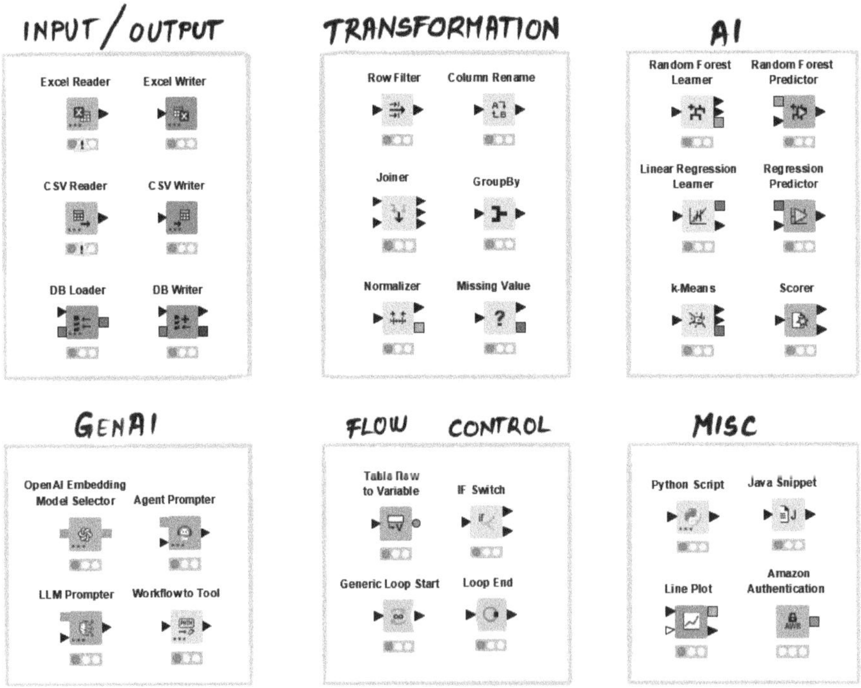


**Figure 7.6** The many types of nodes available in KNIME

This is really all you need to know to get started with KNIME nodes. In the practical spirit of this book, let's skip the theory from here and get our hands dirty: it's time to build something with KNIME and Langflow.

# Generating personalized emails at scale

In this tutorial, we're part of the marketing team at Luminia™, a smart home and wellness brand that sells products such as air purifiers, sleep aids, and ambient lighting through its online store. Our manager, excited by GenAI's potential, has tasked us with an ambitious challenge: designing an application that generates personalized marketing emails in bulk.

Today, our team connects with customers through Direct Email Marketing (DEM) campaigns designed to drive traffic to our product catalogue. These campaigns typically involve sending email messages to the entire customer base. Occasionally, we segment the audience and craft messages for customer clusters—such as premium clients or deal-seekers. We've noticed that these segmented campaigns tend to perform better, as they feel more relevant to the recipients.

**Figure 7.7** Hyper-personalized emails: earning customer love at scale

So, our manager asked the natural next question: what if we could send hyper-personalized emails—each one unique—treating every customer as if they had their own personal shopper? She knows we're into GenAI (she may have spotted a copy of *Grokking AI Applications* on our desk, which definitely increased our credibility), so she asked us to figure out how we could use the data in our CRM system to generate these personalized messages.

Right now, customer data is scattered across multiple files. Specifically, we have two datasets:

- A *Customer Master Data* file in CSV format, which includes information such as name, email address, age, city, and favorite product category.
- A separate Excel file with *Transaction History*, where each row tells us what product was purchased, when, for how much, and by whom.

At the same time, we're committed to following our internal *Customer Email Communication Guidelines*, a document stored in PDF that defines our tone of voice and outlines tested personalization strategies based on customer type. You can now download all the files related to Luminia, as illustrated in figure 7.8, from the page https://tiny.cc/luminia. You will need them very soon.

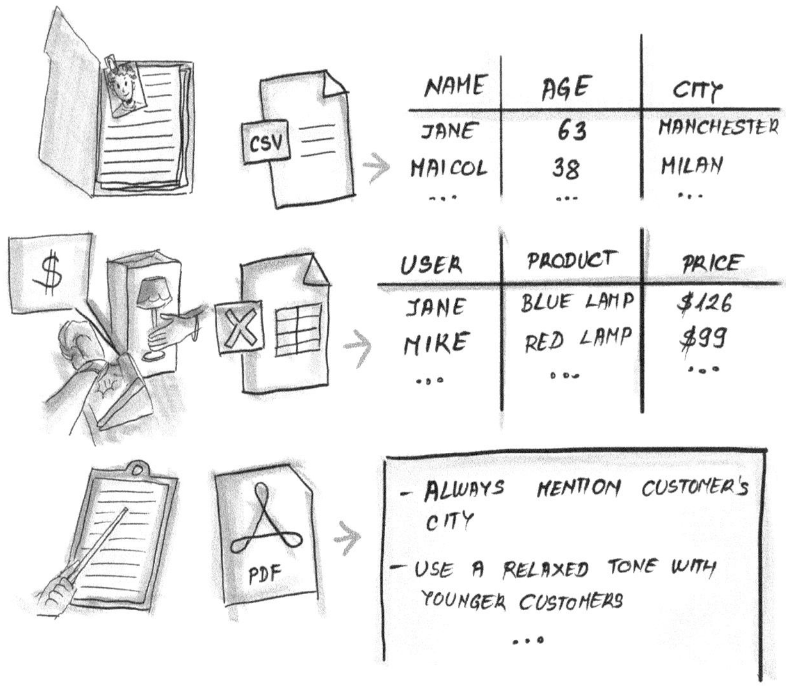


**Figure 7.8** Three files store everything you need to generate the content of your personalized emails.

Our goal is to turn raw customer data into input that an LLM can work with while ensuring that the LLM receives clear, structured instructions aligned with our guidelines. That's where the combination of KNIME and Langflow becomes a game-changer. The system we envision should integrate data processing with KNIME and generative text creation with Langflow.

Our application will follow several key steps, as shown in figure 7.9:

1. First, KNIME processes the input data (customer master and transaction history), and produces a structured, synthetic summary of each customer's status—how much they've spent, what their latest purchase was, and other personal info useful for tailoring a message.
2. We pass this description to Langflow, which enriches it with our brand communication guidelines and generates a composite prompt. The LLM responds with a message that includes a subject line and an email body.

3. Finally, KNIME collects the responses from Langflow and writes them to a new Excel file, which we can plug into our Mail Merge system to send out the campaign at scale.

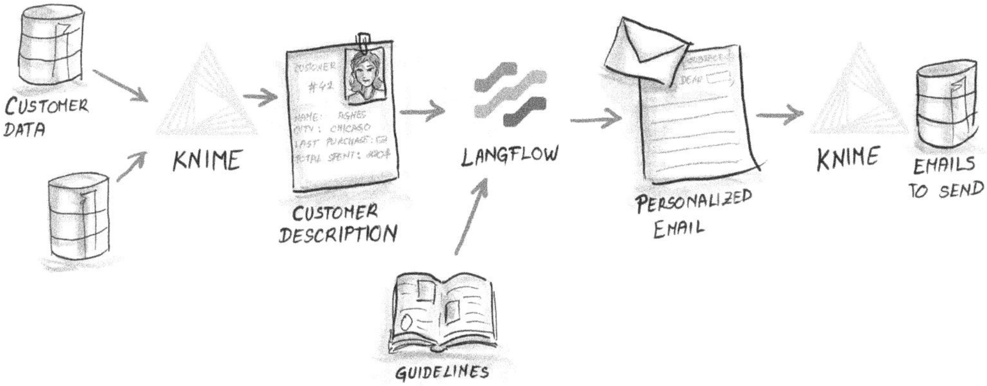


**Figure 7.9** From raw customer data to a list of personalized marketing emails to send

Let's get started with the very first step: transforming our raw data into meaningful customer descriptions.

## Crunching data to build customer descriptions

To execute the initial phase of our application, we must create a KNIME workflow that loads our available data and prepares it in a format suitable for Langflow to process. Let's first open KNIME and create a new workflow; you can go back to figure 7.3 to check the steps. Give it a name, such as `Luminia DEM` or whatever you please.

Of course, the first thing we need to do in our new workflow is load the data. Let's start with the Customer Master Data, which is in CSV format. It won't surprise us to discover that the node we need to load this file is the CSV Reader. In the repository on the left, let's find the node (we can start entering `CSV` in the Nodes repository search box on the left) and then drag and drop it into the central box, as shown in figure 7.10.

Our newly implemented node will display a red traffic light with a nonwelcoming warning icon on top. This is because the node hasn't got everything it needs to run. To configure it, double-click the node or click the little cog icon that appears on top as soon as we select it (you can spot this icon in figure 7.10).

The configuration window of the CSV Reader node (see figure 7.11) will request all you need to open and interpret the data in a CSV file. The most important piece of configuration is to select which CSV file should be read by the node. To do so, just click on the Browse... button on the top right and select the file `luminia_customers.csv` you have previously downloaded.

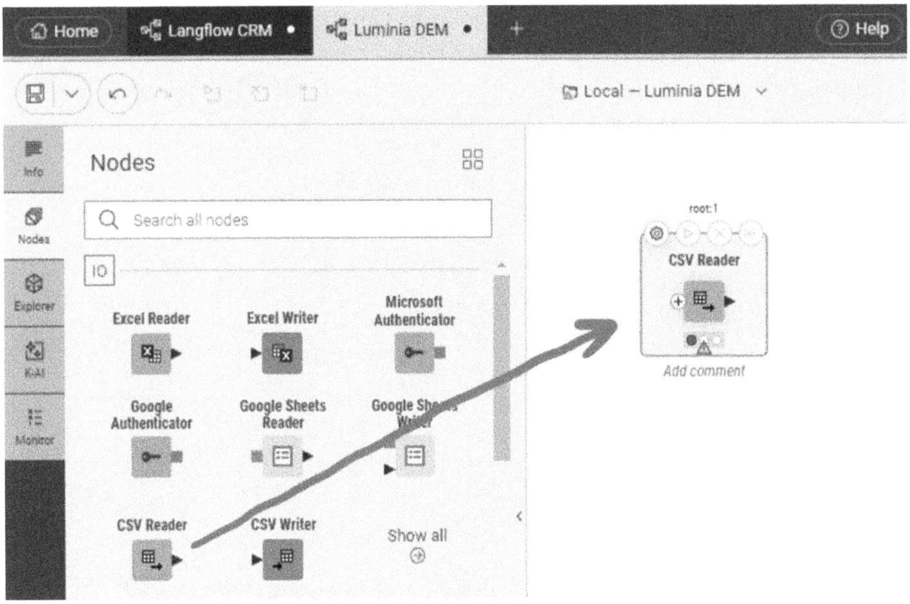


**Figure 7.10** Implementing our very first KNIME node: the CSV Reader

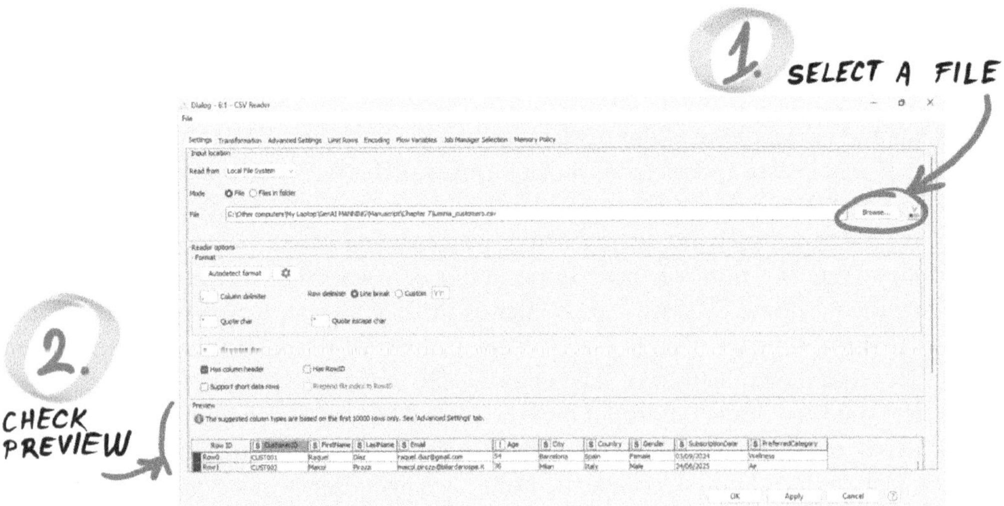


**Figure 7.11** The configuration window of the CSV Reader node

You'll notice that the node has recognized the structure of the file (you can always manually edit the reading format, such as the column delimiters, using the parameters in the middle of the configuration page) and produced a useful preview of the table, which you can find at the bottom of figure 7.11 (2).

This is all you need, at a minimum, to configure this node. For completeness, the node offers additional configuration options that you can access by clicking some of the tabs at the top of the configuration window. For example, if you click the Transformation tab at the top (see figure 7.12), you'll find extra settings that are useful for modifying the structure of the file as you load it. For instance, you can rename and remove columns, as well as change their order. In KNIME, specialized nodes such as Column Renamer, Column Filter, and Column Resorter (check them out in the repository) can perform these steps, but to save time, you can apply them immediately after loading by using this extra settings tab.

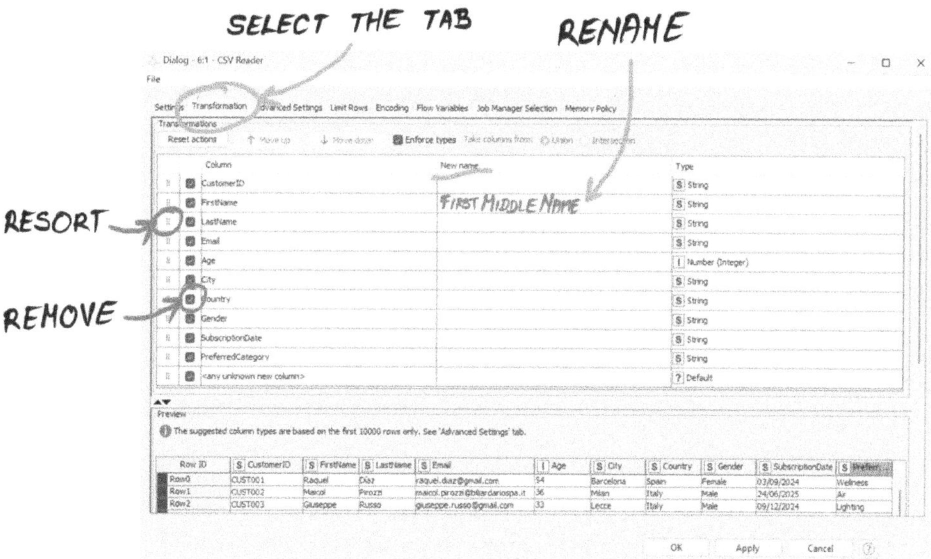


**Figure 7.12** The Transformation tab in the CSV Reader node configuration has extra settings for loading the data the way you need to.

After closing the configuration window (click the OK button at the bottom), you can add a meaningful annotation to the node to help identify its purpose. In this case, let's add a comment such as `Load Customer Master Data` after double-clicking the annotation text box at the bottom of the node.

Let's execute the node: right-click on it and select Execute, or press F7, or just click the play icon appearing on top when you select the node. Once you do so, the traffic light will display a comforting green light: this means that the data has been loaded and is now available at the output port of the node. When the node is selected, you get a handy preview of its main output port. You find it at the bottom of the Workbench window, as shown in figure 7.13. All data seems to be there, so we are ready to move on.

**Figure 7.13** Your first KNIME node did its job: the customer data is ready at the output port of the CSV Reader node.

Let's now load the transactional data, stored in the *luminia_transactions.xlsx* file. Let's explore an alternative way to load data. Open the Windows File Explorer or the macOS Finder at the folder where you put the source data you downloaded earlier, and then simply drag and drop the Excel file onto the KNIME Explorer canvas, somewhere following the CSV Reader node.

KNIME understands you're trying to load an Excel file and automatically provides an Excel Reader node that prepopulates the File location parameter with the path of the file you've just dragged. Yes, you could've taken the traditional approach of dragging an Excel Reader node from the repository and then configuring it as we did with the CSV Reader, but we saved some valuable time this way. The newly implemented node is ready to use, indicated by a yellow status light. You can also double-click it to check its configuration and, most important, ensure that the table preview matches what is shown in figure 7.14, with some transactions at the bottom.

Close the configuration window, edit the annotation label to `Read Transactions`, and execute the node (press F7 or right-click Execute), and you'll have two nodes with green lights whose outputs can now be processed further.

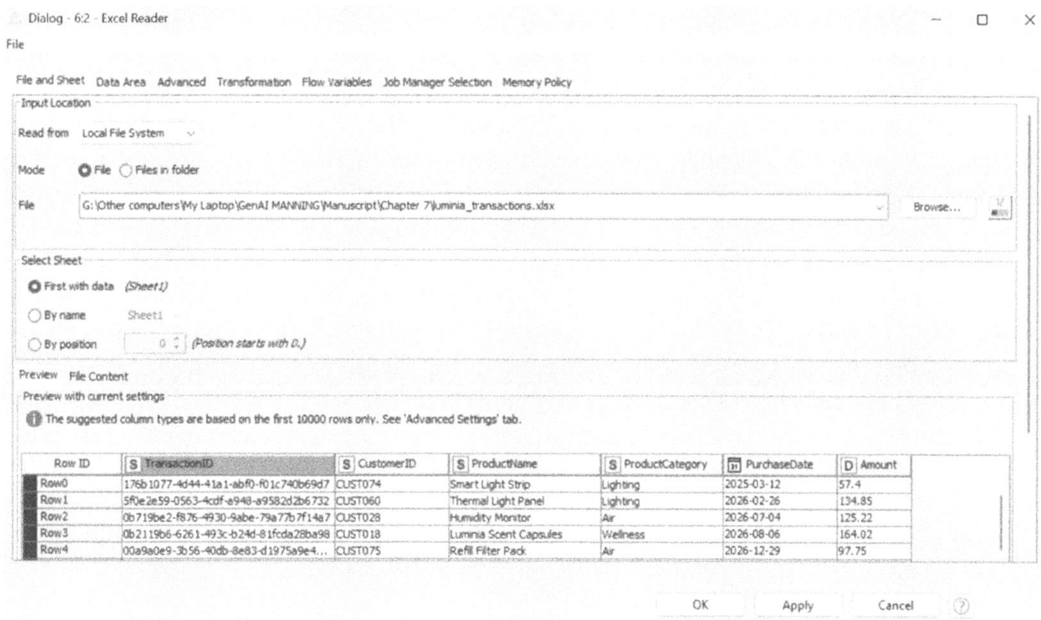


**Figure 7.14** The configuration window of the Excel Reader node. The preview shows some transactions of Luminia products.

To figure out what to do next, let's take a moment to think about what the customer descriptions should look like. We'd like our LLM call to use some key fields to generate a personalized message:

- *First name*—To refer to our customer in the email.
- *City*—To make references to the customer's location context.
- *Age*—To help drive the right tone in the message.
- *Preferred category*—To help maintain relevance to a customer's preferences if they haven't made any purchases yet.
- *Last purchased item*—To refer to an item the customer bought can increase message relevance.
- *Days since last purchase*—To determine whether we need to reactivate a dormant customer.
- *Days since subscription*—To understand whether we need to welcome a new customer or are dealing with an established one.
- *Total spend (in dollars)*—To identify premium customers and trigger loyalty language based on the amount spent by the customer so far.

If we ask ourselves whether we already have this information, ready to use for each customer in our dataset, the answer is, not yet. So, that means that some data transformation is needed.

Because some data points are already present in the Customer Master Data (name, age, city, preferred category, and subscription date), while others are stored in the Transaction History, we need to combine the two tables.

Also, several fields need to be calculated by applying logic to the transaction data. For example, we don't have total spend as a column, but we can compute it by aggregating all the transactions for each customer and summing them. Similarly, we don't have the number of days since the last purchase, but we can calculate it by finding the most recent transaction date for each customer and comparing it with today's date.

This is exactly where KNIME comes into play. We need to build a series of nodes that will combine the two raw datasets and generate a single table with customer-level descriptions containing all the key fields listed previously.

As shown in figure 7.15, we need to implement a workflow that combines the two tables, sorts transactions chronologically, runs the needed aggregations, and calculates the days since the last purchase.

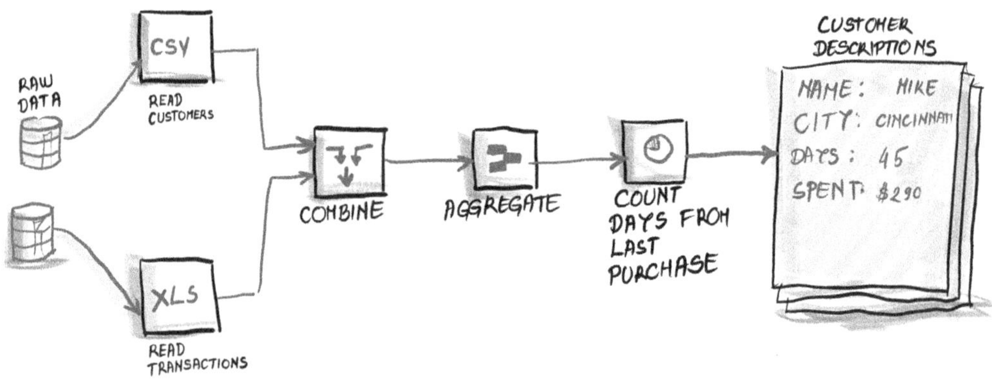


**Figure 7.15** The KNIME workflow, moving from raw data to structured customer descriptions

We've already loaded the Customer Master Data and the Transaction History as two separate tables, using the CSV Reader and the Excel Reader. Now it's time to combine them. This is a classic operation in data analytics called a *join*.

A join allows us to match rows from two tables based on a shared key: a column or a set of columns with matching values across the tables, indicating which rows in both tables refer to the same entity. In this case, the entity is the customer, and the shared key is the column CustomerID. We want to combine the two tables, making sure that the row in Customer Master Data describing a customer gets matched with all and only the rows of the transactions made by that customer. The goal of such a combination is to create a new table that brings together all relevant information from both sources.

Let's see this in action by looking at the following two sample tables (by convention, the tables to combine are called the *left* and *right* tables).

**Customer Master Data (left table)**

| CustomerID | FirstName | Age | City |
|---|---|---|---|
| CUST001 | Rebecca | 53 | Manchester |
| CUST002 | Maicol | 41 | Milan |
| CUST003 | Giulia | 37 | Milan |

**Transaction History (right table)**

| CustomerID | ProductName | PurchaseDate | Amount |
|---|---|---|---|
| CUST002 | Sleep Lamp | 2025-01-25 | 439.96 |
| CUST002 | Essential Oil Diffuser | 2025-03-10 | 288.00 |
| CUST085 | Comfort Bundle Pack | 2025-04-04 | 215.50 |

As you can see, CUST002 appears in both tables (with two purchases), CUST003 appears only in the customer table (no purchases yet), and CUST085 appears only in the transaction file (likely a new record we haven't yet added to our master data).

Depending on the type of join we apply, we might get different results. So we need to decide: which customers do we want to include in the final result?

In our case, we also want to generate emails for customers who haven't made a purchase yet—such as CUST003. That's why we need to include all rows from the left table (Customer Master Data), even if there's no match in the right table (Transaction History). This is called a *left outer join* (because we "preserve" all keys in the left table, even if they aren't matched in the right).

Here's what the result looks like after a left outer join:

| CustomerID | FirstName | Age | City | ProductName | PurchaseDate | Amount |
|---|---|---|---|---|---|---|
| CUST001 | Rebecca | 53 | Manchester | ? | ? | ? |
| CUST002 | Maicol | 41 | Milan | Sleep Lamp | 2025-01-25 | 439.96 |
| CUST002 | Maicol | 41 | Milan | Essential Oil Diffuser | 2025-03-10 | 288.00 |
| CUST003 | Giulia | 37 | Milan | ? | ? | ? |

Note that CUST001 and CUST003 have missing values (represented by a question mark, ?, in KNIME) in the transaction columns because they haven't made a purchase. In contrast, CUST002 appears twice, once for each transaction.

For completeness, we could have decided to run a different type of join. For example, if we wanted to keep only the rows that have a match in both the left and the right table, we would have gone for an *inner* join. In this case, only the two rows related to customer `CUST002` would have appeared in the output. And if we had used a *right outer join*, we'd get `CUST085` even though it doesn't exist in our master data—useful for audits, but not for email generation.

In KNIME, we can use the Joiner node to perform this operation and combine our two tables (the Customer Master Data, the left table, and the Transaction History, the right table) into one. We want all customers to appear in the output, even those with no transactions, so we need to preserve all customers present in the left table: we'll then go for a left outer join.

Find the Joiner in the KNIME node repository and add it to the workflow. Connect the output of the CSV Reader (containing the Customer Master Data) to the first input port of the joiner node (the upper port refers to the left table). Connect also the second table (transactions) to the lower input port (right table). Then, double-click to open its configuration window.

As shown on the left-hand side of figure 7.16, use the Matching Criteria section to specify which columns to match. In our case, both tables have a column named *CustomerID*. Select it as the matching key for both the Top input (left) and the Bottom input (right) tables.

To retain all customer records—even those without matching transactions—we need to select the appropriate output options under Include in Output, as shown on the right-hand side of figure 7.16. Make sure that you only tick:

- *Matching Rows*—To include customers who made purchases
- *Left Unmatched Rows*—To include customers without transactions

Leave Right Unmatched Rows unchecked because we don't need transactions without a customer profile.

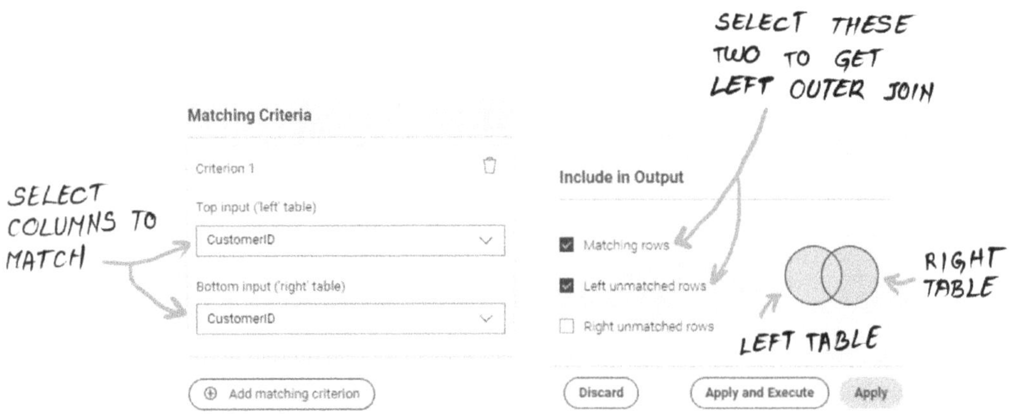


**Figure 7.16** The Joiner node configuration to combine customers with their transactions

That's it! If you click Apply and Execute (or right-click the node and select Execute), you can see the joined table in the output preview at the bottom. It includes all customers and their purchases (if any).

We notice that the rows of the joined table aren't in chronological order. Because we want to spot the latest transaction for each customer, we need to make sure that the latest row with a given *CustomerID* is indeed the most recent purchase made by that customer. Therefore, we need to sort transactions chronologically, from least to most recent. There is a nice KNIME node for this. It won't be a surprise that it's called the Sorter node.

Drag the Sorter node from the repository and place it to the right of the Joiner, and then connect the two. The node configuration (figure 7.17) is straightforward: you need to select the column whose values should be used for sorting and the order, which can be either ascending or descending. In our case, we select PurchaseDate as the column and set Ascending order (from the smallest value, least recent, to the biggest value, most recent).

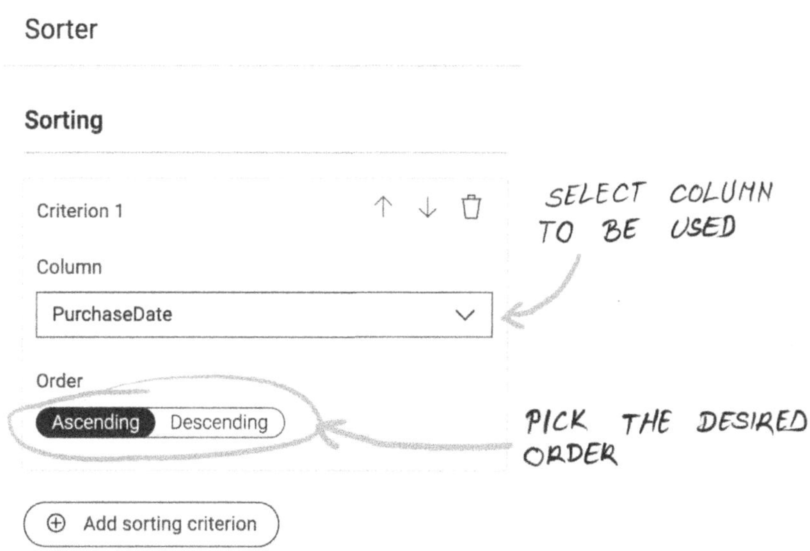


**Figure 7.17** The configuration window of the Sorter node asks you to pick one or more columns to sort on and the sort order.

Notice that the node also lets you set multiple criteria, so you can look at additional columns if there's a tie in one column (multiple rows with the same value). Execute the node, and if you look at the preview, you'll see all rows now nicely sorted from the first transaction to the most recent one.

Let's move to the next step: we need to aggregate rows in the joined table by customer so that we have exactly one row per customer with summarized values. For example, we would need to calculate the total spend of each customer by summing all the Amount values from their transactions. So, the aggregation method will be *Sum*. If you look at the sample table we saw earlier (the output of the left outer join), for customer `CUST002`, we would have a total spend of $727.96, which is the sum of $439.96 and $288.00 (the two individual transaction amounts).

For each customer, we also want to retrieve their last transaction (if present) and the date of that transaction. Since we now have the rows neatly ordered from the least recent to the most recent (thank you, Sorter node!), we can just use an aggregation function that picks the bottom-most row referring to any customer. This aggregation method is called *Last*. For customer `CUST002`, the last of *ProductName* will return `Essential Oil Diffuser`, while the last of *PurchaseDate* will return `2025-03-10`, which is exactly what we want.

The database operation that aggregates multiple rows in a table together is called Group By, and in KNIME, we have a node (GroupBy) that does exactly this. Let's retrieve GroupBy from the KNIME node repository and implement it after the Sorter. Connect the output of the Sorter to its input and double-click on it to get to the configuration window. In the first panel (shown in figure 7.18), you need to define groups. One group will correspond to one row in the aggregated table (the output of this node). So, in this case, we need to define groups by selecting the columns that define the unique value that identifies the entity we are aggregating. In this case, we want to aggregate by customer—one row per customer—so it would suffice to select the *Customer ID* column. Double-click on a column on the right to move it to the left, which means considering it for group definition. Since we want to "carry" other columns of the customer master data that we might need later in the flow, let's select the other columns we want to define as groups. So, let's select name, email, gender, days from subscription, and all other columns as shown in the figure.

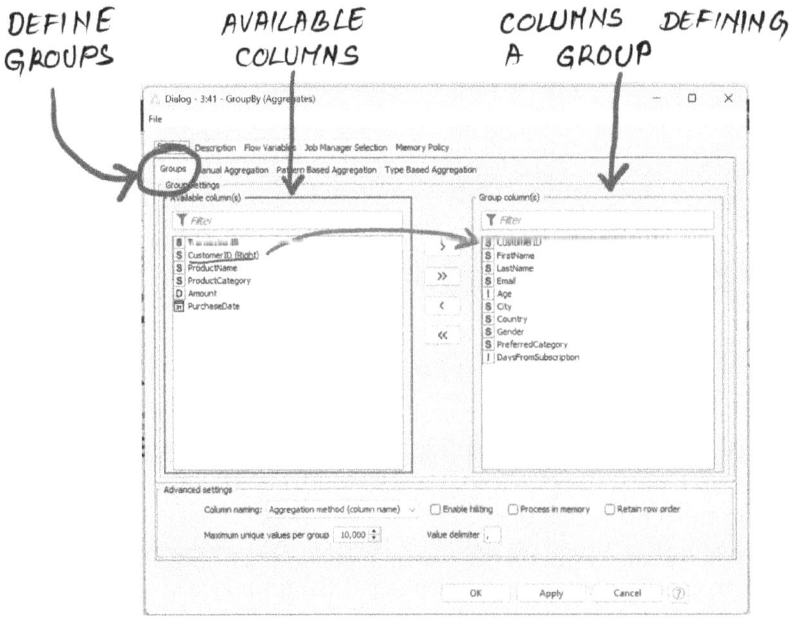


**Figure 7.18** By defining groups, you decide the granularity of your GroupBy aggregation.

Now, let's move to the second panel (click Manual Aggregation at the top). Here, we need to define which columns to use for aggregation and which aggregation method to use. In our case, we need the sum of Amount (for the total spend) and the last instance of ProductName and PurchaseDate. To do so, first double-click Amount and then select Sum as the aggregation method. Then, double-click ProductName and select Last. Do the same for PurchaseDate, as shown in figure 7.19.

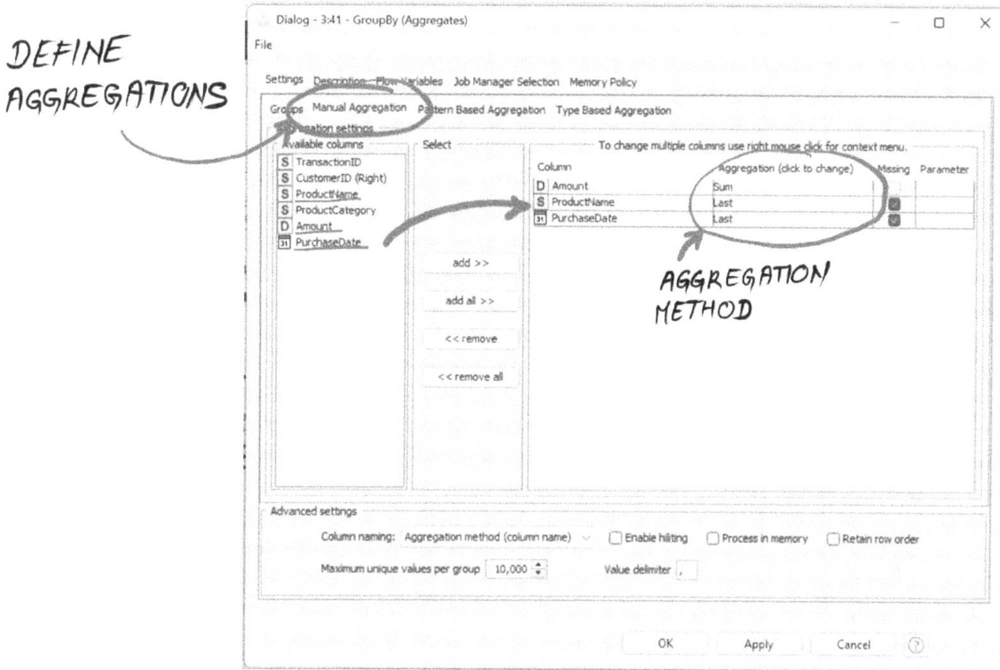


**Figure 7.19** Pick the aggregation method for each column you want to aggregate.

Click the OK button to close the configuration window, run the node (press F7 or right-click Execute), and see the output in the preview at the bottom. As shown in figure 7.20, we now have exactly 10 rows (one per customer, no duplications—sounds good) and, after the columns defining the group (so describing the customer), 3 extra columns reporting their aggregated values: Sum(Amount), Last(ProductName), and Last(PurchaseDate). Notice the null values (question mark icons) in these fields for the customers who have never purchased anything. That makes sense.

Notice that the column *Last(PurchaseDate)* carries individual dates like 2025-10-05, but we want to pass a number that tells us about the recency of the latest transaction to the DEM generator. In fact, LLMs (without any tools at hand) do not know what day it is today, and we should spare them from calculating the interval between two dates. It's better if we ask KNIME to do the calculation and present the LLM directly with the number of days between each *Last(PurchaseDate)* and the current date. Since all

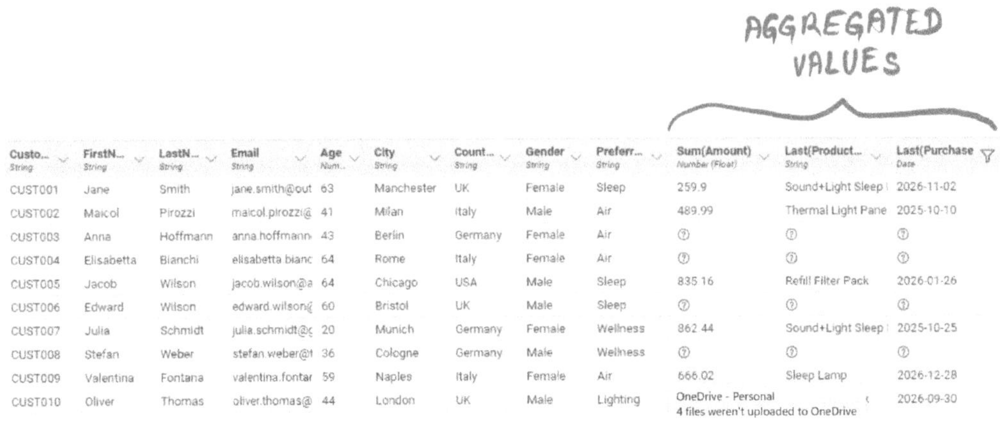


| Custo... String | FirstN... String | LastN... String | Email String | Age Num... | City String | Count... String | Gender String | Preferr... String | Sum(Amount) Number (Float) | Last(Product... String | Last(Purchase Date |
|---|---|---|---|---|---|---|---|---|---|---|---|
| CUST001 | Jane | Smith | jane.smith@out | 63 | Manchester | UK | Female | Sleep | 259.9 | Sound+Light Sleep | 2026-11-02 |
| CUST002 | Maicol | Pirozzi | maicol.pirozzi@ | 41 | Milan | Italy | Male | Air | 489.99 | Thermal Light Pane | 2025-10-10 |
| CUST003 | Anna | Hoffmann | anna.hoffmann | 43 | Berlin | Germany | Female | Air | ? | ? | ? |
| CUST004 | Elisabetta | Bianchi | elisabetta.bianc | 64 | Rome | Italy | Female | Air | ? | ? | ? |
| CUST005 | Jacob | Wilson | jacob.wilson@a | 64 | Chicago | USA | Male | Sleep | 835.16 | Refill Filter Pack | 2026-01-26 |
| CUST006 | Edward | Wilson | edward.wilson@ | 60 | Bristol | UK | Male | Sleep | ? | ? | ? |
| CUST007 | Julia | Schmidt | julia.schmidt@ | 20 | Munich | Germany | Female | Wellness | 862.44 | Sound+Light Sleep | 2025-10-25 |
| CUST008 | Stefan | Weber | stefan.weber@ | 36 | Cologne | Germany | Male | Wellness | ? | ? | ? |
| CUST009 | Valentina | Fontana | valentina.fontar | 59 | Naples | Italy | Female | Air | 666.02 | Sleep Lamp | 2026-12-28 |
| CUST010 | Oliver | Thomas | oliver.thomas@ | 44 | London | UK | Male | Lighting | OneDrive - Personal 4 files weren't uploaded to OneDrive | | 2026-09-30 |

**Figure 7.20** The output of GroupBy: now we have aggregated values by customers.

transactions in our dataset happen between 2025 and 2026, we can set as an assumption that the current date is the 31st of December 2026 and calculate how many days have elapsed between the latest transaction of each user and the end of 2026. To do calculations on dates and times, there is a handy node in KNIME specialized for it.

Let's implement the Date&Time Difference node from the repository and connect its input to the output of the GroupBy node. The configuration window (see figure 7.21) allows us to tell the node:

- Which column to use as the first endpoint in the interval we're calculating. In our case, let's select Last(PurchaseDate) in the First Date&Time column dropdown.
- The second endpoint of the interval. We want to select December 31, 2026, as the fixed end date of our interval.
- Whether we want the node to output a string with the extended interval (in years, months, days) or just a number in a given unit of measure. In our case, we need to select Number as the output type and select Days as the granularity.
- What name should the output column have? For us, `DaysFromLastPurchase`, or anything else you like, would do.

With these settings in place, we can execute the node and see that the new column, containing the number of days between each last purchase and the last day of 2026, has been added, which is great.

We now have all the ingredients for the customer description we wanted to create, so it's just a matter of setting those pieces of information in the format we can send to the LLM. Remember: LLMs take only plain text as input. If we simply send numbers and words without structure, the model may not understand what each piece of data refers to. We therefore need a format that makes explicit which field is which, where the value begins, and where it ends.

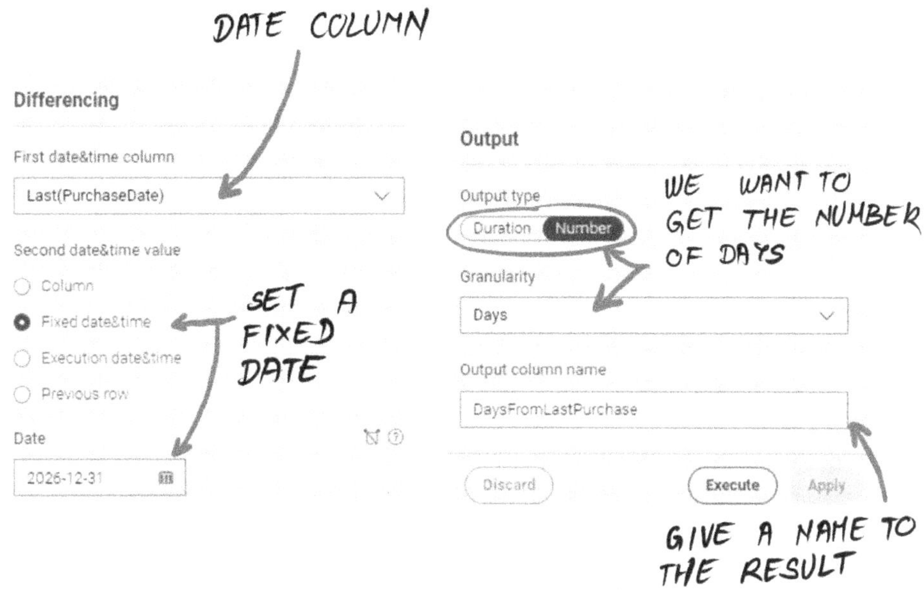


**Figure 7.21** The Date&Time Difference node configuration does the math between times.

In our case, we want to send the LLM a structured description of each user and use a standard format for transferring data between applications as keys and values. JSON is a popular format for this that is well understood by LLMs.

## What is the JSON format?

JavaScript Object Notation (JSON) is a lightweight and widely adopted format for exchanging structured data between applications. It uses braces { }, brackets [ ], and key-value pairs to represent data. For example, a table with two columns—`Name` and `Age`—containing values `Tessa` and `15` becomes `{"Name": "Tessa", "Age": 15}`.

We now need to create a new field that will contain, in the form of a JSON string, all and only the customer information we want to pass to the LLM. This field will include the relevant columns as key–value pairs (for example, *FirstName*, *Age*, *DaysFromSubscription*, *Sum(Amount)*, and so on).

To do this in KNIME, we use the Columns to JSON node. This node combines the selected fields into a single JSON object. Implement the Columns to JSON node and, following the guide in figure 7.22, configure it properly. You can name the output column as `Customer_data` and remove the columns you don't want to be used in the JSON element (the LLM doesn't need, for instance, *CustomerID* or *LastName* to do its job), by double-clicking on them from the list on the right (or using the chevron '<' button to move them across). You should only be left with *FirstName*, *Age*, *City*, *Country*, *Gender*, *PreferredCategory*, *DaysFromSubscription*, *Sum(Amount)*, and *DaysFromLastPurchase*.

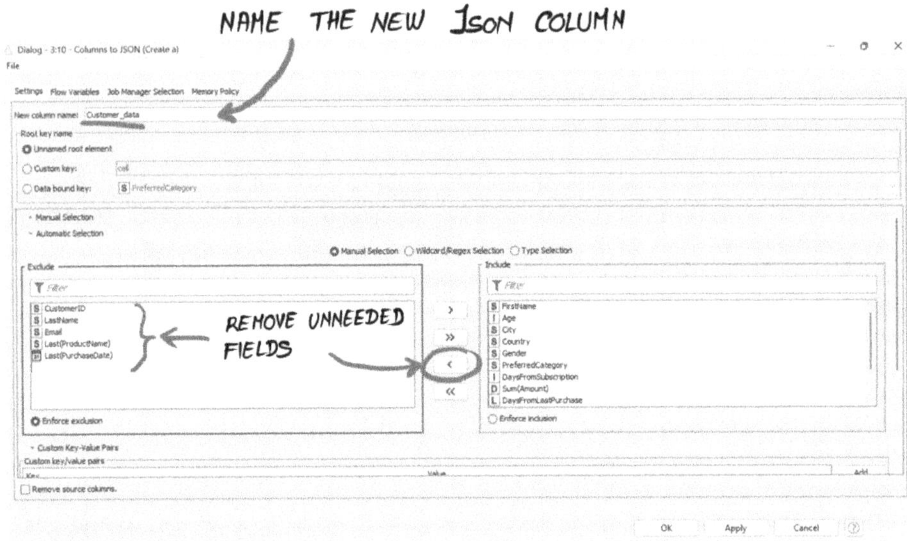


**Figure 7.22** The Columns to JSON node generates a single object embedding all the columns you need.

There's one more conversion we need to manage. Because we want to send only text to the LLM, we need to convert the JSON column we just created into its plain, string-only version. This is a technical step—just a conversion of the KNIME column format to allow the next nodes to work.

The simplest way to do so is to implement a node called String Manipulation (find it in the repository) and use it to define a formula that converts the JSON format into a string. After doing the wiring, open its configuration and just type `string($Customer_data$)` into the expression field, then select Replace Column at the bottom and pick the *Customer_data* column in the dropdown menu so that you basically "replace" the old JSON-typed column with its string version. Use figure 7.23 as a guide.

## The mighty expression nodes in KNIME

The String Manipulation node in KNIME is very powerful. It lets you write small formulas that transform the content of your fields—for example, replacing characters, counting how many characters a word has, or capitalizing names. In KNIME, these formulas are called expressions. They're written in KNIME's own built-in expression language (not Python or Java—it's a native, formula-based syntax specific to KNIME), and you can pick from a large list of ready-made functions in the configuration window. Check all the available functions in the central list in the configuration window. In addition, try the Math Formula node—it lets you define operations between numeric columns in a very similar way.

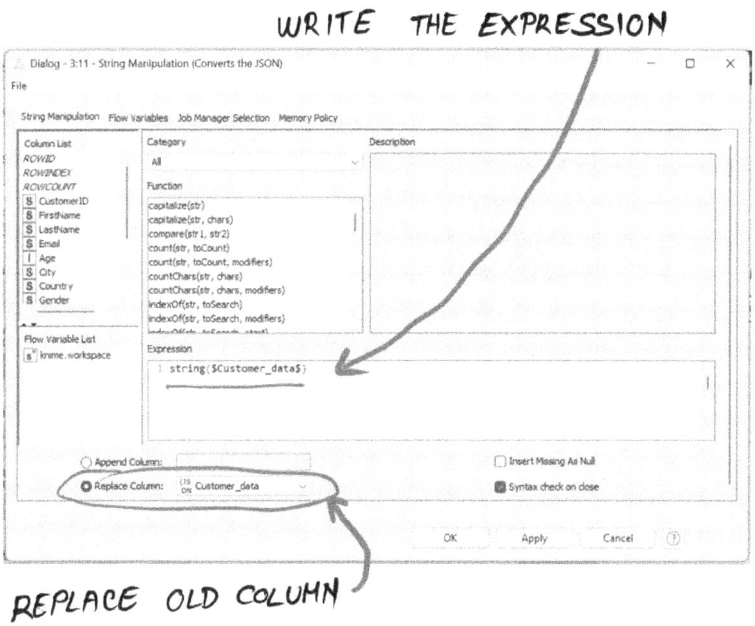


**Figure 7.23** The String Manipulation node lets you apply any sort of transformation to strings.

If you execute the node and check the table preview at the bottom, you'll notice that the last column of your table is now a nice string with the JSON-formatted description of your customer that includes all of its key features, such as name, age, total spend, and so on. This is what the LLM needs to do its magic.

## Generating customer-specific emails

Now it's time to change gears and move to the Langflow part of our application. Our goal is to create a flow that takes JSON as input and follows the official Luminia™ brand guidelines to act as a virtual copywriter, generating a personalized subject line and email body for each customer.

Before implementing the flow, it's good practice to sketch the structure first—something you should be used to now. If we had to sketch what we're about to build, it would look something like figure 7.24.

At a high level, here's the plan:

1. A Read File component loads the Luminia Guidelines PDF.
2. A Prompt Template component formats a structured system message, including both the brand rules and the customer input.
3. The JSON input is passed to an LLM, which generates the subject and body of the email, using the output of the Prompt Template component as a system message.

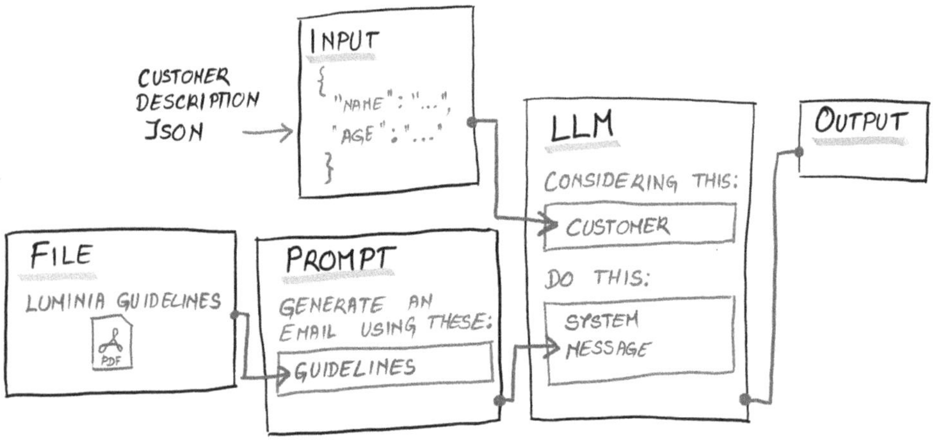


**Figure 7.24** The workflow for turning customer descriptions into emails

Open a new flow in Langflow, and let's implement a Read File component. Click on the Select files button and upload the `Luminia Guidelines.pdf`—you can find it on the same page at tiny.cc/luminia.

Next, let's implement the Prompt Template component. This will format the instruction we want to send to the LLM. It should use our standard prompting structure, acting as a senior copywriter with knowledge of brand tone and voice. We should mention that the customer data will be provided and "attach" the Luminia guidelines, leaving a variable in curly brackets (like `{guidelines}`) as a placeholder. We should also explain the type of output format we would like. Let's go for JSON this time as well, since LLMs are good at understanding JSON inputs and producing JSON outputs.

If we put it all together, we should use a template like this:

```
Act as a senior copywriter for Luminia.
Your task is to generate a personalized marketing email that includes:

• A short, engaging subject line
• A concise body tailored to the customer profile (under 120 words)

Follow the brand rules strictly and reference the customer data provided. Just
generate the subject and the body as a JSON object. The names of the keys must
be: 'subject' and 'body'.

------------------------------------------------
### CUSTOMER GUIDELINES
{guidelines}
------------------------------------------------
```

Once you save this prompt, Langflow will recognize the variable and add a new input port to this component. You can now connect the output of the Read File component to the guidelines input of the Prompt Template component so that the contents of the PDF get injected into the LLM calls.

Now, let's implement the usual Chat Input → OpenAI → Chat Output sequence of components. Add a Chat Input component to allow for some text to get into our flow: this will become our "connection" to KNIME. Then, implement the OpenAI component and complete the wiring: we need the Chat Input component to enter as Input, while the Prompt output should enter as a System Message. Don't forget to configure the OpenAI (or any other provider of your choice) component using your API key and select the model you would like to test. Finally, add a Chat Output component to display the response and connect it to the output of the LLM.

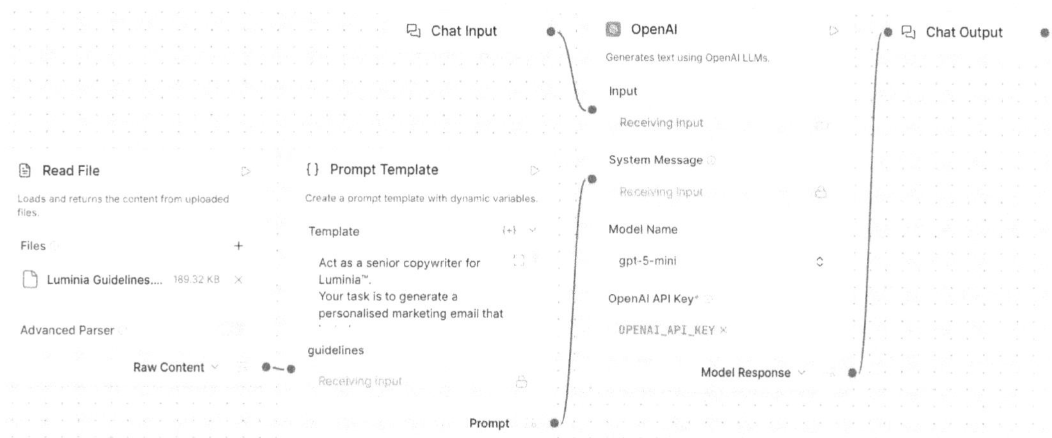


**Figure 7.25** The Langflow flow that takes a customer JSON profile and generates a subject and email body according to Luminia's brand guidelines

Let's test it! Open the Playground and manually enter a JSON-formatted customer profile, like the one you see in figure 7.26. You can copy/paste a sample value from the Customer_data component in KNIME or enter any data as you like.

Now that our Langflow flow is working and tested in the Playground, the final step is making it callable from KNIME—or any external application. To do so, we need to expose our flow and essentially publish it in a way that can be reached by other applications, such as KNIME. We'll do this through APIs, interfaces that let applications speak to each other in a structured manner.

What conditions must be met for the Langflow and KNIME integration to function properly? We need to expose the flow on a machine that the external application, KNIME, can reach. To establish the API connection, the essential parameters include the Server URL (similar to the address of a building) and the API Key for authentication (acting as a key to access the building).

User

```
{
 "FirstName" : "Maicol",
 "Age" : 41,
 "City" : "Milan",
 "Country" : "Italy",
 "Gender" : "Male",
 "PreferredCategory" : "Air",
 "DaysFromSubscription" : 704,
 "Sum(Amount)" : 489.99,
 "Last(ProductName)" : "Thermal Light Panel",
 "DaysFromLastPurchase" : 447
}
```

AI gpt-4o-mini

{ "subject": "Maicol, elevate your Milanese lifestyle", "body": "Hi Maicol, we hope you're enjoying the ambiance created by your Thermal Light Panel. As Milan continues to inspire with its elegance, we invite you to explore our latest air quality innovations designed to enhance your home. Discover how our smart air purifiers can complement your stylish living space. Your comfort deserves the best—explore now!" }

**Figure 7.26** Sample input and output from the Langflow flow. This user has no excuses not to buy a new product.

The simplest setup is to have Langflow and KNIME running on the same machine. But they could also be on two separate machines. In either case, KNIME needs the URL of the machine where Langflow is running.

We'll explore more details about deploying Langflow and connecting to it remotely—enabling seamless integration with other applications—in the next chapter. For now, we'll keep things simple and work with a local setup: in this exercise, we assume that KNIME and Langflow run on the same machine. This means that Langflow will be reachable locally via the conventional local server URL, which will look something like `http://localhost:7860`. Notice that Langflow runs on a specific port (7860 by default), which is why `:7860` is added at the end of the URL.

To discover the Server URL and Flow ID of your application, follow the steps shown in figure 7.27. With your flow open, click the Share menu (you'll find it right beside the Playground button, 1), then select API access (2).

Langflow will show the code you can use to connect programmatically to your flow from any application. Since we stay "low code," we are just interested in two parameters. Using figure 7.27 as a guide, you can recognize in the Python code (3) what the connection URL is. More specifically, you will be able to recognize the Server URL (starts with `http` and ends with a port number, by default, is 7860) and the Flow ID, which is a long set of characters identifying the specific flow you are working on (4). Our Luminia email generator will have a different Flow ID than the HealthyChef flow, although the server URL might be the same (our local computer).

The next piece is authentication. When we connect to external services through an API, we need an API key. Langflow also needs to verify the key when it accepts API connections. So, we need to generate an API key that KNIME can use to connect.

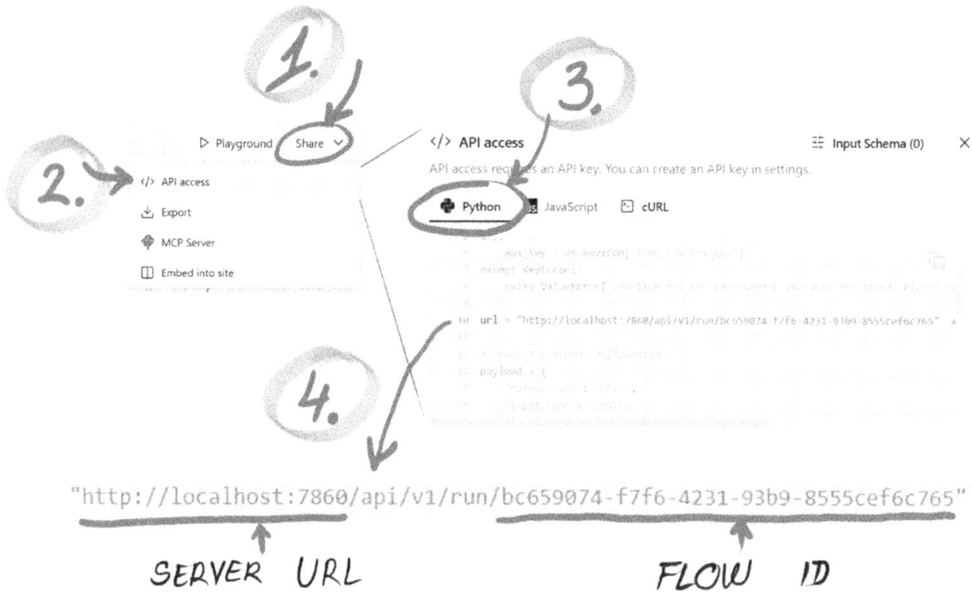


**Figure 7.27** Where to find your server URL and flow ID

This is easy to do by following the steps shown in figure 7.28. You need to go to Settings (1) by clicking the user icon in the top right corner. Then select the Langflow API Keys section on the left (2): you will be shown all the previously generated keys (if any). Lastly,

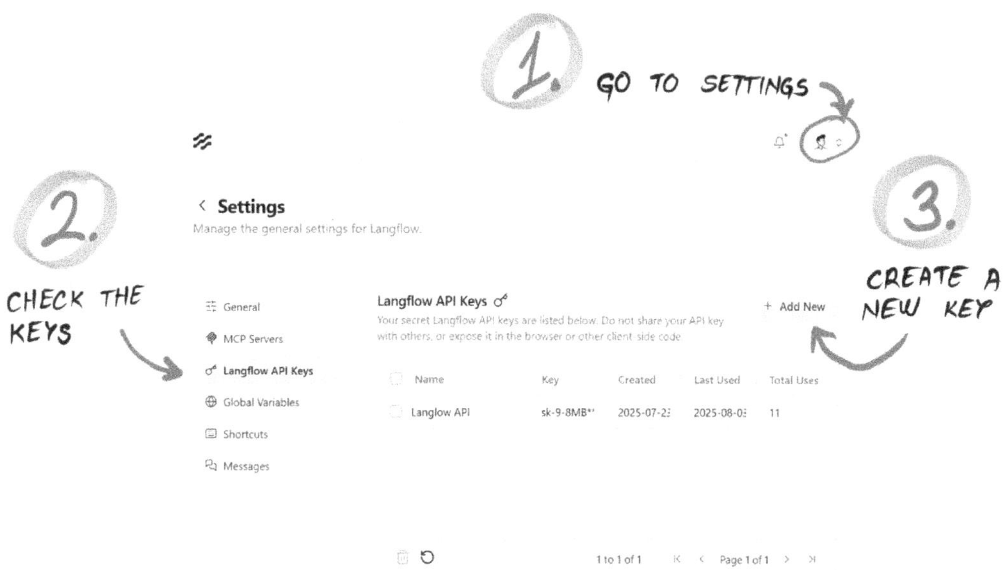


**Figure 7.28** How to generate a Langflow API key

click the Add New button on the right (3): you will be able to add a description of your new key, confirm it, visualize the new key, copy and paste it, and save it for future use. Beware that you will not be able to read the key again for security reasons, so you need to save the key somewhere safe and accessible. If you lose this secret key, you'll need to generate a new one.

## Automating email generation

Now that we have the connection parameters and a Langflow API key generated, we can finally attempt the connection from KNIME so that it can repeat the email-generation process autonomously. So, let's go back to KNIME, keeping the Langflow application open if it's on our local machine, as it needs to "answer" our calls when we knock at its door.

Fortunately, in KNIME, there is a special node that lets us connect to Langflow: it's called Langflow Runner. Since it is custom-built, you will not find it in the node repository like the other ones, but you can easily drag and drop it from KNIME's hub webpage. Search for Langflow Runner on the KNIME community Hub website (at hub.knime.com) or just go to tiny.cc/langflowrunner. As shown in figure 7.29, you'll see a node icon at the top right. If you resize your browser so that both the Hub and the KNIME workspace are visible, you can simply drag and drop the node onto the canvas.

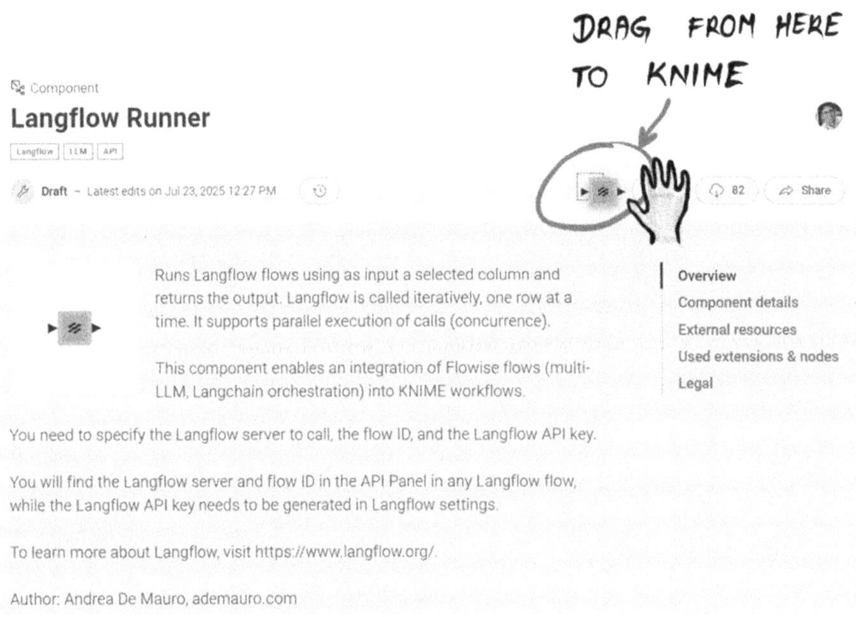


**Figure 7.29** Langflow Runner in KNIME Hub: Drag it into your workspace.

Now that the Langflow Runner is in your KNIME Workflow, we can connect it with the previous node (String Manipulation) and double-click on it to set all parameters correctly. As you can see in figure 7.30, we can finally enter the Server URL (if you are running Langflow locally, this is likely to be `http://localhost:7860`), the Flow ID you got from the Share menu/API Access, and the Langflow API Key you took from the Settings page in Langflow.

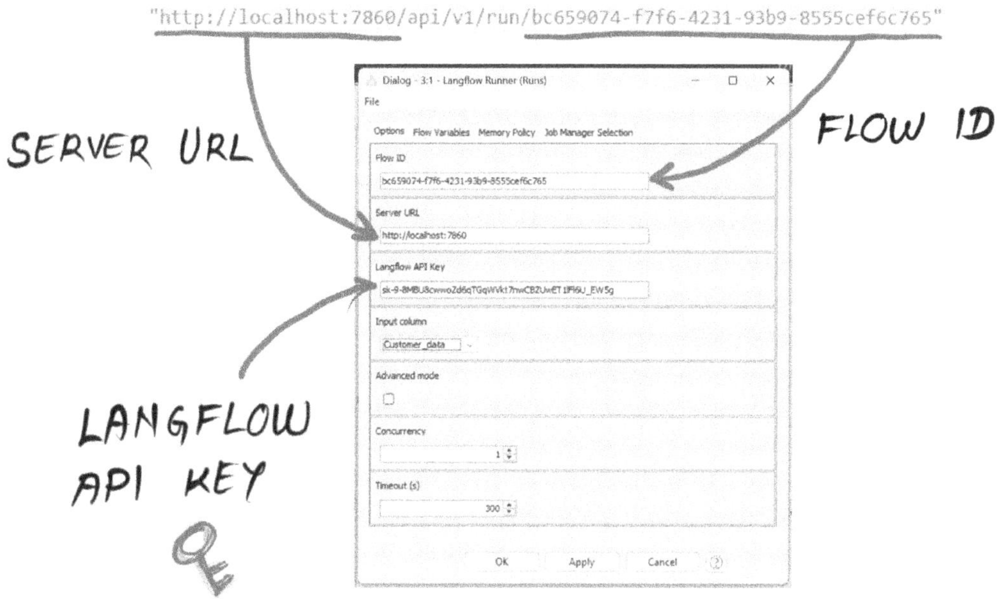


**Figure 7.30** Configuration window of Langflow Runner in KNIME

You can select Customer_data as the input column (this is the string that will be "sent" to Langflow, as the Chat Input) and click OK to close the window.

In a real-world scenario, you could easily send thousands of customer records to Langflow in one run, and KNIME will handle this scale without problems—even in its base, open source version. But since this is a book exercise, waiting for all records to be processed would take several minutes and generate many LLM calls, which would slow down your learning.

To make things faster while developing the application, we'll filter the input table before going to Langflow by implementing a Row Filter node. This node lets you set criteria to keep or remove the rows you want. For instance, you could filter out rows for customers whose names start with "A" or whose age is greater than 42. Here, for simplicity, we'll just keep the top two rows of the table.

Now, implement the Row Filter node and place it between String Manipulation and Langflow Runner, as shown in figure 7.31 (1). Then, select it and set its condition so that Row Number is less than or equal to 2 (2). If you run the node, you'll find that only two customers are kept, which lets us minimize waiting time and token usage while we develop our application.

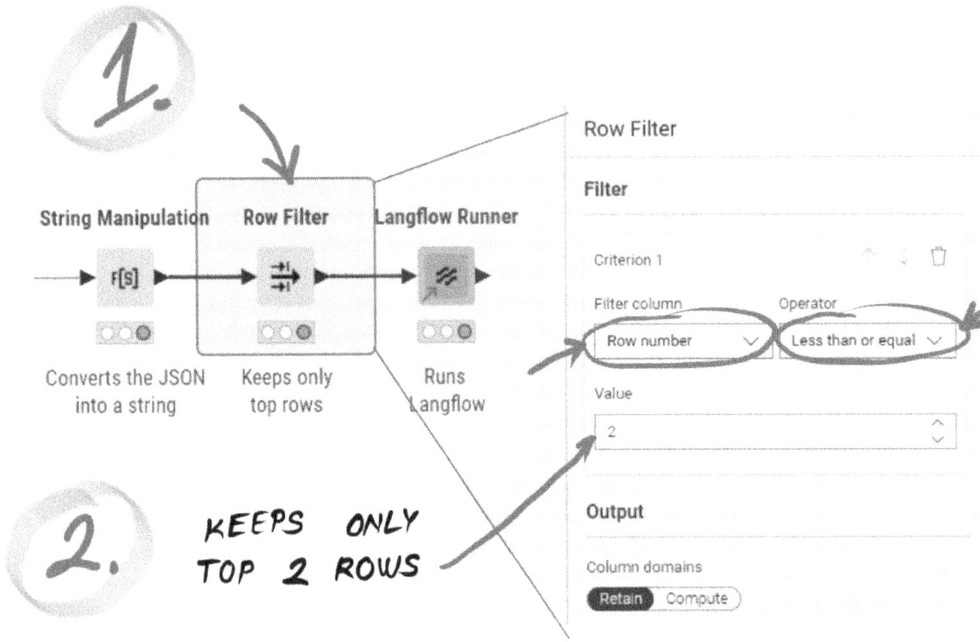


**Figure 7.31** The Row Filter node lets you set criteria for keeping only the rows you need in a table.

It's time to run the Langflow Runner and watch the magic happen. When executed, each value in the Customer_data column is sent one by one to the Langflow email generator flow. The LLM generates output, and KNIME adds it to the table as a new column called Response.

Double-click any cell in the Response column preview, and you'll see the resulting string—a nicely formatted JSON object with the email subject and body. It works!

**Figure 7.32** KNIME + Langflow: the spell that turns raw data points into ready-to-send emails

## Storing the emails to be sent

This KNIME workflow could now be extended further depending on how we'd like the generated emails to be stored or processed. Let's imagine that we want the subject and body to be saved in an Excel file, together with all the other aggregated customer information. Maybe this Excel file could be used to send emails en masse, using the mail merge functionality in Word or another method.

To do this, we need to add three final nodes to our workflow:

- *String to JSON*—This node converts the Response column (a string) into a JSON-typed column. This is the reverse of the conversion we did earlier with the String Manipulation node. The only configuration needed is to select Response as the input column to convert.
- *JSON to Table*—With this node, we disaggregate the various fields in the JSON into separate fields in our table. In this case, the subject and body become two separate string columns. This is basically the reverse process of Columns to JSON, but now applied to the response fields. This node doesn't require any specific configuration—you can keep the default one.
- *Excel Writer*—This node saves the full table into an Excel file. Configure the node by specifying the file path and name of the Excel file to be created.

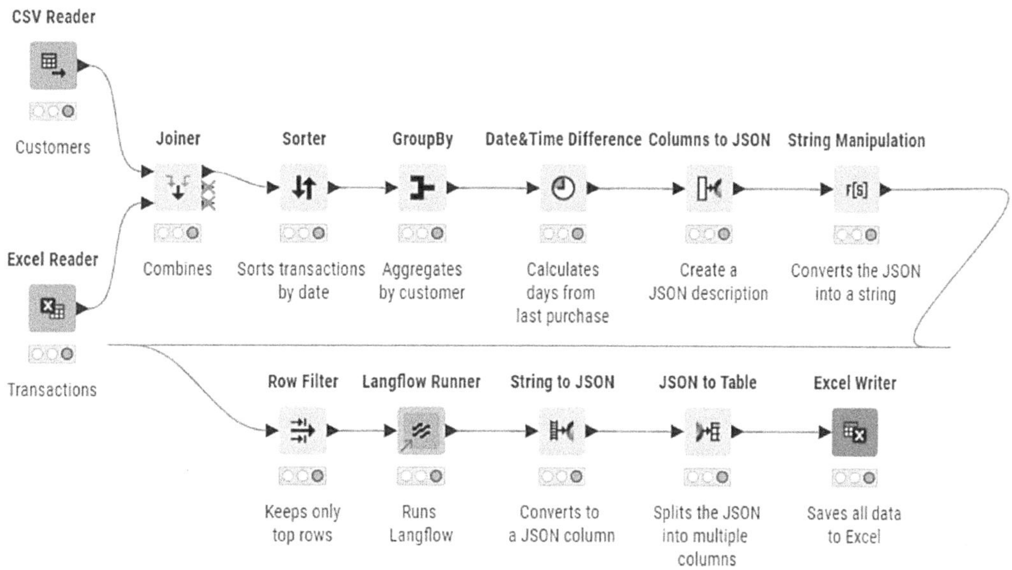


**Figure 7.33** The full KNIME workflow can generate hyper-personalized emails for all of our customers.

After you add these three nodes, you'll have the final workflow shown in figure 7.33. Now you have a repeatable routine that loads raw data (the latest customers and transactions) and creates an Excel file with the freshly generated emails to send to them. You can see a preview of some columns in the output Excel file in figure 7.34.

This brings an impressive automation capability to the Luminia™ marketing team. If they wanted to send a weekly email to all their customers (or a portion of them), they could rerun this flow (leaving filenames as they are) and obtain an updated Excel file with the new emails to send.

| | A | B | C | D | P | Q |
|---|---|---|---|---|---|---|
| 1 | **CustomerID** | **FirstName** | **LastName** | **Email** | **subject** | **body** |
| 2 | CUST001 | Jane | Smith | jane.smith@outlook.com | Jane, enhance your sleep experience | Hello Jane, we hope you're enjoying your Sound+Light Sleep Kit. As a valued member of our Luminia family, we wanted to share our latest sleep-enhancing products that could elevate your nightly routine even further. Discover the new additions designed to promote restful sleep and comfort in your home. Explore your upgrade today! |
| 3 | CUST002 | Maicol | Pirozzi | maicol.pirozzi@gmail.com | Maicol, enhance your space with Luminia | Hi Maicol, we hope you're enjoying your Thermal Light Panel! As a valued member of our Luminia family, we invite you to explore our latest air quality solutions designed to elevate your home environment. Discover how our smart air purifiers can complement your wellness journey. We appreciate your loyalty and look forward to supporting your comfort needs. Explore now! |

**Figure 7.34** The Excel file with the subject and body of the emails to be sent to Luminia™ customers

## Taking it to the next level

Hopefully, this exercise left you with a load of ideas for applying this approach to your business area and improving what we did with Luminia™. Here are some ideas to think about that could improve what we did:

- We left the LLM free to craft a personalized message without specifying any campaign-specific content to add, such as the arrival of new products or a discount offer. If needed, we could have injected more specific information into the Luminia Guidelines files (or into a separate one to add to the prompt template in Langflow) with the key messages to add to the email—maybe even leaving it to the reasoning power of the LLM to decide which offer to communicate, depending on the known customer information.
- We got our customer data from some files and saved the email messages to another file. We could have loaded the data directly from a database or even from a cloud-based CRM system such as Salesforce (there are KNIME nodes that can connect to Salesforce objects, making the loading step much easier). The email could also have been sent directly within the KNIME workflow (check the Send Email node in the repository).
- We could fully automate a process of this kind. By using the KNIME Business Hub or a KNIME Pro personal account (there's a fee to unlock the cloud-based resources), we could schedule this KNIME workflow to run regularly, like every Friday at 2 PM. Of course, Langflow will also have to be reachable by KNIME, so it should be hosted somewhere (more to come on this in the next chapter). Think about the automation opportunities when we have KNIME and Langflow operating together without human intervention at any time during the day.

These are just some ideas for making this work better. All in all, this exercise has shown the power of creating a complex, GenAI-powered application that can be integrated into any data ecosystem and automate important pieces of work. Now it's up to you to think about the next killer application of the KNIME and Langflow kit!

## What if we coded it?

In this chapter, we turned a Langflow flow into a deployable GenAI service. Instead of interacting with the model through a chat interface, we exposed the logic as an HTTP API that can be called by any external system.

The following script mirrors the Langflow design directly. The PDF Loader component becomes a `PyPDFLoader`, used to load and inject the Luminia™ brand guidelines into the prompt. The Prompt Template is implemented as a `ChatPromptTemplate` combining system instructions and a customer profile passed as JSON. The OpenAI component maps to a standard `ChatOpenAI` invocation.

What changes compared to previous chapters is the execution model. Instead of a chat loop, the core generation logic is wrapped inside a FastAPI endpoint. The Langflow "entry point" becomes a POST `/generate-email` route that accepts a generic customer profile and returns a structured JSON response containing the email subject and body. This mirrors how a Langflow flow can be exposed as an API, but makes the boundary explicit in code. In the initial comment in the code, you'll also find a guide on how to test the API call from your terminal.

```
"""
Install dependencies once (pinning versions to match Langflow):

    pip install "langchain==0.2.7" "langchain-openai==0.1.14" \
        "langchain-community==0.2.7" pypdf fastapi uvicorn python-dotenv

Before running the service:
- keep `Luminia Guidelines.pdf` next to this script
- make sure OPENAI_API_KEY is available in `.env`

Start the API locally:

    uvicorn CH7_LuminiaDEM:app --reload

Send a test request:

    curl -X POST http://localhost:8000/generate-email \
         -H "Content-Type: application/json" \
         -d '{ "profile": { "name": "SANTOSHI", "segment": "LIGHTS", "recent_
purchase_days_ago": 30 } }'
"""
```

```
import os
import json
from typing import Any, Dict
```

manage environment variables and file paths.

JSON encoding/decoding for customer profiles and model output.

Typing hints for dictionary-based profiles.

```
from dotenv import load_dotenv
from fastapi import FastAPI
from pydantic import BaseModel
```

FastAPI framework to expose a simple HTTP endpoint.

Pydantic model for validating incoming request bodies.

Chat model wrapper used throughout the book.

```
from langchain_openai import ChatOpenAI
from langchain_core.prompts import ChatPromptTemplate
from langchain_community.document_loaders import PyPDFLoader
```

Prompt template builder (system + human messages).

Convenience loader to extract text from the Luminia guidelines PDF.

```
# --- Configuration -------------------------------------------------------------
```

Folder where this script lives.

```
BASE_DIR = os.path.dirname(os.path.abspath(__file__))
GUIDELINES_PATH = os.path.join(BASE_DIR, "Luminia Guidelines.pdf")

# os.environ["OPENAI_API_KEY"] = "REPLACE_WITH_YOUR_KEY"
load_dotenv()
```

Full path to the Luminia™ brand guidelines PDF file.

Load `.env` so the OpenAI key stays outside the source code.

```
llm = ChatOpenAI(model="gpt-4o-mini", temperature=0.2)
```

Initialize the LLM "magic black box" of the email generator.

```
# --- Load and prepare guidelines text ------------------------------------

loader = PyPDFLoader(GUIDELINES_PATH)
docs = loader.load()
guidelines_text = "\n\n".join(page.page_content for page in docs)
```

Load the PDF guidelines using the LangChain document loader.

Concatenate all PDF pages into one guidelines string.

```
PROMPT_TEMPLATE = """
Act as a senior copywriter for Luminia.

Your task is to generate a personalized marketing email that includes:
- A short, engaging subject line
- A concise body tailored to the customer profile (under 120 words)

Follow the brand rules strictly and reference the customer data provided.
Just generate the subject and the body as a JSON object.
The names of the keys must be: 'subject' and 'body'.
```

```
---------------------------------------------------
### CUSTOMER GUIDELINES
{guidelines}
---------------------------------------------------
""".strip()

prompt = ChatPromptTemplate.from_messages(
    [
        ("system", PROMPT_TEMPLATE),
        ("human", "{customer_json}"),
    ]
)

# --- Core helper: turn a profile into subject+body -----------------------


def generate_email_from_profile(profile: Dict[str, Any]) -> Dict[str, str]:
    """Call the LLM to generate a JSON email (subject+body) for one customer."""
    customer_json = json.dumps(profile, ensure_ascii=False, indent=2)
    messages = prompt.format_messages(
        guidelines=guidelines_text,
        customer_json=customer_json,
    )
    response = llm.invoke(messages)
    text = response.content.strip()

    # We expect a JSON object like {"subject": "...", "body": "..."}.
    try:
        data = json.loads(text)
    except json.JSONDecodeError:
        # If parsing fails, return everything in the body and a generic subject.
        return {
            "subject": "Luminia special offer",
            "body": text,
        }

    subject = data.get("subject", "Luminia special offer")
    body = data.get("body", text)
    return {"subject": subject, "body": body}

# --- FastAPI app and request model ----------------------------------------


class CustomerProfile(BaseModel):
    """A generic customer profile wrapper."""
    profile: Dict[str, Any]


app = FastAPI(title="Luminia Email Generator")
```

System-level instructions for the copywriter, including the {guidelines} slot.

Prompt object combining system message and customer JSON as human input.

Serialize the incoming customer profile as JSON text for the model.

Inject guidelines and customer JSON into the prompt.

Call the OpenAI chat model to generate the email.

Get the raw text output from the model.

Parse the expected JSON with 'subject' and 'body', with a simple fallback.

Pydantic schema: the API expects {"profile": {...customer fields...}}.

FastAPI application object.

```
@app.post("/generate-email")
async def generate_email(payload: CustomerProfile) -> Dict[str, str]:
    """
    Accepts a JSON customer profile and returns a brand-compliant
    Luminia email with 'subject' and 'body' keys.
    """
    return generate_email_from_profile(payload.profile)

# --- Optional: quick local test without HTTP ----------------------------

if __name__ == "__main__":
    # Simple CLI test: type a minimal profile and see the result.
    sample_profile = {
        "name": "Alex",
        "segment": "loyal_customer",
        "last_purchase_days_ago": 45,
        "preferred_channel": "email",
        "interests": ["smart lighting", "energy savings"],
    }
    print("Sample profile:", json.dumps(sample_profile, indent=2))
    email = generate_email_from_profile(sample_profile)
    print("\nGenerated email JSON:\n", json.dumps(email, indent=2, ensure_
ascii=False))

    print(
        "\nTo start the API server, run from the terminal:\n"
        "  uvicorn CH7_Luminia_Email_API:app --reload\n"
        "Then POST to http://localhost:8000/generate-email with a JSON body 
like:\n"
        '{ "profile": { ... your customer data ... } }'
    )
```

API endpoint logic: run the core helper and return its JSON result.

Optional local test and a hint on how to start the FastAPI server.

## Summary

- Integrating GenAI into a data ecosystem means moving beyond conversational AI to applications where inputs come from databases, files, or other systems rather than directly from humans.
- KNIME complements Langflow by handling data extraction, transformation, aggregation, and integration with external systems, while Langflow focuses on the LLM-driven generative logic.
- KNIME workflows are built from nodes—visual building blocks—used to load, join, sort, aggregate, and transform data into the structured formats LLMs require.
- This KNIME–Langflow integration can be extended with dynamic campaign content injection, direct CRM connectivity, automated email sending, and scheduled executions for full end-to-end marketing automation.

# 8 Deploying and orchestrating GenAI apps

## In this chapter

- deploying applications so they can be accessed by others through websites and APIs
- understanding the role of agent protocols (MCP, A2A, ACP) in orchestrating GenAI systems
- monitoring and debugging your GenAI apps using observability tools such as LangSmith
- building an agent using an MCP server and embedding it on your personal website

Up to now, we've been happily running our GenAI applications on our own machines. That's fine for experimenting, but sooner or later, you want your creations to be used by others—colleagues, customers, or strangers visiting a website. To make this possible, your applications must be accessible from the outside. You do so by *deploying* them somewhere so they can stay "always on."

You'll also often want them to be interoperable, meaning that a Langflow flow can call other applications, agents can interact with one another, and other applications can call yours. Designing such a collaboration to be reliable requires properly *orchestrating* the various parts.

You already had a taste of these topics in chapter 7, when KNIME invoked a Langflow flow through an API. Here, we take it a step further and put all the pieces together, so you have the levers to both deploy your creations and make them interoperable. We'll talk about practical things—protocols, servers, clients, URLs—one small step at a time with simple examples you can follow.

A quick disclaimer before we begin: deployment involves complex technologies, such as cloud platforms, which evolve rapidly. As a result, some details might change by the time you read this. Don't worry. Treat this chapter as your conceptual map: once the big picture is clear, any up-to-date guide will be easy to adapt. Let's start.

# Deploying your GenAI app

Deployment is simply making our app accessible beyond our laptops. Locally, Langflow runs as long as the computer is on and connected—this is a suitable setup for exploring and developing our app. But if we want the assistant to answer users 24/7 while they browse our website—or to be invoked by another application at any time—we need to run Langflow on an always-on machine with a stable, publicly reachable address, either a static IP address or a domain name pointing to it.

That machine can be our own hardware, a virtual server we manage (on which we install and maintain Langflow), or a hosted service that runs Langflow. In any case, the idea remains the same: the flow should be accessible so that people and systems can consistently reach it.

## Selecting the best deployment method

To make this easy to visualize, you have three practical options:

- Self-host on your own hardware.
- Run a self-managed virtual machine (VM) in the cloud.
- Use a managed hosting service (for example, Hugging Face Spaces).

The first option, self-hosting, involves purchasing, setting up, and maintaining dedicated hardware on which you install Langflow. This approach may be suitable for specific cases (consider companies that require strict privacy and have the resources to manage their own infrastructure), but it's expensive and operationally complex. Instead of buying your own hardware, you can rent it by using cloud providers.

### Demystifying cloud computing

Cloud computing involves renting computing resources—such as CPU, memory, storage, and networking—over the internet, rather than buying and maintaining physical machines. You hire capacity when you need it, scale it up or down, and pay for what you use. This rental model lets a project be available worldwide without building a data center.

The second option is a self-managed virtual machine (VM) on a cloud provider, such as Google Cloud Platform (GCP), Microsoft Azure, or Amazon Web Services (AWS). A VM is like a remote computer that you can access through a terminal or a virtual screen-sharing application. You can set up a VM on any cloud platform (paying for certain resources and reserving them for a period of time, with a credit card if needed), install Langflow, configure it (for instance, you'll need to set up the environment's firewall to allow outside connections), wire your domain, and keep the system healthy over time. You gain very good control and flexibility, but you also assume ownership of updates, security, and other operational complexities. We won't explore this option further in this book, but you can find tutorials on how to do this online.

The third (and simplest) route is to use ready-made hosting services. Such services let you start an instance of Langflow on a remote computer and access it from a unique public URL so you can start developing with it, as we are doing in this book.

Many cloud hosting services, including Render, Railway, and Hugging Face Spaces, offer a preconfigured Langflow environment. To give you a rough idea of costs, at the time of writing, you can typically run a small Langflow instance with around 4 GB of RAM and some persistent disk space (storage that's preserved across restarts and isn't wiped when the service is restarted) for roughly $5 to $60 USD per month, depending on the provider, region, and usage limits.

In our case, we'll opt for what is, at the time of writing, the simplest and most cost-effective option: Hugging Face, which also offers a very generous free tier you can use to follow along. Keep in mind that cloud prices and configurations change quickly, so these numbers are only indicative. You should always double-check the current pricing when you set up your own deployment.

### Deploy anything on the cloud

Services such as Render, Railway, and Hugging Face Spaces let you run *any* application by providing compute, memory, and optional persistent storage space. You pay for the uptime and resources you use. For example, if you wanted to host a dedicated vector database to support a retrieval-augmented generation (RAG) pipeline (as seen in earlier chapters), you could deploy it using this approach to improve performance and reliability.

## Setting up a Hugging Face Space

Hugging Face is a popular hub in the AI and data science world, widely used to publish models, datasets, and small demo applications. It also offers a simple app-hosting platform called *Spaces*, mainly designed for experimentation and showcasing work publicly. A Space is a small environment where your app runs under a public URL with a clear control panel for configuration, which is exactly what we need for this chapter.

The feature that matters most for us is space duplication. You can copy an existing Langflow Space, give it a name, and make it your own in a couple of clicks.

Let's test this out. Go to https://tiny.cc/langflow-master, click the menu on the top right (1), and select Duplicate This Space (2), as shown in figure 8.1. If you don't have a Hugging Face account, you'll need to create a free one now by following the instructions after clicking Sign Up.

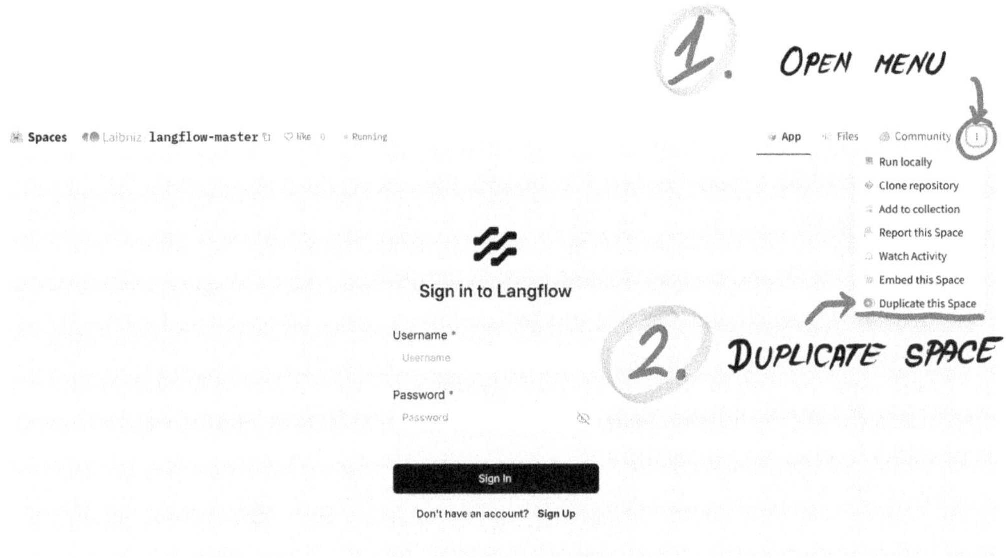


**Figure 8.1** You can duplicate any Langflow space and make it your own.

During the duplication process, you'll be asked to set up some parameters—called environment variables and secrets—related to your new space. Following the example in figure 8.2, you need to:

- Set the name of your Space (1) at the top.
- Set the username and password (2) you'll use as an admin of the tool by filling in the `LANGFLOW_SUPERUSER` and `LANGFLOW_SUPERUSER_PASSWORD` fields, and set a random string in the `LANGFLOW_SECRET_KEY` field to prevent others from reversing the encryption used to protect global variables stored in Langflow's internal database.
- Then click the Duplicate Space button (3) at the bottom, wait a few minutes, and you'll have a personal Langflow environment deployed at a publicly accessible URL.

Cloud services typically incur costs because they require maintenance and operation, consuming disk space, memory, and computational power. If you use this free Hugging Face Space, you should consider certain limitations. First, you're using a minimal configuration, so it might be slower than what you experience on your own machine. Additionally, the disk space you use isn't persistent, meaning that whenever the space

**Figure 8.2** When duplicating a Hugging Face Space, you need to set a few parameters.

restarts (and it automatically restarts every few hours if it isn't being used), the disk is wiped, and you start from scratch, losing your flows. This setup is acceptable if you're developing your flows to learn about GenAI, as we do in this book, but if you intend to use them regularly, you'll need to pay at least for a persistent disk (a few dollars per month) or move to more robust, and expensive, hosting options that allow you to control resources more extensively.

## Sharing your Playground with anyone

Now that we have a deployed instance of Langflow, we can test that other users can connect to it. To do so, we'll use a simple yet powerful Langflow capability: sharing its playground, allowing end users to interact with our app.

The easiest way to explain it is to try it. First, we need to create a flow in our deployed environment so we can share its Playground. You can either create any flow you like from scratch in the new environment or import a flow you've already built locally on your computer.

For example, let's duplicate the HealthyChef™ flow you built in chapter 3. Go to your local implementation of Langflow (the one you've used until this chapter), open the HealthyChef™ flow, and export its definition by opening the Share menu at the top right and clicking Export, as illustrated in figure 8.3.

You'll be asked to confirm its name and definition, and whether to include your API keys in the file (not recommended, to keep keys safe). Once you're done, you'll be able to download a .json file that contains the definition of the Healthy Chef™ flow, component by component.

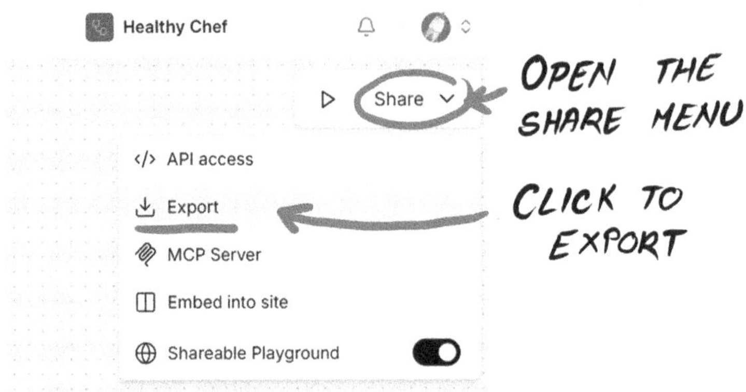


**Figure 8.3** You can export any flow definition as a file from the Share menu.

You can now upload this flow to the deployed instance of Langflow in your Hugging Face Space by clicking the Upload a Flow button (shown in figure 8.4) on the left side of the home page.

After you complete this step, the flow will appear in the project list in the center. Once you open it, you should find precisely the same flow (you might be asked to update some components if the Langflow code was updated in the meantime; this is normal).

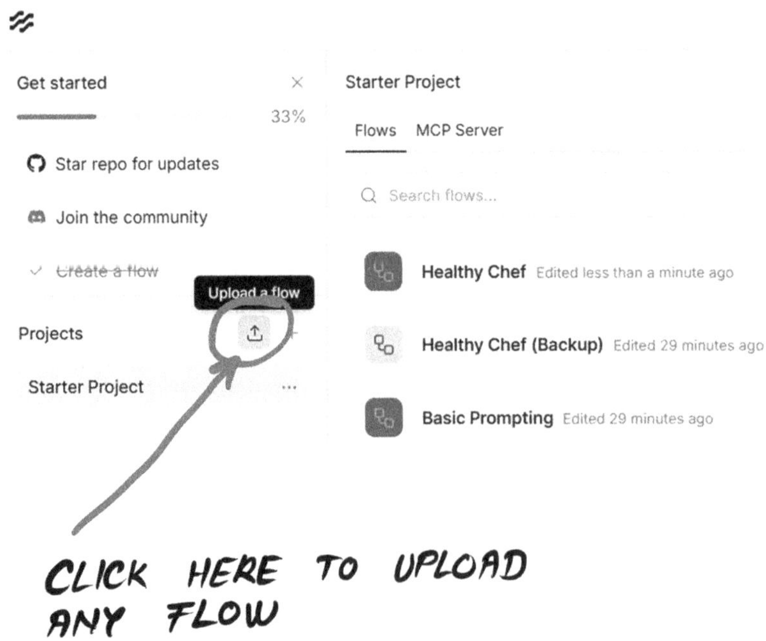


**Figure 8.4** You can import any external flow by uploading its definition file.

Because we plan to use them later, you can transfer all the flows you've built so far locally to your new deployed instance of Langflow by exporting and importing them as described earlier.

Now we're good to go and share the Playground with whoever we like. Just click on the Share menu (1) at the top right (this time, of course, from the Hugging Face deployed instance) and enable the Shareable Playground option (2) at the bottom, as you can see in figure 8.5.

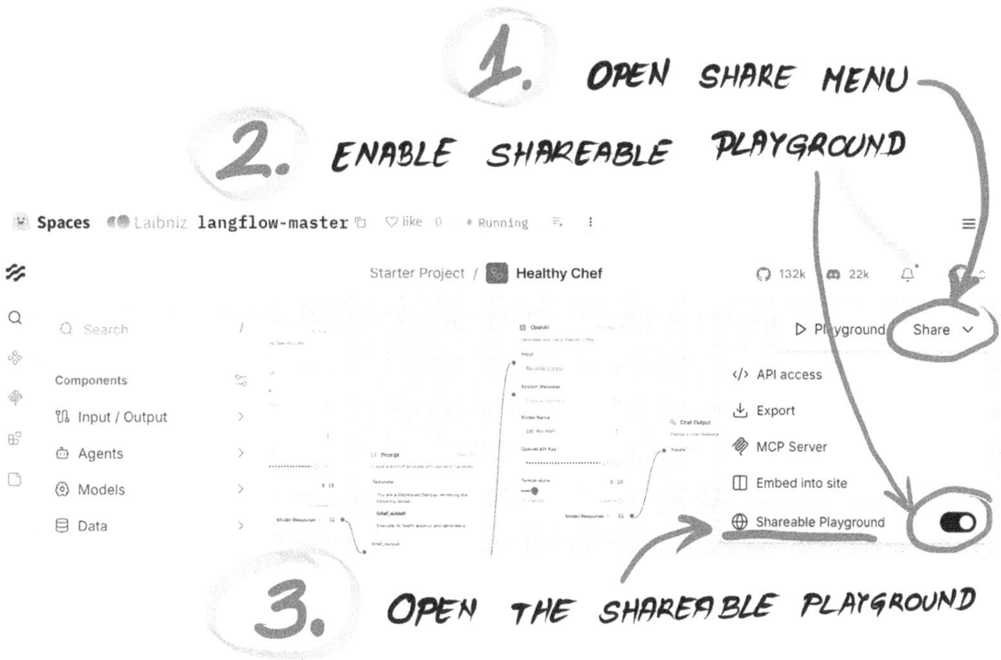


**Figure 8.5** Share a Langflow Playground with anyone you like.

All that's left is to click the Shareable Playground label, and you'll be directed to a URL with a Playground interface up and running, as shown in figure 8.6. If you copy that URL from your address bar and open it on your mobile device or share it with a friend, you'll see that this Playground can now be accessed from any device.

You made it! Other people can now use your deployed GenAI app 24/7 as long as the Hugging Face Space is active.

By deploying Langflow on an always-on server, we enable many usage scenarios for our GenAI apps. As we'll see later in the chapter, we can embed our chat UI on our website. We can also let other applications connect with our GenAI app from anywhere.

Remember what we did in chapter 7 when we let KNIME "call" a Langflow app that was running on our computer? Well, now we can enable virtually any external application (not necessarily running on our machine) to interact with Langflow apps through

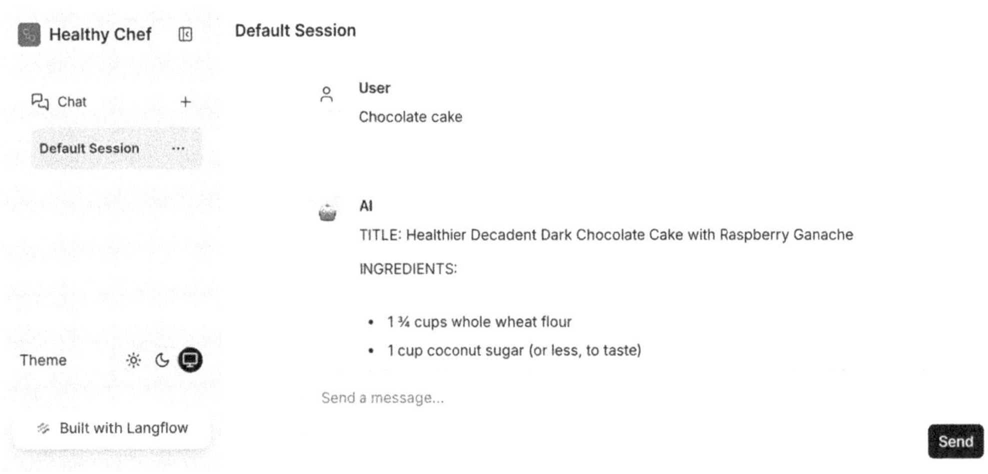


**Figure 8.6** A shared Playground interface that can now be shared with anyone

the API, as shown in previous chapters. The URL will no longer be localhost, as in chapter 7, but the external URL of the deployed Langflow instance. Follow the same steps, using the new base URL and settings.

**Figure 8.7** After deployment, HealthyChef™ can be reached by many users at once from different devices. Quite a shift!

Now that we understand how to deploy Langflow on a cloud server, we can focus on the interoperability of GenAI systems and agent orchestration.

# Orchestrating GenAI apps

Up to now, you've made your AI assistants reachable. The next step is making them sociable.

We've already seen that APIs are a good way to connect applications. You can certainly wire one app to another with an API connector and get neat, deterministic behavior: one API call is followed by one API answer—that's it.

But what if you want a GenAI app to use the thinking power of a large language model (LLM) to decide which other apps it needs and when, based on the specific user's goal? That brings us back to the idea from chapter 5: agents and tools. Remember that in the context of agents, a "tool" is simply a callable capability—often implemented as a function, flow, or external application—that the agent can invoke when needed. It would be much more potent if an app could "make use" of another app the way an agent uses a tool—selecting it when helpful, passing the right inputs, and handling the result.

Inside a company, this dynamic interoperability matters even more. To automate real processes—actual tasks and transactions—your GenAI assistant must connect to existing enterprise systems such as ticketing platforms, enterprise resource planning (ERP) systems (such as SAP), Customer Relationship Management (CRM) systems (such as Salesforce), analytics tools, or knowledge repositories.

A simple way to think about this is to create tools that specialize in these connections. Each tool is a standardized method for communicating with a single system. Assistants then call the tools they need—for example, checking an invoice in the ERP system (using the ERP tool) and using information from the CRM system (via the CRM tool) to draft an email to the customer about that invoice.

Instead of building a separate connector for every assistant, you create standard tools that many assistants can call. These tools should stay up-to-date with the systems they front: when a system changes, you update the tool once, and all assistants keep working.

In short, keep the tools close to the systems they serve, let them evolve together, and allow multiple assistants to reuse them. This removes the middle layer between assistants and underlying systems, replacing it with a thin, shared tool layer. To make that work reliably, we need the right agent orchestration protocols.

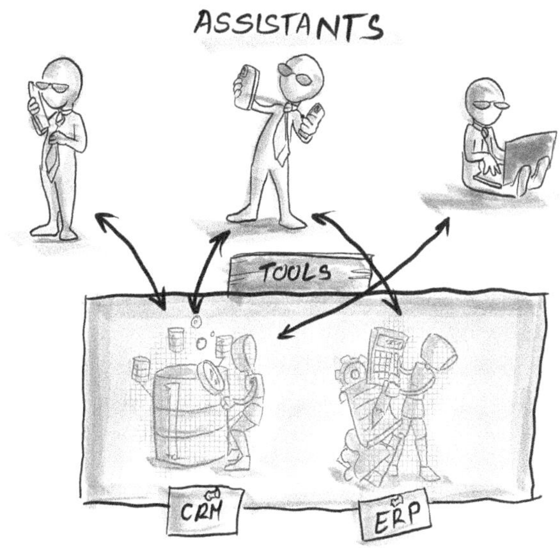


**Figure 8.8** Many assistants can use many tools at once, much like in-the-flesh employees do in a real office.

## Agent orchestration protocols

Agent orchestration protocols let you set a standard way agents and tools can work together. The landscape of agent orchestration is moving fast, and while there isn't a single standard that covers all needs, the following three protocols cover most of them:

- *Model Context Protocol* (MCP)—This open standard lets a server expose tools—think actions such as "search knowledge base for topic X" or "get orders for customer Y"—in a consistent way, and lets clients (tool-calling agents) discover and call those tools. If you like analogies, MCP has been described as the USB-C of agent tools: a standard plug for many peripherals.
- *Agent-to-Agent* (A2A) *protocol*—This focuses on how agents talk to one another directly, negotiate tasks, and coordinate over time. Developed by Google, this standard regulates how agents exchange messages with each other, enabling effective collaboration.
- *Agent Communication Protocol* (ACP)—This is another open effort to standardize agent messaging so teams can share and reuse agents across projects and organizations. The goal is the same: less brittle integration, more portability.

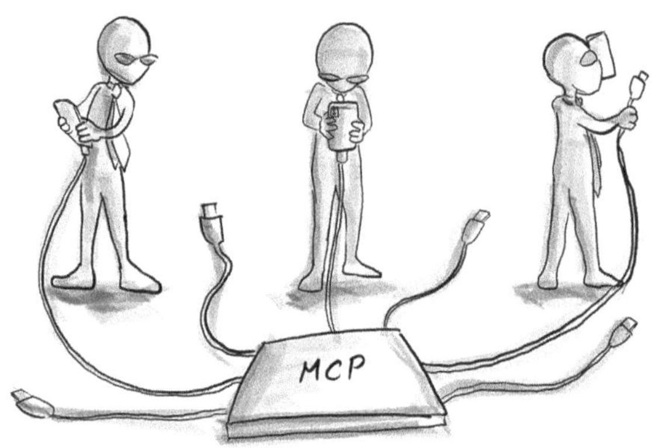


**Figure 8.9** MCP servers act like USB-C hubs for agents: one universal plug with many possible tools.

Let's focus on MCP because it's immediately practical. If a flow becomes a tool and is exposed by an MCP server, every assistant that understands MCP can find and call it. If your connectors to systems are exposed the same way, you can manage tools separately from assistants: the tool layer stays close to the systems and their life cycles, while assistants remain free to choose the right tool at the right time. That separation is powerful in a company.

Here's a concrete scenario involving multiple departments. The finance team maintains invoices in an ERP, the customer care team works within a ticketing system, and the sales team uses a CRM. Let's imagine you're tasked with building GenAI virtual assistants to support those three teams. The assistants might need to connect to multiple systems to perform their tasks.

Instead of running three parallel projects (one for each team and system), you can publish a thin set of stable tools behind MCP—such as `fetch_invoice`, `create_ticket`, and `get_customer_timeline`—and register them on your Langflow MCP server. The customer-service assistant, the finance assistant, and any other agent we build in the future can then use the same tools. If the ERP changes (and it often does), you update one tool in one place, and everyone benefits.

Compliance is easier too: by exposing just the few safe calls you want assistants to make, you create a natural policy boundary. Tools are documented, access is controlled, and logs can be centralized so that every access to important data is tracked and auditable.

**Figure 8.10** Through the MCP server, different assistants can reuse the same tools to create one unified interface for many underlying systems.

## Wait a minute . . . couldn't I just use APIs?

Yes, you could expose every system through traditional APIs, and agents could call them. But APIs were designed for deterministic software, where the client must know the exact route, the exact payload, and the exact structure in advance.

MCP adds a layer of flexibility that fits the agentic way of working: tools can be discovered dynamically, described in natural language, and selected by the agent based on context. Instead of wiring each assistant to each API endpoint manually, MCP standardizes how tools are exposed and keeps them close to the systems they represent. Update the tool once, and every assistant immediately benefits.

## Enabling MCP in Langflow

After so many protocols, now for the good news: Langflow can easily expose your flows as tools on an MCP server by default. This means that all the flows we've built so far can be instantly "toolified" and made available to any agent we need to build through a single MCP server. Let's see this in action.

Open your deployed Langflow (for example, on your Hugging Face Space) and import the flows you previously built locally, following the steps explained earlier. Then select your project and switch to the MCP Server tab (1). Figure 8.11 shows exactly what this looks like for our "AI Apps Made Easy" project (you can rename the project to whatever you like by clicking the three dots on the right of the project name). Every flow we've built in the book so far appears as a tool in the middle list (one flow = one tool). The gray labels are the tool names: Healthy_Chef, Hello_World, Pizzeria_Assistant, and so on. The tool's input is the text received at the Chat Input component, and the tool's output is the text returned at the Chat Output component. On the right, Langflow shows a ready-to-use client configuration that includes everything another agent needs to contact your MCP server: the server address, the headers it expects (such as the API Key), and a copyable snippet you can paste into an integrated development environment (IDE) or agent client. At the top of the panel, you can set the authentication method and, if needed, generate an API key.

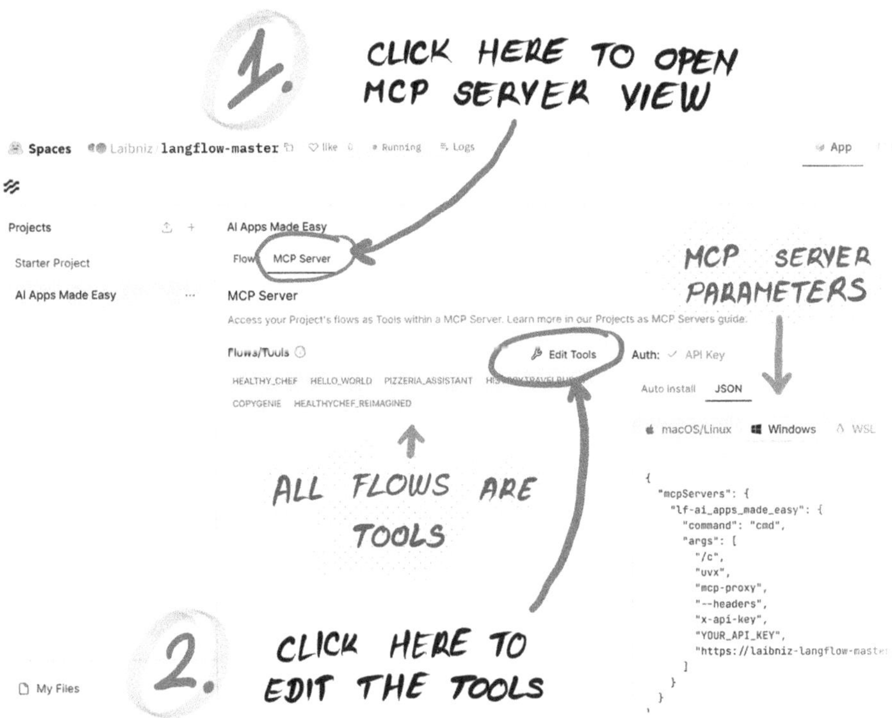


**Figure 8.11** Project-level MCP server view. All flows inside the project become tools.

Click Edit Tools (2) to curate what you expose. This opens the window shown in figure 8.12. On the left, you can enable or disable each flow as a tool with a simple checkbox. On the right, you can edit two important fields: Tool Name and Tool Description. Think of the description as the tool's manifest—the short text agents read to decide whether to call the tool and what to ask it. Keep it crisp and specific: what the tool does, what input it expects, what it returns, and any limits. This is the same principle you met in chapter 5, when we discussed how agents choose tools.

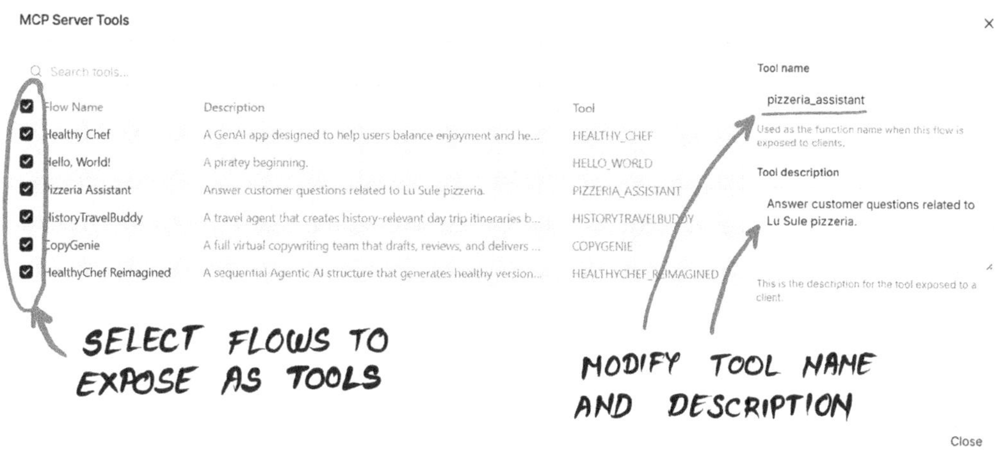


**Figure 8.12** MCP Server Tools dialog. The description acts as the tool's manifest and guides agents' decisions.

With this in place, your project becomes a small interoperability hub: flows are now callable tools, and other assistants—inside or outside Langflow—can discover and use them without hand-built, point-to-point integrations.

In the tutorial that follows, you'll see this in action. We'll expose a couple of flows as tools on your MCP server, let another assistant discover and call them, and make the experience visible to people on a web page—while you watch the whole dance in your observability dashboard.

## Setting up a culinary travel agent

In this tutorial, we're going to bring together everything we've learned about MCP servers and deployment by working through another food-based example.

Imagine you work for a travel agency that specializes in creating unique culinary-oriented itineraries—trips that are about both the places you visit and the flavors you experience along the way. Your goal is to build a multifaceted virtual assistant that can craft a travel plan and enrich it with a matching recipe, so travelers can get a "taste" of their destination before they even leave home. Our client, the founder of this travel agency, would like to embed this personal assistant on the home page of her agency. She's convinced that such a gadget will stimulate the appetite of her prospective customers. Ideally, the assistant will also let users share the itinerary via email, so they can spread the news and hopefully attract new visitors.

As we start thinking about the "capabilities" of such an assistant, we notice something familiar that can potentially save us a lot of time: we've already built flows that do parts of this job. We have a flow that generates recipes (HealthyChef™ from chapter 3) and another that creates travel itineraries (HistoryTravelBuddy™ from chapter 5). We've also previously used a simple tool to send emails (used by the CopyGenie™ team in chapter 6).

How about we "reuse" the abilities that we've already created and mix them in a single flow where an agent can "pull" them as needed? This is where the MCP server comes into play. In practice, MCP turns each flow in your Langflow project into a discoverable tool that an agent can invoke when needed. By making this happen, our HungryTraveler agent can simply plug in these pre-made abilities and mix them to perform a new, more complex task.

This is reminiscent of the hierarchical agent structure we introduced in chapter 6, where a "parent" agent used a "child" agent as a tool. Here, the parent agent (HungryTraveler™) acts as a supervisor, and its child agents connect to it through an MCP server, exposing their "abilities" as tools.

This project is more involved than the previous ones because it brings multiple agents and tools together. It's even more important to understand what's happening behind the scenes at each step, so we can quickly debug, troubleshoot, and improve it. That's why we'll also introduce the concept of observability into the mix.

We need to see how our assistant is orchestrating these calls, and for that, we'll introduce a new development tool, LangSmith, which we'll explore shortly and which gives us complete visibility into each step.

Before we get our hands dirty, it makes sense to sketch out what we need to build. The core of the assistant will be an agent, like the ones we've built over the past few chapters. Such an agent will need specialized tools:

- *A tool that generates itineraries based on user preferences*—We'll call HistoryTravelBuddy™ for that. We can make this connection happen through an MCP server.
- *A tool that generates recipes inspired by some keywords*—We can call HealthyChef™. In this case as well, the connection can go through an MCP server.
- *A tool that sends email*—Here, we can just use the same Gmail component tool (through Composio) that we've used earlier. There's no need to use MCP for that, since we have a component that can act directly as a tool.

All in all, we need two tools (which were originally flows) exposed via the MCP server, plus a third "local" tool for sending emails, connected directly to the HungryTraveler™

agent. Guided by its system message, HungryTraveler™ can decide which tool to call and in what order, assemble what's needed, and send everything to the user via email at the right time. As you can see in figure 8.13, HungryTraveler™ has a lot to do, but building it will be much faster than we'd think, thanks to the interoperability made available by the MCP server setup.

**Figure 8.13** How the HungryTraveler™ agent uses MCP to reuse existing agents and do its tasty job

## Setting up the MCP server

As seen earlier in the chapter, we'll gather the flows we've previously created—such as the healthy recipe generator and the itinerary builder—into one project and configure the MCP server so that our new agent can call them as tools.

For this step, we can refer to figures 8.11 and 8.12 shown earlier. We need to ensure that at least our HistoryTravelBuddy™ and HealthyChef™ are included in the project. Then, select the MCP Server tab and configure the exposed tools by clicking the Edit Tools button.

We also need to ensure that each flow (made available as a tool) has a clear, descriptive label. If you recall from the earlier steps, each tool's description must tell the agent exactly when to use it. For example, the HealthyChef™ flow should be described as "Generates healthy recipes based on user inputs," so our agent knows what it's for. Similarly, HistoryTravelBuddy™ should have "A travel agent that creates history-relevant itineraries by enriching them with historical facts," as a description, or something similar.

These descriptions matter because, unlike traditional APIs, MCP sends them to the agent, allowing the LLM to interpret the purpose of each tool and choose the right one based on context.

We don't want to confuse our agent with too many choices, so let's expose only the two flows we actually need and unselect all the others. The final configuration should look like the one in figure 8.14, where we expose only the required tools and make sure they are adequately described.

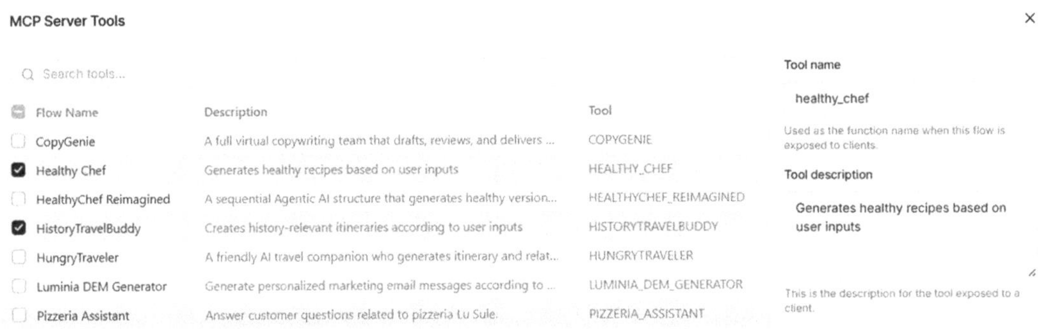


**Figure 8.14** Let's keep only the flows we need, with the right tool descriptions.

Once this is done, you can close the window and, from the MCP Server tab, first check the authentication setting. If you want calls to your MCP server to be authenticated (recommended), click Edit Auth and select API Key; alternatively, select None to skip authentication. Then, you can follow the three steps illustrated in figure 8.15 to obtain all the connection parameters of your MCP server:

1. Within the JSON panel on the right, select macOS/Linux (because the Hugging Face Space is running on Linux, this is the right format to use).
2. Click the Generate API Key button. (Skip this step if you chose no authentication.)
3. Copy the connection string by clicking on the last icon on the left.

This string has all you need to enable any agent out there to connect and make use of your tools.

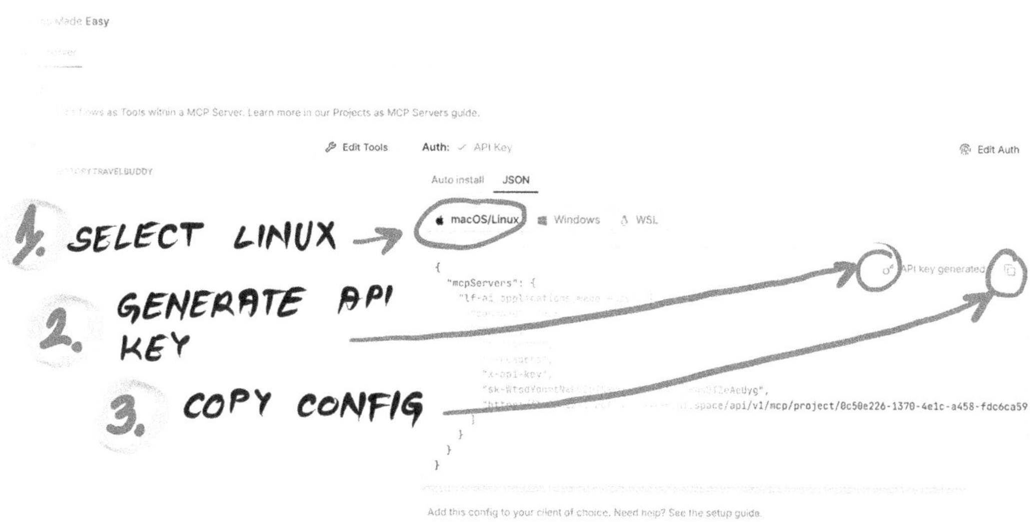


**Figure 8.15** Generate an API key and copy the connection string of our MCP server.

It's time to create a new flow and try connecting with our newly created MCP server using a special component in Langflow that can connect to any MCP server and pull the available tools it exposes.

Select the Flow tab and then click the New Flow button, as usual. Once you're in a blank flow, follow the three steps shown in figure 8.16:

1. Select the MCP panel from the icons on the left side of the screen.
2. Click the Add MCP Server button.
3. Paste your JSON configuration string into the field that appears and then click Add Server.

You'll have to do this config step only once: the MCP server is now saved, and you can reuse it as many times as needed. Once added, a new entry appears in the MCP panel—this is your MCP Tools component. You can drag and drop it onto the canvas just like any other component. It acts as the gateway between your flow and the MCP server: once placed on the canvas, it connects to the server, retrieves the list of available tools, and lets you select which one to invoke—all from a simple dropdown inside the component.

At this point, we can test whether we can connect to our server properly. To do so, follow the steps shown in figure 8.17. Select a tool (1), add a prompt (2; how about asking for a recipe inspired by Venice?), run the component (click the play button on top, 3), and then inspect the output (button on the bottom right, 4). If everything works, after just a few seconds, you should be able to enjoy a recipe that recalls the city of canals.

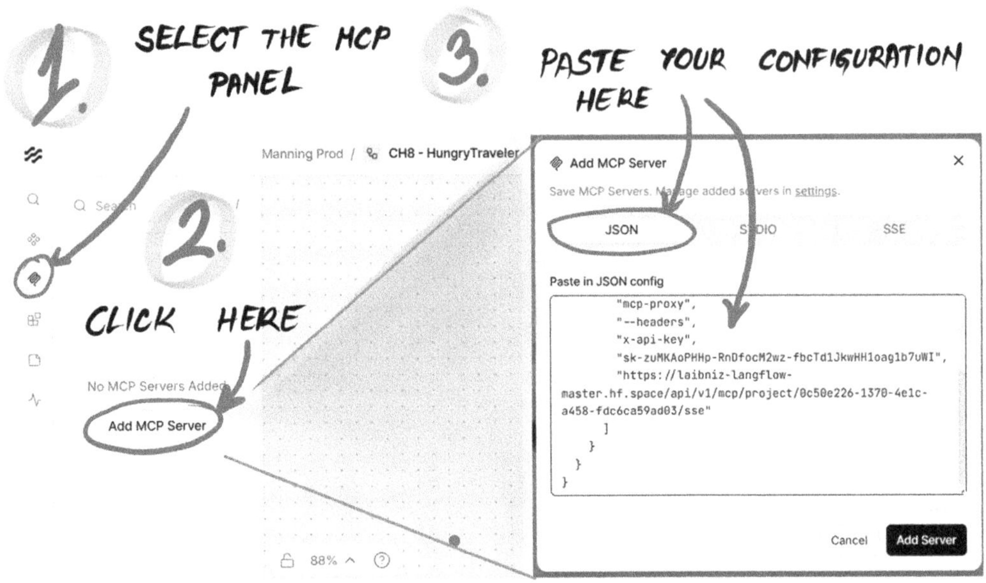


**Figure 8.16** Configure your MCP server by pasting the connection string.

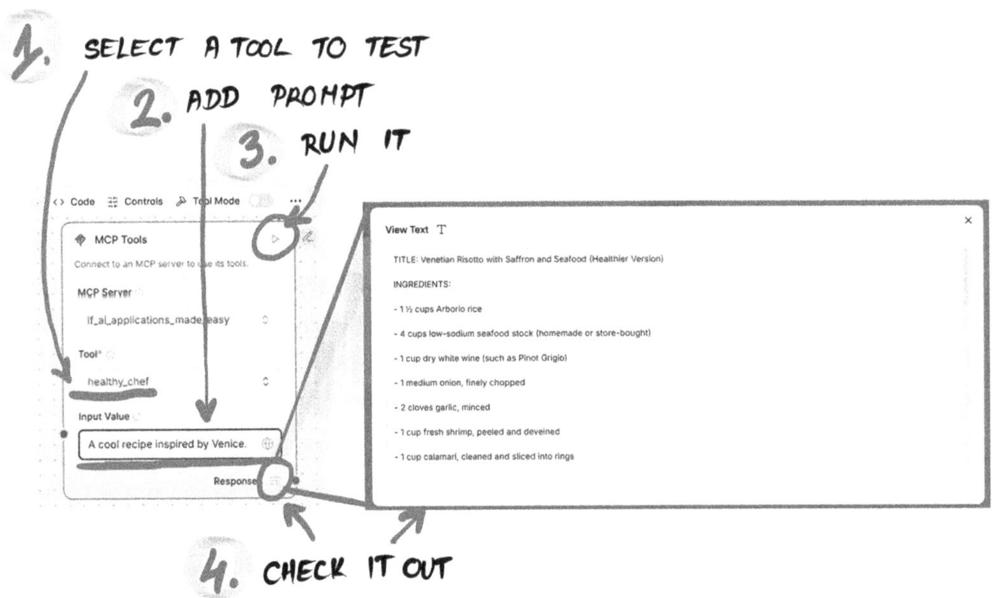


**Figure 8.17** You can test any tool from the MCP server by sending an input prompt and checking the response.

If you receive a message like "invalid API key," don't worry. This is because after uploading the flow on the Hugging Face server, you've probably missed reentering the API keys. Just go back to the individual flows and check that all the keys are there, and then test them in the Playground.

Because we want our agent to freely choose which tool to call and how, we need to toolify the MCP server component. Just click the Tool Mode selector to enable it, and we're good to "serve" the tools to our agent.

We need another tool to let users send emails. Here, we can reuse the Gmail component already introduced in chapter 6. You can refer to that chapter for detailed instructions, but in short, you just need to follow these four steps:

1. Add the Gmail component.
2. Add the Composio API key.
3. Enable the Tool Mode.
4. Select Send Email as the only action permitted by the tool.

Now we have all we need to create our agent. Implement an agent component, select the provider and model, and add the usual API key. Then, we'll define the agent instructions for our HungryTraveler agent. These instructions guide the agent on how to behave and use the tools. For example, we can ask the agent to generate a travel itinerary first, then a recipe, and finally send an email.

Here's a possible version of the instructions we can give our agent:

> You are HungryTraveler, a friendly AI travel companion who loves mixing food and adventure. You have tools available to generate recipes, create travel itineraries, and send emails.
>
> Guide the user through a short conversation to learn where they want to go, what they enjoy, and who's traveling with them. Then generate an itinerary and a recipe inspired by the generated itinerary, and finally ask for the email address(es) to send everything to in a nice HTML email. Identify yourself as HungryTraveler in the signature at the bottom of the email body.
>
> Keep your tone warm, playful, and to the point.

Of course, we also need to add the usual Chat Input and Chat Output components, connecting them to the agent's Input and Response connectors, respectively. With the full flow built, we're ready to test HungryTraveler, as shown in figure 8.18.

## Observing underlying interactions with an observability tool

This time, there is a lot going on! We have built an agentic system where an agent is leveraging tools made available through an MCP server. Actually, those tools are other Langflow flows that run whenever those tools are invoked. It would be nice to understand what is

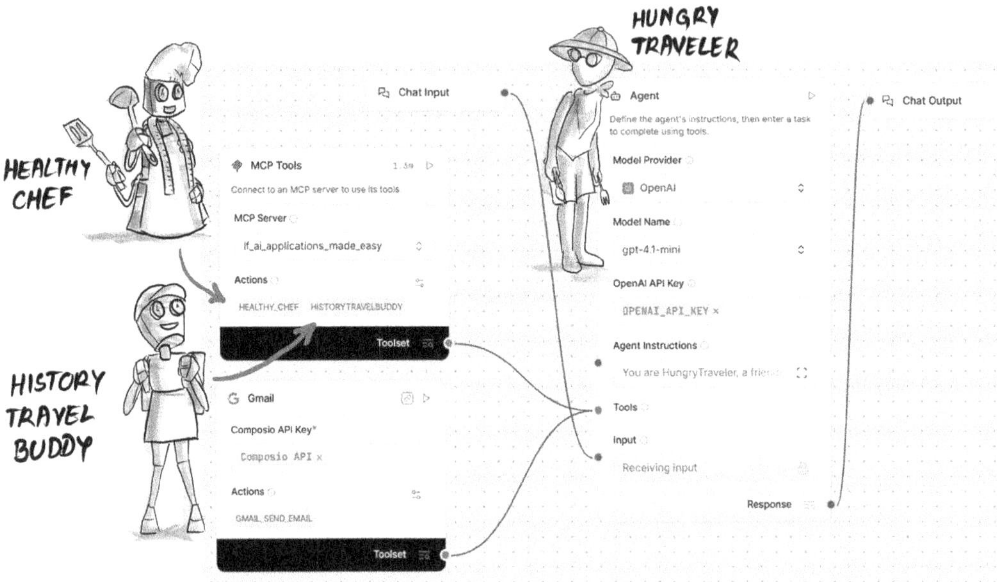


**Figure 8.18** HungryTraveler flow. We're reusing chefs and travel agents as tools made available through an MCP server.

happening at each interaction. For instance, we would like to see which tools are called, when, and in what order, and how the supervisor agent (the core of HungryTraveler™) manages responses and requests. We could follow some of this in the interactive chat Playground, but sometimes we need more details. This is when we need observability systems.

In an AI context, observability means recording data at every stage of your application's process. When a user makes a request, several actions occur: a prompt is generated, one or more calls are made to an LLM, the result is parsed, and additional tools, such as calculators or web search APIs, might be used. Good observability also helps you assess whether the model's outputs are valid (or drifting into hallucination), monitor token usage and costs, and verify that each tool is behaving as expected.

An effective observability system tracks the whole process as a *trace*—a detailed record of a request's complete journey, illustrating the connections between operations, their inputs and outputs, and essential metadata such as latency and token counts.

Observability systems such as Langfuse, LangWatch, and LangSmith can analyze those traces and let you "observe" what's happening in your GenAI app while you develop it and also, at scale, when you put it in production—meaning you make it available to your end users.

Let's take as an example the home automation agent we encountered in chapter 5. The agent was helping the user sleep comfortably through a series of reasoning steps, tool calls, and responses. As you can see in figure 8.19, an observability tool can analyze the traces left by the agent through its course of actions and put together a list or, better, a timeline view—called a *waterfall chart*—with the sequence of steps: interpreting the user request, calling first the thermometer tool, then calling the AC tool, and finally formulating a response to the user.

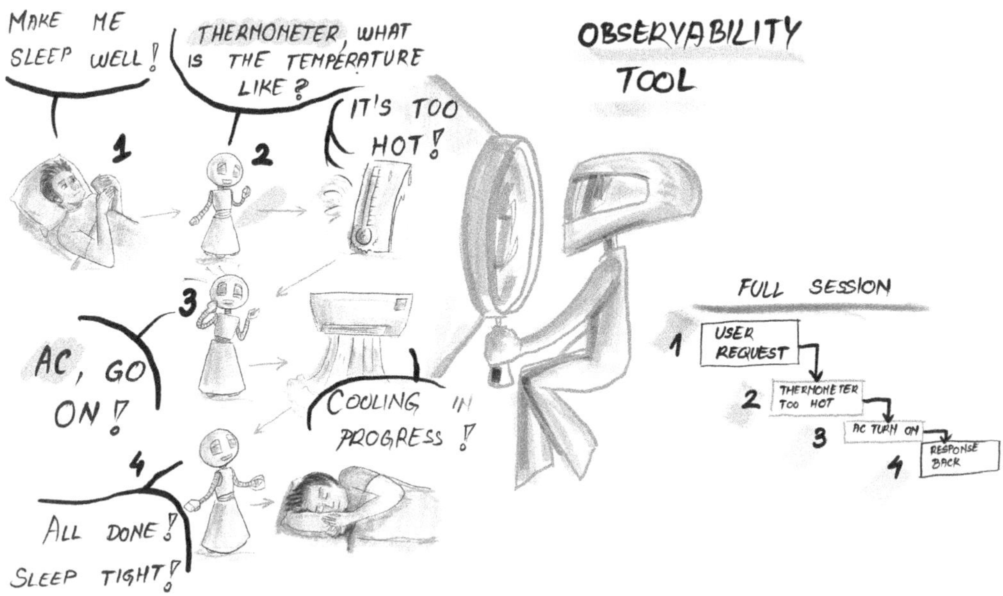


**Figure 8.19** The behavior of an agent can be visualized through an observability tool.

The good news is that Langflow comes ready with everything you need to seamlessly connect its operations with a third-party observability tool after some minimal configuration.

In this book, we'll use a comprehensive observability tool called LangSmith, developed by the creators of LangChain, the open source development framework on which Langflow is based. Its free tier is pretty generous, and you can definitely manage all your initial visibility needs without buying a subscription.

To use LangSmith, you first need to sign up at https://smith.langchain.com and create an API key. After you do so, follow the instructions in figure 8.20: go to settings (1), click on the + API Key (top right, 2), enter any text as a description (3), and click Create API Key (4) at the bottom. You'll be issued a key that you can copy and paste somewhere safe. To connect LangSmith with Langflow, you need to add some environment variables to Langflow. The steps to do so differ depending on the environment where Langflow sits. In this case, because we're running on Hugging Face Space, click Settings (1) on the Hugging Face bar at the top, and then add the variables (2) following the guide shown in figure 8.21.

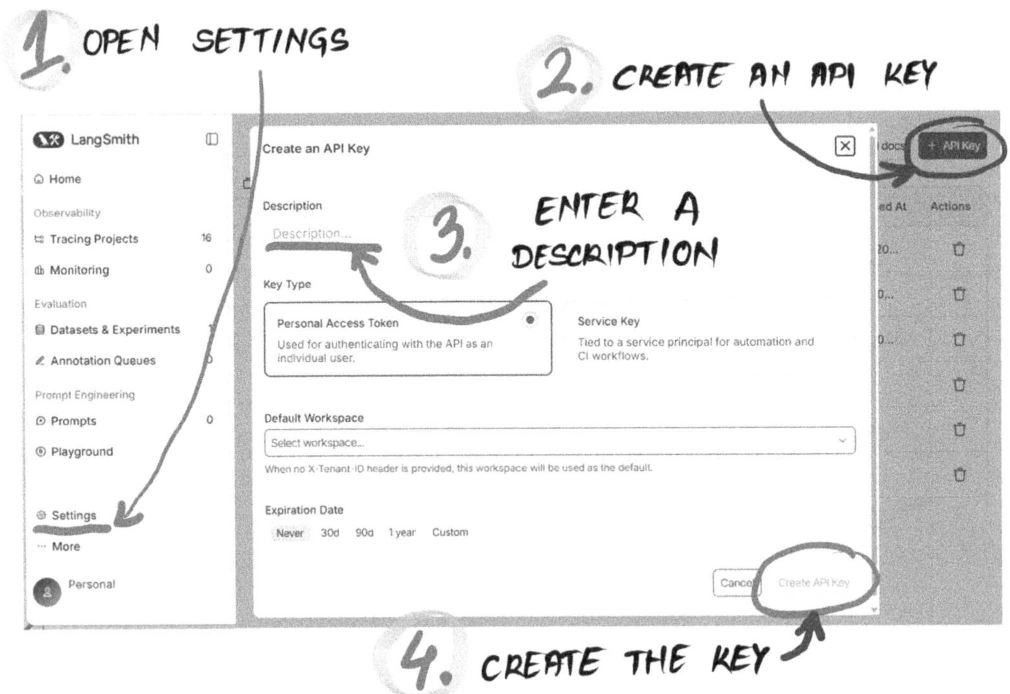


**Figure 8.20** After signing up, create an API key to connect with LangSmith.

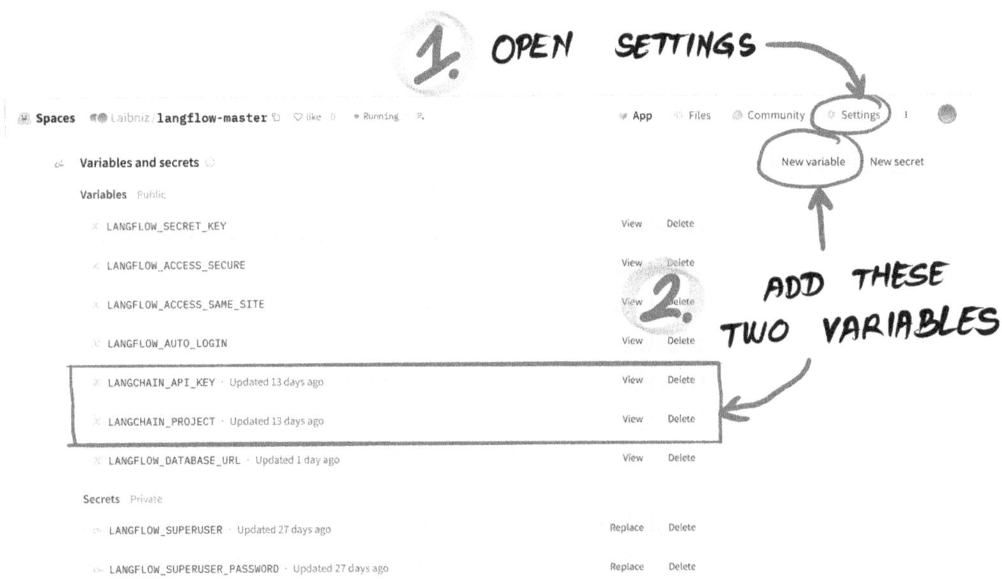


**Figure 8.21** Setting environment variables in a Hugging Face Space

The variables required to connect with LangSmith are `LANGCHAIN_API_KEY` (paste the API key you created in LangSmith here) and `LANGCHAIN_PROJECT` (any name will do). Be aware that changing these variables might trigger a restart of the space. If you're on a free tier, this means you may lose the current flows, so be sure to export the flow so you can import it back after the system has started up.

## Setting environment variables locally

To set environment variables in your local installation, you'll need to change the content of the .env file in the installation folder and add a couple of rows:

```
LANGCHAIN_API_KEY="your_key"
LANGCHAIN_PROJECT="your_project_name"
```

You can check the up-to-date online documentation to find out about this step.

Now that LangSmith is set up, you can test it out. We can start our chat in the Playground and ask, for example, for an itinerary to visit Rajasthan in northwestern India—the land of the maharajas—with our partner and our child. Given its instructions, HungryTraveler will greet us and ask for some more details, such as the number of days we have available and the email address to send the itinerary and recipe to, as shown in the example in figure 8.22.

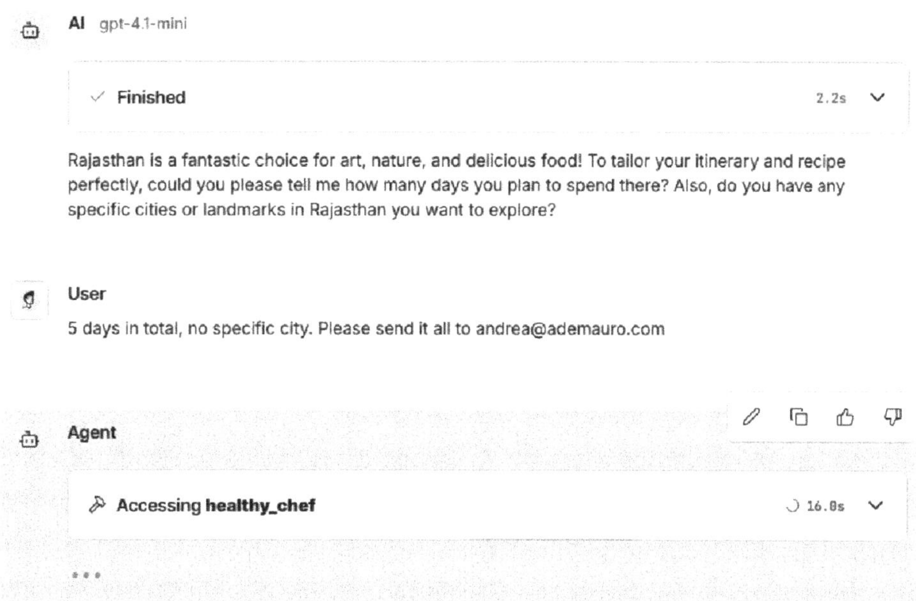


**Figure 8.22** Let's get a good Rajasthani itinerary and recipe to prepare us for the journey.

At this point, we can open LangSmith and check out what's going on. We'll see a "live" list of traces. In our case, HungryTraveler™ triggers the run of two additional flows (HealthyChef™ and HistoryTravelBuddy™), so we'll have three traces in the list. All of these flows are, in fact, running from the same machine (the Hugging Face Space), so Langflow is instructed to send traces to LangSmith for each of them.

If we click the HungryTraveler list item, we're greeted with a detailed Trace view (figure 8.23), which is full of interesting facts. On the left, we see a Waterfall chart telling us what's going on step-by-step under the hood. First, a Chat Input is provided by the user, which starts the trace; then, after a few initialization steps in which the MCP tools component checks for the available tools on the server, the agent thinks about what to do. It has a few tools available (see the right side of the figure) and decides to call the `history_travel_buddy` tool (exposed by our MCP server), which triggers the HistoryTravelBuddy™ flow. We can check the inputs and outputs of this call to determine the exact request that HungryTraveler made to the travel agent. Following the waterfall chart, we can see how HungryTraveler decides to invoke HealthyChef™ and then, lastly, the Gmail tool. By clicking on all the instances, we could find out every detail about each step, spotting imperfections that we can improve with a better prompt, a tool description, or maybe by changing the LLM model guiding the agent.

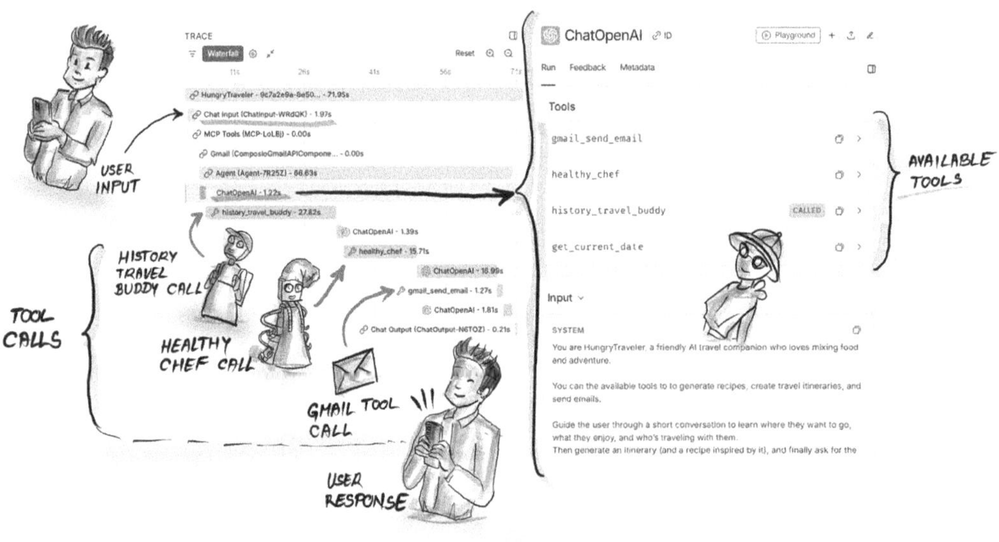


**Figure 8.23** This LangSmith trace shows how HungryTraveler operated—and it did well!

To make this more concrete, imagine that in a different scenario from figure 8.23, we discover something unexpected: HungryTraveler had generated the itinerary and the recipe *in parallel*, instead of waiting to produce the recipe only *after* the itinerary is finalized. This type of problem is almost impossible to spot from the chat interface alone, but

LangSmith makes it immediately visible in the trace. By inspecting the sequence of tool calls, we can understand exactly where the agent's reasoning went off track.

Fixing it is then a matter of adjusting the agent's instructions—for example, by explicitly stating that the recipe must be generated after the itinerary, or by reinforcing this with prompt-enhancement techniques (such as double-down clarifications, as we learned in chapter 3). This small scenario illustrates the real value of observability: it lets us see how an agent thinks and behaves, diagnose subtle bugs, and iteratively refine the system through the fascinating mix of art and science required when developing GenAI apps.

Thanks to LangSmith, we now have full visibility into what's happening. Think about all the bugs you can fix this way. If our application were already in production and offered to many end users, we could use LangSmith to check the usage rate, average token consumption, and other helpful statistics to control performance over time.

After checking LangSmith, we open our inbox and find a nice email from HungryTraveler (figure 8.24), confirming that the full flow worked.

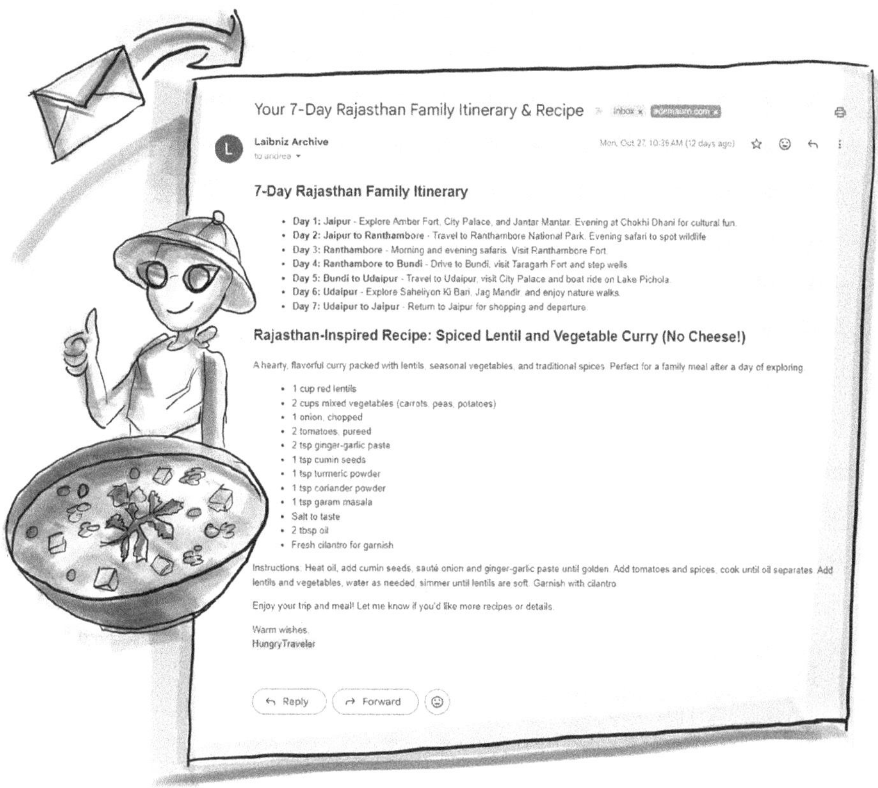


**Figure 8.24** You've got mail! HungryTraveler created a delicious itinerary and recipe combo.

## Publishing our assistant on a website

At this point, there's only one thing left: publish HungryTraveler on a web page to make it ready to have a chat with our visitors. The simplest way to do this is to use the Langflow chat widget—an embeddable JavaScript code snippet that adds basic chat functionality to a web page and uses Langflow APIs to connect with a deployed flow.

To get the HTML code to embed, click Share (1) > Embed into Site (2), as shown in figure 8.25. You'll be given the HTML code to copy (3) and paste onto any web page to add the chat widget.

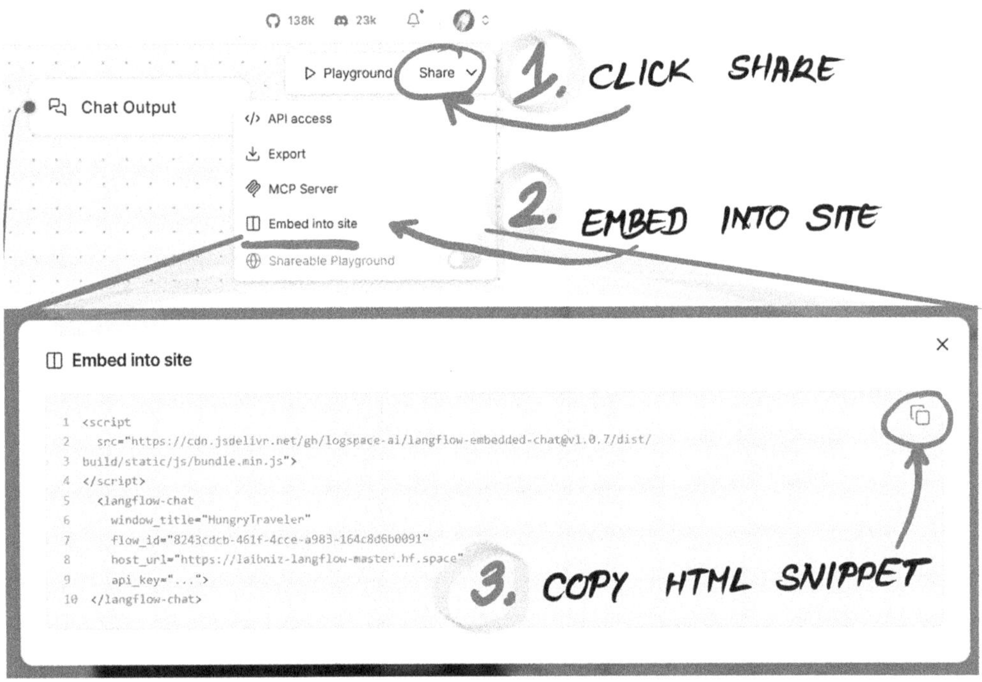


**Figure 8.25** You can embed the chat widget onto any web page by copying and pasting some HTML code.

If your website is based on WordPress, you can follow the steps shown in figure 8.26: open the editor of any page, add a Custom HTML block, paste the code you got from Langflow (make sure you add the Langflow API keys—you can follow the instructions in chapter 7 to do so), preview, and publish.

This logic applies to any CMS or site builder: locate the area where you can add raw HTML to the page and insert the snippet there.

If the widget's appearance feels too plain or requires some customization (like the welcome message on top), you can use the little configurator tool you find at tiny.cc/LangflowConfig. This tool allows you to preview and style the embedded chat without

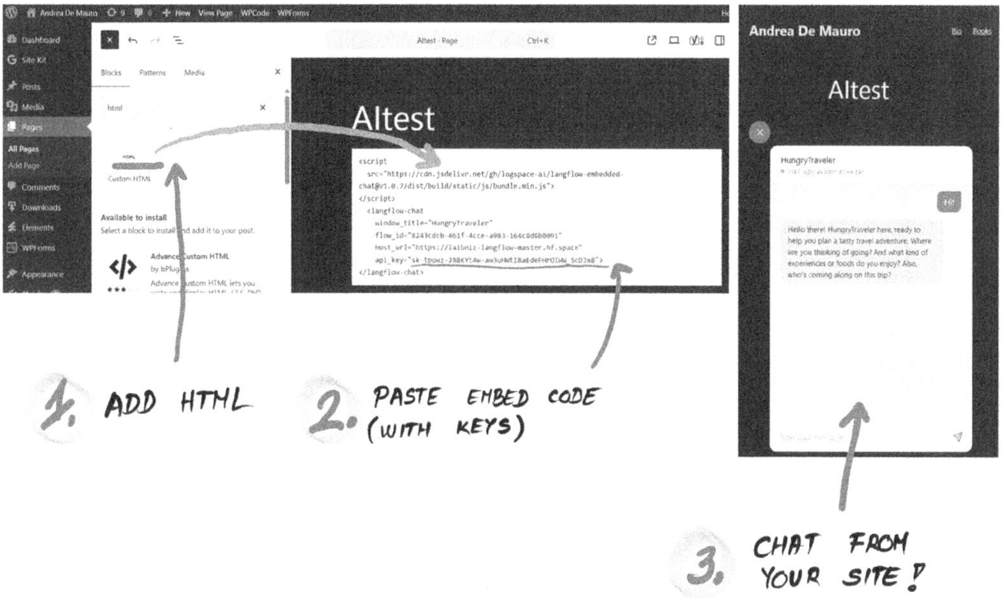


**Figure 8.26** How to add a Langflow assistant to a WordPress page

requiring any specific code. Point it to your flow, provide the host and your Langflow API key, tweak colors and labels, load the preview, and copy the ready-to-paste snippet. This saves time and helps match the look to your site's theme.

We're open for business! HungryTraveler™ is now deployed and ready to chat with the public. With LangSmith in place, we can also monitor how the assistant is used over time and review some of its answers. (Just remember to inform your users that their conversations may be reviewed by humans for quality and debugging purposes.)

For completeness, there are more robust ways to integrate a Langflow chat onto a website, such as a server-side integration that calls the Langflow REST API from your backend (see chapter 7) to avoid exposing keys in HTML pages. But if you need something deployed and tested quickly by a prospective user, the embed option works well.

## What if we coded it?

In this chapter, we introduced agent interoperability through MCP. In Langflow, this means exposing flows as tools via an MCP server, which Langflow instantiates automatically, and allowing other agents—or flows—to discover and call those tools through a standard protocol.

The following two scripts implement the same setup directly in Python: one creates an MCP server from scratch, and the other connects to it as a client and invokes its tools.

The first script shows how to define tools and build an MCP server using a Python module called FastMCP. A Langflow "tool" becomes a Python function decorated with `@server.tool`, and the server metadata (name and instructions) is defined when instantiating the `FastMCP` object.

The script supports two execution modes. When called with numeric arguments, it behaves as a simple calculator that can be invoked from the terminal for quick testing. Otherwise, it starts an MCP server over `stdio` (that is, the server waits for requests sent directly by another program, without opening a network port), making the `add(a, b)` tool available to any MCP-compatible client.

```
"""
Install dependencies once:

    pip install fastmcp

To test quickly:
1. Run `python CH8-MCPserverCreation.py 4 5` to verify the calculator logic.
2. Run `python CH8-MCPserverCreation.py` to start the MCP server over STDIO.
"""
import sys
from fastmcp import FastMCP

server = FastMCP(
    name="Calculator MCP Server",
    instructions="Simple MCP server exposing basic calculator tools.",
)

@server.tool()
async def add(a: float, b: float) -> float:
    """Add two numbers and return the result."""
    return a + b

if __name__ == "__main__":
    if len(sys.argv) == 3:
        a = float(sys.argv[1])
        b = float(sys.argv[2])
        print(a + b)
    else:
        server.run()
```

Import FastMCP, a small library used to define MCP servers in Python.

Mark this function as a tool that other agents can call.

A simple calculator tool that adds two numbers and returns the result.

If numbers are provided, run as a calculator; otherwise, wait for tool calls.

The second script mirrors how Langflow connects to an external MCP server. It launches the calculator server as a subprocess, performs the MCP handshake, lists the available tools, and invokes the `add` tool programmatically.

In Python, this is handled by the MCP client utilities: `StdioServerParameters` defines how to start the server, `stdio_client` opens the communication channel, and `ClientSession` manages the interaction. Listing tools corresponds to the discovery step in Langflow, while `call_tool()` mirrors invoking the MCP tool from an agent.

```
"""
Install dependencies once:

    pip install fastmcp mcp

Run the client script while the server script is available in the same folder.
The script will:
- start the MCP server as a subprocess,
- list its exposed tools,
- call the `add(a, b)` tool and print the result.
"""
import asyncio
import sys
```

asyncio is used because the MCP client runs asynchronously.

ClientSession represents the connection to the MCP server.

```
from mcp.client.session import ClientSession
from mcp.client.stdio import StdioServerParameters, stdio_client
```

These utilities start the server script and connect to it.

main function that runs the MCP client logic.

```
async def main() -> None:
    server_params = StdioServerParameters(command=sys.executable, args=["CH8-
MCPserverCreation.py"])
```

Launch the calculator MCP server as a background process.

Open a session to talk to the server.

```
    async with stdio_client(server_params) as (read, write):
        async with ClientSession(read, write) as session:
            await session.initialize()
```

Initialize the connection before making requests.

Ask the server which tools it exposes.

```
            tools_response = await session.list_tools()
            tools = tools_response.tools
            print("Available tools on the server:")
            for tool in tools:
                print(f"- {tool.name}: {tool.description or '(no
description)'}")

            result = await session.call_tool("add", {"a": 4.0, "b": 3.0})
```

Call the "add" tool with example inputs.

Read the numeric result returned by the tool.

```
            print("\nRaw MCP tool result:")
            print(result)

            value = None
            if getattr(result, "structuredContent", None):
                value = result.structuredContent.get("result")

            print(f"\n4 + 3 = {value}")
```

Run the client when this file is executed directly.

```
if __name__ == "__main__":
    asyncio.run(main())
```

## Summary

- For others to use a Langflow flow, we need to deploy it in an always-on environment, not just on our local computer.
- Suitable deployment options are self-hosting on a publicly available server, running a virtual machine, or using a managed hosting solution compatible with Langflow.
- We can duplicate an existing Hugging Face Space running Langflow and make it our own by changing its configuration—later, we can easily upgrade computing resources if needed.
- Agent orchestration protocols allow agents and tools to collaborate seamlessly. For example, by creating an MCP server, we can publish a set of tools for use by multiple remote agents simultaneously.
- We can embed a chat widget to let users interact with a flow directly from a website simply by pasting a small HTML snippet onto any web page.

## Now what happens?

It's been a long journey—but what a journey! Across these eight chapters, we've filled our backpack with a powerful toolkit. We began by exploring the foundational concepts behind modern generative AI, learning how large language models—our magic black boxes—work, what they excel at, and where their limitations lie. We saw how they differ from traditional deterministic systems and how to harness their inherently probabilistic nature.

We discovered how retrieval-augmented generation (RAG) breathes new life into existing knowledge, connecting LLMs with documents that might have been sleeping for years in a corporate repository or a forgotten folder on your laptop. We ventured into the world of agents—autonomous decision-makers that can use tools, call upon other agents, and collaborate in complex, agentic structures to perform sophisticated tasks that require specialization.

We learned how APIs allow our GenAI applications to interact with the broader data ecosystem—fetching data from a CRM, updating knowledge bases, or automating reasoning workflows. Finally, we explored what it takes to deploy and orchestrate these creations, making them accessible to real users in real time.

All of these ideas were tool-agnostic. Langflow has been our primary companion, but along the way, we've discovered how to extend it with analytics platforms such as KNIME, observability tools like LangSmith, and external integrations such as Composio and SerpApi. We've become autonomous GenAI creators—able to design, prototype, test, and deploy complete applications with agility and confidence. This blend of imagination and execution is what can truly empower us: our creativity can now move *as fast as* our ability to make it real.

With this mix of practical tools and conceptual understanding, we now hold both a map and a compass for navigating a landscape that expands by the day. You should feel proud of your journey—I'm certainly proud to have walked this path with you.

Needless to say, AI is evolving at a pace rarely seen in human history. It will likely evolve in directions that are difficult to predict now. Still, I'd like to share three tips that, during previous hype cycles (think of Big Data a dozen years ago!), have personally helped me stay relevant and benefit professionally.

### 1. Practice, practice, practice—now, not later

First, you've got to keep practicing what you've learned, and you need to start now. We're all busy, and there's a high risk that we store the book on a shelf, let it gather dust, and carry on with our routine priorities, slowly but steadily forgetting what we've learned.

Since you've got all the content fresh now, this is the best time to carry on. Was there a chapter that left you with an idea for a possible extension you wanted to try? Is there anything that needs revision? This is the time to revisit that chapter, perhaps read it again, and run the tutorial one more time, changing the "case" and the aim. If you're energized about what you've learned, you can amplify the value by starting a quicker reread of the full book now, and when you find a tutorial, run it again on a different case.

If you're working in a company, think about the pain points of your daily job that you and your colleagues struggle with. Is there any way a GenAI capability can help? Consider incorporating some of the documentation into a live system with a custom RAG. Or maybe you can automate some tasks with a set of agents that "mimic" the way your team should operate?

If you're a student or a freelancer, go out and hunt for cases. Discuss the potential of GenAI with your customers and explore opportunities to develop a quick prototype for a helpful application. If you don't have a customer right now, apply it to your personal life. Perhaps you'd like to add a virtual assistant to your website? Or is there an association you're part of or volunteer with that can benefit from your new skills?

The point is to look for specific opportunities, make a list, and go for them. Act while the knowledge is fresh. Inspiration fades faster than you think—do it now, don't wait a few weeks.

### 2. Venture beyond Langflow

The second piece of advice is to go beyond what you've learned by exploring other tools and experimenting with them. As mentioned when we introduced Langflow, it isn't the only low-code platform for "doing" GenAI.

For instance, take a look at n8n.io. It's a low-code platform that resembles Langflow, letting you connect nodes through a visual interface similar to Lego bricks. It offers more than 400 nodes, integration with external services (including WhatsApp, so you can make your creation available on a WhatsApp Business account), and scheduling options to trigger a flow regularly over time. You can download and install the community edition of n8n for free, as we did with Langflow, or use a cloud-hosted edition for a fee.

Another one is Flowise, which is very similar to Langflow and n8n. Check it out.

In other words, what you've learned in Langflow can be immediately reused in other environments, since most of what we covered is agnostic to the specific environment.

And, for those who code, needless to say, everything we've seen can be reproduced as code, offering unlimited customization and expansion capabilities, with total control over performance for a production-grade deployment.

My advice is to invest a few hours or days picking one of these non-Langflow environments, installing it, or creating a free account and playing with it to appreciate the differences and similarities. Keep exploring new GenAI development capabilities, as they'll keep popping up for sure. In general, never fall in love with one single environment or programming language, because they always come and go, and you need to develop the flexible muscles to adapt over time.

**3. Stay curious—forever**

The third point I wanted to make is to stay curious. I hope this book is the beginning of a series of books, courses, and readings you're going to make. This space is changing so quickly that you can't stop now from learning about new techniques, models, and applications. My advice is to make learning a habit and prioritize some time in your weekly schedule, protecting it as a core component of your activities. Maybe a 3-hour slot on every Friday afternoon could work? Some prefer investing half an hour every day?

Pick other books. Manning's catalog is so rich on GenAI—have a look at it. I'm biased but a genuine fan of Manning books' quality, and after going through the production process with Manning professionals, I can guarantee you'll find top-level content in every single one of their books.

Online platforms such as Coursera and DeepLearning.AI, led by Andrew Ng—one of the most inspiring teachers I know—offer bite-sized, free courses that will keep your skills sharp and your curiosity alive.

I wrote this book to empower you—to help you move from *talking about AI* to *making AI happen*. You now possess the knowledge, tools, and mindset to create, experiment, and innovate.

I can't wait to see what you build next. And I'd love to stay in touch—you'll find my contact details below. Feel free to connect with me on LinkedIn, where I regularly share reflections, tutorials, and stories that may spark your next idea.

Good luck with the next steps of your journey into AI and beyond. May you reach your goals—and have plenty of fun in the process.

To stay in touch, you can contact me on my website (ademauro.com), by email (andrea@ademauro.com), or through LinkedIn (linkedin.com/in/andread).

—Andrea De Mauro

# index

## A



## B



## C

## H



## I



## J



## K



## L

## M



## N



## O



## P



## Q



## R

## S



## T



## U



## V



## W



## Z

*(continued from back cover)*

Compact by design, this fast-paced book includes eight fully illustrated chapters that build intuition through engaging, memorable, and relatable real-world scenarios. As you read, you'll experience a shift from AI as the familiar conversational chatbot to AI as an essential part of your application and, further, to the design of multi-agentic teams with specialized roles and supervised coordination.

And you'll enjoy every page of the journey!

**"An essential guide for anyone looking to operationalize AI across the business."**
**—Guy Peri, McCormick & Company**

**"The perfect primer if you are starting your journey in building Generative AI applications."**
**—John K. Thompson**
**Author of *The Path to AGI***

**"Succeeds where many AI books fail—it teaches transferable thinking, not just today's tooling."**
**—Michael Berthold, Data and AI strategist, author, and speaker**

**"A rare book that is simultaneously practical, conceptually elegant, and strategically relevant."**
**—Nino Letteriello, FIT Academy**

**"Whether you write code or strategy, you'll come away with a working mental model and the confidence to actually build something."**
**—Dave Mariani, AtScale**

**"Stands out for its clarity and pedagogical depth."**
**—Domenico Vistocco**
**University of Naples Federico II**

**"Strikes the perfect balance between theory and practice."**
**—Shalini Kurapati, Clearbox AI**